MILL's
UTILITARIANISM

MILL'S
UTILITARIANISM

Critical Essays

Edited By
DAVID LYONS

ROWMAN & LITTLEFIELD PUBLISHERS, INC.
Lanham • Boulder • New York • Oxford

ROWMAN & LITTLEFIELD PUBLISHERS, INC.

Published in the United States of America
by Rowman & Littlefield Publishers, Inc.
4720 Boston Way, Lanham, Maryland 20706

12 Hid's Copse Road
Cummor Hill, Oxford OX2 9JJ, England

British Library Cataloguing in Publication Information Available

Library of Congress Cataloging-in-Publication Data

Mill's Utilitarianism : critical essays / edited by David Lyons.
     p.   cm.—(Critical essays on the classics)
  Includes bibliographical references and index.
   ISBN 0-8476-8783-X (cloth : alk. paper)—ISBN 0-8476-8784-8
(pbk. : alk. paper)
    1. Mill, John Stuart, 1806–1873. Utilitarianism.
  2. Utilitarianism.   I. Lyons, David, 1935– . II. Series.
B1603.U873M55   1997
171'.5—dc21   97-29038
                                    CIP

ISBN 0-8476-8783-x (cloth : alk. paper)
ISBN 0-8476-8784-8 (pbk. : alk. paper)

Printed in the United States of America

♾ ™ The paper used in this publication meets the minimum requirements of
American National Standard for Information Sciences—Permanence of Paper for
Printed Library Materials, ANSI Z39.48–1984.

For Mili and Leo

CONTENTS

Preface   ix

Acknowledgments   xiii

1 The Interpretation of the Moral Philosophy of J.S. Mill   1
    J.O. Urmson

2 What is Mill's Principle of Utility?   9
    D.G. Brown

3 Mill's Act-Utilitarianism   25
    D.G. Brown

4 Human Rights and the General Welfare   29
    David Lyons

5 John Stuart Mill on Justice and Fairness   45
    F.R. Berger

6 What's the Use of Going to School?   67
    Amy Gutmann

7 Mill's "Proof" of the Principle of Utility   85
    Henry R. West

8 How Thinking about Character and Utilitarianism Might Lead to
    Rethinking the Character of Utilitarianism   99
    Peter Railton

9 John Stuart Mill and Experiments in Living   123
    Elizabeth S. Anderson

10 Mill's Deliberative Utilitarianism   149
    David O. Brink

Further Readings   185

Index   187

About the Contributors   195

PREFACE

John Stuart Mill's essay on utilitarianism first appeared in 1861 as a series of three articles and was published as a book in 1863. It has inspired a substantial literature, both critical and interpretive.

Not long ago, Mill's detractors seemed to outnumber his defenders. Critics claimed that this renowned logician's principal work in ethics had irremediable flaws. An embarrassing fallacy was perceived at the heart of his so-called "proof" of the principle of utility. Mill's distinction between "higher" and "lower" pleasures was seen as generating contradictions and as an unprincipled deviation from the utilitarian tradition he professed to embrace.

Recent scholarship offers a different picture. Scholars have proposed new readings of Mill's essay as well as of the theories that he helped to develop. Where some critics have perceived confusion, new readers have discovered subtlety and respect for the complexity of our moral concepts. Mill's essay has lately resumed its place as the classic statement to which all students of utilitarianism must refer. Mill's avowed utilitarian creed, that the "greatest happiness" is the "foundation of morals," remains of course a leading contender in moral theory. This volume collects a distinguished sample of recent studies, which focus mainly (but not exclusively) on Mill's own distinctive contribution.

A reappraisal of Mill's essay was inevitable. Classic works must periodically be read afresh, in light of new theoretical developments. Rich philosophic writing is hard to grasp at once. It may be ahead of its own time, and even of prevailing views in subsequent times.

Mill's essay merits reading free of the presumption that its ideas must fit into some standard theoretical pigeonhole. We cannot assume, for example, that Mill believes the morality of an action is determined solely by the difference that the individual action makes to the general welfare (as "act-utilitarianism" insists). Nor should we simply shift to the presumed alternative and suppose that Mill must mean that the morality of acts is determined solely by its conformity to welfare-promoting rules (as "rule-utilitarianism" holds).

Although Mill's essay retains the language of "pleasure" and "pain," his understanding of it, his approach to applying the utilitarian criterion, and his view of its implications are all different from the conceptions that are associated (fairly or otherwise) with his philosophical godfather, Jeremy Bentham, and that have often been identified with utilitarianism. We are not seen by Mill as calculating maximizers of utility, nor does Mill wish we were. We are urged to experiment with life. Mill calls on us to challenge conventional wisdom and to reform social mores and institutions. Most importantly, perhaps, Mill's essay stands apart from most other classical and contemporary presentations of utilitarianism by recognizing the vital role in moral thought of justice, fairness, rights, and obligations. Mill offers intriguing accounts of these ideas in utilitarian terms.

★   ★   ★

Mill's essay can be read by itself for the theories it expresses or suggests. To achieve a fuller understanding of Mill's moral ideas, it should be read with some of his other works, such as the essays on Bentham, *On Liberty,* and Book VI of *A System of Logic,* "On the Logic of the Moral Sciences."

To understand better the man who did the writing, one must learn about Mill's life. Born in 1806, John Stuart was a prodigy. He was tutored at home, along strict lines that his father, James Mill, derived from Bentham's teachings. While still in his teens, Mill studied law with John Austin, the English jurist, who was also a follower of Bentham; he edited for publication Bentham's *Rationale of Judicial Evidence;* and he became active in the intellectual and political life of the period.

Most of Mill's substantial body of published work, on a wide range of scholarly and political subjects, was written and published while he was employed full time by the British East India Company, from 1823 until 1858.

Mill had a close friendship for many years with Harriet Taylor, whom he met in 1830. After her husband died, Mill and Taylor married, in 1851. Mill credited Taylor with considerable influence on the development of his thought, not least his essays *On Liberty* (1859) and *The Subjection of Women* (1869). Taylor died in 1858.

Mill was elected to Parliament in 1865, where he continued his life-long work for democratic reforms. After losing reelection in 1868, he retired to Avignon, where he died in 1873.

In his *Autobiography,* Mill recounts a debilitating depression that he suffered in 1826–27. He felt himself then incapable of emotion, a deficiency he came to associate with the principles that had guided his upbringing. The transformation that Mill experienced in recovering from this depression seems linked to his enhanced appreciation of the range of human sensibilities and his enriched conception of human flourishing, which are reflected in the philosophical essays for which he is best known, *Utilitarianism* and *On Liberty*.

ACKNOWLEDGMENTS

The editor and publisher thank the authors and publishers of the following essays for permission to reprint them in this volume:

Chapter 1, "The Interpretation of the Moral Philosophy of J.S. Mill," by J.O. Urmson, originally appeared in *Philosophical Quarterly* 3 (1953): 33–39.

Chapter 2, "What is Mill's Principle of Utility?", by D.G. Brown, originally appeared in *Canadian Journal of Philosophy* 3 (1973): 1–12.

Chapter 3, "Mill's Act-Utilitarianism," by D.G. Brown, originally appeared in *Philosophical Quarterly* 24 (1974): 67–68.

Chapter 4, "Human Rights and the General Welfare," by David Lyons, originally appeared in *Philosophy & Public Affairs* 6 (1977): 113–129.

Chapter 5, "John Stuart Mill on Justice and Fairness," by F.R. Berger, originally appeared in *New Essays on John Stuart Mill and Utilitarianism*, edited by Wesley E. Cooper, Kai Nielsen and Steven C. Patten (Guelph, Ontario: Canadian Association for Publishing in Philosophy, 1979), *Canadian Journal of Philosophy* Supplementary Volume 5 (1979): 115–136.

Chapter 6, "What's the Use of Going to School?", by Amy Gutmann, originally appeared in *Utilitarianism and Beyond*, edited by Amartya Sen and Bernard Williams (Cambridge: Cambridge University Press, 1982), 261–277. © Maison des Sciences de l'Homme and Cambridge University Press, 1982. Reprinted with the permission of Cambridge University Press.

Chapter 7, "Mill's 'Proof' of the Principle of Utility," by Henry R. West, originally appeared in *The Limits of Utilitarianism*, edited by Harlan B. Miller and William H. Williams (Minneapolis: University of Minnesota Press, 1982), 23–34. © 1982 by the University of Minnesota.

Chapter 8, "How Thinking about Character and Utilitarianism Might Lead to Rethinking the Character of Utilitarianism," by Peter Railton, originally appeared in *Midwest Studies in Philosophy*, Volume XIII, edited by Peter A. French, Theodore E. Uehling, Jr., and Howard K. Wettstein. © 1983 by the University of Notre Dame Press, Notre Dame, Indiana. Used by permission of the publisher.

Chapter 9, "John Stuart Mill and Experiments in Living," by Elizabeth S. Anderson, originally appeared in *Ethics* 102 (1991): 4–26. © 1991 by the University of Chicago [publisher].

Chapter 10, "Mill's Deliberative Utilitarianism," by David O. Brink, originally appeared in *Philosophy & Public Affairs* 21 (1992): 67–103. © The Johns Hopkins University Press.

★   ★   ★

When I began the daunting project of selecting a handful of articles from a very large and rich scholarly literature, I turned to several scholars for suggestions, and I am grateful to them for responding to my appeal (though I should mention that none was perfectly impartial, as none suggested that I include his or her own work). My thanks go to Wendy Donner, Ray Frey, Maria Morales, Wayne Sumner, and Henry West. Thanks also to Joshua Shafer for editorial assistance.

· 1 ·

THE INTERPRETATION OF THE MORAL PHILOSOPHY OF J.S. MILL

J.O. Urmson

It is a matter which should be of great interest to those who study the psychology of philosophers that the theories of some great philosophers of the past are studied with the most patient and accurate scholarship, while those of others are so burlesqued and travestied by critics and commentators that it is hard to believe that their works are ever seriously read with a sympathetic interest, or even that they are read at all. Amongst those who suffer most in this way John Stuart Mill is an outstanding example. With the exception of a short book by Reginald Jackson,[1] there is no remotely accurate account of his views on deductive logic, so that, for example, the absurd view that the syllogism involves *petitio principii* is almost invariably fathered on him; and, as Von Wright says, 'A good systematic and critical monograph on Mill's Logic of Induction still remains to be written'.[2] But even more perplexing is the almost universal misconstruction placed upon Mill's ethical doctrines; for his *Utilitarianism* is a work which every undergraduate is set to read and which one would therefore expect Mill's critics to have read at least once. But this, apparently, is not so; and instead of Mill's own doctrines a travesty is discussed, so that the most common criticisms of him are simply irrelevant. It will not be the thesis of this paper that Mill's views are immune to criticism, or that they are of impeccable clarity and verbal consistency; it will be maintained that, if interpreted with, say, half the sympathy automatically accorded to Plato, Leibniz, and Kant, an essentially consistent thesis can be discovered which is very superior to that usually attributed to Mill and immune to the common run of criticisms.

One further note must be made on the scope of this paper. Mill, in his *Utiliatrianism* attempts to do two things; first, he attempts to state the place of the conception of a *summum bonum* in ethics, secondly, he attempts to give an account of the nature of this ultimate end. We shall be concerned

1

only with the first of these two parts of Mill's ethical theory; we shall not ask what Mill thought the ultimate end was, and how he thought that his view on this point could be substantiated, but only what part Mill considered that the notion of an ultimate end, whatever it be, must play in a sound ethical theory. This part of Mill's doctrine is logically independent of his account of happiness.

Two Mistaken Interpretations of Mill

Some of Mill's expositors and critics have thought that Mill was attempting to analyse or define the notion of right in terms of the *summum bonum*. Thus Mill is commonly adduced as an example of an ethical naturalist by those who interpret his account of happiness naturalistically, as being one who defined rightness in terms of the natural consequences of actions. Moore, for example, while criticising Mill's account of the ultimate end says: 'In thus insisting that what is right must mean what produces the best possible results Utilitarianism is fully justified'.[3] Others have been less favourable in their estimation of this alleged view of Mill's. But right or wrong, it seems clear to me that Mill did not hold it. Mill's only reference to this analytic problem is on page 27 (of the Everyman edition, to which all references will be made), where he refers to a person 'who sees in moral obligation a transcendent fact, an objective reality belonging to the province of "Things in themselves" ', and goes on to speak of this view as an irrelevant opinion 'on this point of Ontology', as though the analysis of ethical terms was not part of ethical philosophy at all as he conceived it, but part of ontology. It seems clear that when Mill speaks of his quest being for the 'criterion of right and wrong' (p. 1), 'concerning the foundation of morality' (p. 1) for a 'test of right and wrong' (p. 2), he is looking for a 'means of ascertaining what is right or wrong' (p. 2), not for a definition of these terms. We shall not, therefore, deal further with this interpretation of Mill; if a further refutation of it is required it should be sought in the agreement of the text with the alternative exposition shortly to be given.

The other mistaken view avoids the error of this first view, and indeed is incompatible with it. It is, probably, the received view. On this interpretation Mill is looking for a test of right or wrong as the ultimate test by which one can justify the ascription of rightness or wrongness to courses of action, rightness and wrongness being taken to be words which we understand. This test is taken to be whether the course of action does or does not tend to promote the ultimate end (which Mill no doubt says is the general happiness). So far there is no cause to quarrel with the received view, for it is surely correct. But in detail the view is wrong. For it is further suggested that for Mill this ultimate test is also the immediate test; the rightness or wrongness of any particular action is to be decided by considering whether it promotes the ultimate end. We may, it might be admitted, on Mill's view sometimes act, by rule of thumb or in a hurry, without actually raising this question; but the actual justification, if there is one, must be directly in terms of consequences, including the consequences of the example that we have set. On this view, then, Mill holds that an action, a particular action, is right if it promotes the ultimate end better than any alternative, and otherwise it is wrong. However we in fact make up our minds in moral situations, so far as justification goes no other factor enters into the matter. It is clear that on this interpretation Mill is immediately open to two shattering objections; first, it is obviously and correctly urged, if one has, for example, promised to do something it is one's duty to do it at least partly because one has promised to do it and not merely because of consequences, even if these consequences are taken to include one's example in promise-breaking. Secondly, it is correctly pointed out that on this view a man who, *ceteris paribus,* chooses the inferior of two musical comedies for an evening's entertainment has done a moral wrong, and this is preposterous.[4] If this were in fact the view of Mill, he would indeed be fit for little more than the halting eristic of philosophical infants.

A REVISED INTERPRETATION OF MILL

I shall now set out in a set of propositions what I take to be in fact Mill's view and substantiate them afterwards from the text. This will obscure the subtleties but will make clearer the main lines of interpretation.

A. A particular action is justified as being right by showing that it is in accord with some moral rule. It is shown to be wrong by showing that it transgresses some moral rule.

B. A moral rule is shown to be correct by showing that the recognition of that rule promotes the ultimate end.

C. Moral rules can be justified only in regard to matters in which the general welfare is more than negligibly affected.

D. Where no moral rule is applicable the question of the rightness or wrongness of particular acts does not arise, though the worth of the actions can be estimated in other ways.

As a terminological point it should be mentioned that where the phrase 'moral rule' occurs above Mill uses the phrase 'secondary principle' more generally, though he sometimes says 'moral law'. By these terms, whichever is preferred, Mill is referring to such precepts as 'Keep promises', 'Do no murder', or 'Tell no lies'. A list of which Mill approves is to be found in *On Liberty* (p. 135).

There is, no doubt, need of further explanation of these propositions; but that, and some caveats, can best be given in the process of establishing that these are in fact Mill's views. First, then, to establish from the text that in Mill's view particular actions are shown to be right or wrong by showing that they are or are not in accord with some moral rule. (i) He says with evident approbation on p. 2: 'The intuitive, no less than what may be termed the inductive, school of ethics, insists on the necessity of general laws. They both agree that the morality of an individual action is not a question of direct perception, but of the application of a law to an individual case. They recognise also, to a great extent, the same moral laws'. Mill reproaches these schools only with being unable to give a unifying rationale of these laws (as he will do in proposition B). (ii) He says on page 22: 'But to consider the rules of morality as improvable is one thing; to pass over the intermediate generalisations entirely, and endeavour to test each individual action directly by the first principle, is another. It is a strange notion that the acknowledgement of a first principle is inconsistent with the admission of secondary ones'. He adds, with feeling: 'Men really ought to leave off talking a kind of nonsense on this subject which they would neither talk nor listen to on other matters of practical concernment'. (iii) Having admitted on p. 23 that 'rules of conduct cannot be so framed as to require no exceptions', he adds (p. 24) 'We must remember that only in these cases of conflict between secondary principles is it requisite that first principles should be appealed to. There is no case of moral obligation in which some secondary principle is not involved; and if only one, there can seldom be any real doubt which one it is, in the mind of any person by whom the principle itself is recognised'. This quotation supports both propositions A and D. It shows that for Mill moral rules are not merely rules of thumb which aid the unreflective man in making up his mind, but an essential part of moral reasoning. The relevance of a moral rule is the criterion of whether we are dealing with a case of right or wrong or some other moral or prudential situation. (iv) The last passage which we shall select to establish this interpretation of Mill (it would be easy to find more) is also a joint confirmation of propositions A and D, showing that our last was not an *obiter dictum* on which we have placed too much weight. In the chapter entitled 'On the connection between justice and utility', Mill has maintained that it is a distinguishing mark of a just act that it is one required by a specific rule or law, positive or moral, carrying also liability to penal sanctions. He then writes this important paragraph (p. 45), which in view of its importance and the neglect that it has suffered must be quoted at length: 'The above is, I think, a true account, as far as it goes, of the origin and progressive growth of the idea of justice. But we must observe, that it contains, as yet, nothing to distinguish that obligation from moral obligation in general. For the truth is, that the idea of penal sanction, which is the essence of law, enters not only into the conception of injustice, but into that of any kind of wrong. We do not call anything wrong, unless we mean to imply that a person ought to be punished in some way or other for doing it; if not by law, by the opinion of his fellow-creatures; if not by opinion, by the reproaches of his own conscience. This seems to be the real turning point of the distinction between morality and simple expediency. It is a part of the notion of Duty in every one of its forms, that a person may rightfully be compelled to fulfil it. Duty is a thing which may be exacted from a person, as one exacts a debt. Unless we think that it may be exacted from him, we do not call it his duty. . . . There are other things, on the contrary, which we wish that people should do, which we like or admire them for doing, perhaps dislike or despise them for not doing, but yet admit that they are not bound to do; it is not a case of moral obligation; we do not blame them, that is, we do not think that they are proper objects of punishment. . . . I think there is no doubt that this distinction lies at the bottom of the notions of right and wrong; that we call any conduct wrong, or employ, instead, some other term of dislike or disparagement, according as we think that the person ought, or ought not, to be punished for it; and we say, it would be right to do so and so, or merely that it would be desirable or laudable, according as we would wish to see the person whom it concerns, compelled, or only persuaded and exhorted, to act in that manner'. How supporters of the received view have squared it with this passage I do not know; they do not mention it. If they have noticed it at all it is, presumably, regarded as an example of Mill's inconsistent eclecticism. Mill here makes it quite clear that in his view right and wrong are derived from moral rules; in other cases where the ultimate end is no doubt affected appraisal of conduct must be made in other ways. For example, if one's own participation in the ultimate end is impaired without breach of moral law, it is (*Liberty,* p. 135) imprudence or lack of self respect, it is not wrong-doing. So much for the establishment of this interpretation of Mill, in a positive way, as regards points A and D. We must now ask whether there is anything in Mill which is inconsistent with it and in favour of the received view.

It is impossible to show positively that there is nothing in Mill which favours the received view against the interpretation here given, for it would require a complete review of everything that Mill says. We shall have to be content with examining two points which might be thought to tell in favour of the received view.

(*a*) On p. 6 Mill says: 'The creed which accepts as the foundation of morals, Utility, or the Greatest Happiness Principle, holds that actions are right in proportion as they tend to promote happiness, wrong as they tend to promote the reverse of Happiness'. This seems to be the well-known sentence which is at the bottom of the received interpretation. Of course, it could be taken as a loose and inaccurate statement of the received view, if the general argument required it. But note that strictly one can say that a certain action tends to produce a certain result only if one is speaking of type- rather than token-actions. Drinking alcohol may tend to promote exhilaration, but my drinking this particular glass either does or does not produce it. It seems, then, that Mill can well be interpreted here as regarding moral rules as forbidding or enjoining types of action, in fact as making the point that the right moral rules are the ones which promote the ultimate end (my proposition B), not as saying something contrary to proposition A. And this, or something like it, is the interpretation which consistency requires. Mill's reference to 'tendencies of actions' at the top of p. 22 supports the stress here laid on the word 'tend', and that context should be examined by those who require further conviction.

(*b*) Mill sometimes refers to moral rules as 'intermediate generalisations' (e.g., p. 22) from the supreme principle, or as 'corollaries' of it (also p. 22). These are probably the sort of phrases which lead people to think that they play a purely heuristic role in ethical thinking for Mill. As for the expression 'intermediate generalisation', Mill undoubtedly thinks that we should, and to some extent do, arrive at and improve our moral rules by such methods as observing that a certain type of action has had bad results of a social kind in such an overwhelming majority of cases that it ought to be banned. (But this is an over-simplification; see the note on p. 58 on how we ought to arrive at moral rules, and the pessimistic account of how we in fact arrive at them in *Liberty*, p. 69–70). But this account of the genesis of moral rules does not require us to interpret them as being anything but rules when once made. It really seems unnecessary to say much of the expression 'corollary'; Mill obviously cannot wish it to be taken literally; in fact it is hard to state the relation of moral rules to a justifying principle with exactitude and Mill, in a popular article in *Fraser,* did not try very hard to do so.

MORAL RULES AND THE ULTIMATE END

We have already been led in our examination of possible objections to proposition A to say something in defence of the view that Mill thought that a moral rule is shown to be correct by showing that the recognition of that rule promotes the ultimate end (proposition B). A little more may be added on this point, though it seems fairly obvious that if we are right in saying that the supreme principle is not to be evoked, in Mill's view, in the direct justification of particular right acts, it must thus come in in an indirect way in view of the importance that Mill attached to it. And it is hard to think what the indirect way is if not this. (i) On p. 3 Mill reproaches other moral philosophers with not giving a satisfactory account of moral rules in terms of a fundamental principle, though they have correctly placed moral rules as governing particular actions. It would be indeed the mark of an inconsistent philosopher if he did not try to repair the one serious omission which he ascribes to others. (ii) Mill ascribes to Kant (p. 4) the use of utilitarian arguments because, Mill alleges, he in fact supports the rules of morality by showing the evil consequences of not adopting them or adopting alternatives. Thus Mill is here regarding as distinctively utilitarian the justification or rejection of moral rules on the ground of consequences. He could hardly have wished to suggest that Kant would directly justify, even inadvertently, particular actions on such grounds. But it is perhaps not to the point to argue this matter more elaborately. If anyone has been convinced by what has gone before, he will not need much argument on this point; with others it is superfluous to make the attempt.

In What Fields are Moral Rules of Right and Wrong Applicable?

The applicability of moral rules is, says Mill, 'the characteristic difference which marks off, not justice, but morality in general, from the remaining provinces of Expediency and Worthiness' (p. 46). Mill says little or nothing in *Utilitarianism* about the boundary between morality and worthiness (surely it would be better to have said the boundary between right and wrong on the one hand and other forms of both moral and non-moral appraisal on the other?). It seems reasonable to suppose that he would have recognised that the use of moral rules must be confined to matters in which the kind of consequences is sufficiently invariable for there not to be too many exceptions. But this is a pragmatic limitation; Mill does have something to say about a limitation in principle in *Liberty* which I have crudely summarised in my proposition C—moral rules can be justifiably maintained in regard only to matters in which the general welfare is more than negligibly affected.

It is important to note that Mill in *Liberty* is concerned with freedom from moral sanctions as well as the sanctions of positive law. The distinction between self-regarding and other actions is regarded by him as relevant to moral as well as to political philosophy. The most noteworthy passage which bears on the scope of moral rules is on page 135. Here he mentions such things as encroachment on the rights of others as being 'fit objects of moral reprobation, and, in grave cases, of moral retribution and punishment'. But self-regarding faults (low tastes and the like) are 'not properly immoralities and to whatever pitch they are carried, do not constitute wickedness. . . . The term duty to oneself, when it means anything more than prudence, means self-respect or self-development'. Self-regarding faults render the culprit 'necessarily and properly a subject of distaste, or, in extreme cases, even of contempt', but this is in the sphere of worthiness not of right and wrong.

So much then for Mill's account of the logic of moral reasoning. It must be emphasized that no more has been attempted than a skeleton plan of Mill's answer, and that Mill puts the matter more richly and more subtly in his book. Even on the question of general interpretation more store must be laid on the effect of a continuous reading in the light of the skeleton plan than on the effect of the few leading quotations introduced in this paper. It is emphatically not the contention of this paper that Mill has given a finally correct account of these matters which is immune to all criticism; an attempt has been made only to give a sympathetic account without any criticism favourable or unfavourable. But I certainly do maintain that the current interpretations of Mill's *Utilitarianism* are so unsympathetic and so incorrect that the majority of criticisms which have in fact been based on them are irrelevant and worthless.

NOTES

1. *An Examination of the Deductive Logic of J. S. Mill* (1941).
2. *A Treatise on Induction and Probability* (1951), p. 164.
3. *Principia Ethica,* reprinted 1948, p. 106.
4. For one example of this interpretation of Mill and the first and more important objection, see Carritt, *The Theory of Morals,* Ch. IV.

· 2 ·

WHAT IS MILL'S PRINCIPLE OF UTILITY?

D.G. Brown

In a recent article[1] I gave reasons for attributing to Mill a restricted view of the demands of morality, according to which no conduct would be *prima facie* wrong unless it was harmful to others. This interpretation of Mill raises the problem of reconciling such a view of morality with the principle which Mill calls the Principle of Utility. I tried to show that a reconciliation was possible by invoking the reminder, for which we are indebted to Alan Ryan[2] and D. P. Dryer[3], that Mill conceived of the Principle of Utility as a very abstract principle, and said that it governed not just morality but the whole of the Art of Life. I concluded that, whatever the subject matter of Mill's Principle of Utility might be, it was not the rightness and wrongness of actions. But I pointed out that neither Ryan nor Dryer provided a satisfactory formulation of the principle, and that this was an enterprise of some difficulty. The purpose of this article is to establish what Mill's Principle of Utility actually is.

My conclusion is roughly that, in Mill, the Principle of Utility is the principle that happiness is the only thing desirable as an end. This will be old news to some readers of Mill. But historical accidents of the way Mill has been discussed give some occasion for being insistent about the matter. Those who have debated the status of Mill's 'proof' of utility have often arrived at such a formulation as mine, in terms of desirability, in order to state the proposition that Mill wished in some way to offer to us. But they have not generally been equally interested in Mill's view on the moral rightness and wrongness of actions. Nor have they generally said much about the role the Principle of Utility is supposed to have in determining rightness and wrongness. On the other hand, those who have been interested in criteria of moral right and wrong, and have engaged in attacking or revising classical utilitarianism, have commonly written as though they assumed Mill's Principle of Utility to state a criterion of rightness and wrongness. Nor have they generally raised the question whether such a principle appeared to be at stake in Mill's 'proof'. Perhaps for reasons such as these, it is rare to find a commentator of either predilection who undertakes at any point to give simply a statement of the Principle of Utility together with a reference to the text.

There are also some unavoidable hazards. I will argue that any attempt to identify Mill's supreme principle is subject to two kinds of indeterminacy in the principle, one kind relatively superficial, the other kind going deep. The first kind consists in a certain arbitrariness in selecting one particular formulation from among fifteen possible formulations which Mill seems committed to regarding as equivalent. The deeper indeterminacy reflects the incompleteness of Mill's account of practical reasoning. That theory assigns a special role to the Principle of Utility, a role which requires us to place an unusual interpretation on the wording of the principle. In consequence, even after choosing the formulation which says that happiness is the only thing desirable as an end, we are required to interpret these words in such a way that the principle will fulfill the demands of the theory. Since, as I will argue, it is problematic how and whether the principle can fill its role, it remains problematic what interpretation to place on Mill's formulation of it. It is therefore indeterminate in this respect also what Mill's Principle of Utility is.

1. FORMULATIONS IN *UTILITARIANISM*

It will be wise to deal first with the passage which has probably misled many of Mill's readers into thinking that the Principle of Utility simply undertakes to say what actions are right or wrong.

The second chapter of *Utilitarianism*[4] called 'What utilitarianism is', gets down to business with the following paragraph:

> The creed which accepts as the foundation of morals, Utility, or the Greatest Happiness Principle, holds that actions are right in proportion as they tend to promote happiness, wrong as they tend to produce the reverse of happiness. By happiness is intended pleasure, and the absence of pain; by unhappiness, pain, and the privation of pleasure. To give a clear view of the moral standard set up by the theory, much more requires to be said; in particular, what things it includes in the ideas of pain and pleasure; and to what extent this is left an open question. But these supplementary explanations do not affect the theory of life on which this theory of morality is grounded—namely, that pleasure, and freedom from pain, are the only things desirable as ends; and that all desirable

things (which are as numerous in the utilitarian as in any other scheme) are desirable either for the pleasure inherent in themselves, or as means to the promotion of pleasure and the prevention of pain.[5]

I was convinced myself for many years that the first sentence of this passage constituted the primary official statement of the Principle of Utility. Mill has already explicitly identified the Principle of Utility with the Greatest Happiness Principle.[6] It is natural to suppose that here Mill identifies both of these with the doctrine that actions are right or wrong in proportion as they tend to promote happiness or the reverse, and this in turn with what he calls 'this theory of morality'. In addition, the chapter opens by speaking of 'those who stand up for utility as the test of right or wrong'.

We must concede that one of the main things, at least, that the essay sets out to do is to give a criterion or test of right and wrong. Further, we have in this passage the official announcement, however obscurely put, of the essay's main doctrine on this question. This doctrine is said, quite naturally, to be a moral theory which sets up a moral standard.

But it does not follow that the Principle of Utility, of utilitarianism, is identical with this moral doctrine. What Mill says is that his creed holds this doctrine. I take this, less oddly put, to be the assertion that a person whose creed this is holds this moral doctrine, where the creed itself is or includes the acceptance of Utility as the foundation of morality. Mill's language in presenting the moral doctrine allows us with equal propriety to interpret him either as stating his ultimate principle or as saying what application a holder of it will make to the particular subject of morality. The passage is therefore consistent with the suggestion that the Principle of Utility is the principle governing all appraisal of action. If the principle supplies the foundation of prudence, aesthetics, and morality alike, then it can be said in the last of these three roles to ground, or to imply, or to issue in, the given theory of morality.

Once we grasp this possibility, we can see what to do with the rest of the passage. In what sense is Utility the foundation of morals? In the sense which is at once explained, namely that the theory of morality is grounded on a theory of life; and the Principle of Utility is the theory of life. But that theory is actually stated. So we learn from this passage after all what the Principle of Utility is. It is the principle that pleasure and freedom from pain are the only things desirable as ends.

It is satisfying to extract a true view of the Principle of Utility from the paragraph which is so often taken to support a false view. But it remains to show that this interpretation stands up throughout the essay. On the whole it stands up well. Unfortunately we must also reckon with Mill's habit of interchanging doctrines he regards as equivalent, without deciding whether he has merely restated a position or has derived a consequence from it. I think that Mill, without leaving us doubtful whether or not he holds a given view, often renders it indeterminate just which view bears a particular name or answers to a particular description.

A second official-looking formulation occurs in this same chapter on what utilitarianism is:

> According to the Greatest Happiness Principle, as above explained, the ultimate end, with reference to and for the sake of which all other things are desirable (whether we are considering our own good or that of other people) is an existence exempt as far as possible from pain, and as rich as possible in enjoyments, both in point of quantity and quality. . . . This, being, according to the utilitarian opinion, the end of human action, is necessarily also the standard of morality. . . .[7]

This passage does, with a qualification, confirm my interpretation. The qualification concerns the parenthesis about self and others; my consideration of it must wait for section 3. But at least this passage makes the Principle of Utility a proposition about the ultimate end for the sake of which all other things are desirable. The version I have already offered is a proposition about what things are desirable as ends. It is evident that Mill regards the corresponding phrases as interchangeable. To say of something that it is the only thing desirable as an end is to say of it that it is the ultimate end for the sake of which all other things are desirable. Similarly, he regards the complicated description of a kind of existence given in this passage as no more than an expanded form of reference to 'pleasure, and freedom from pain'.

In a similar way we can see that when Mill comes, in the famous chapter on the sort of proof of which the Principle of Utility is susceptible, to set out the proposition to be recommended, he intends to state a third version interchangeable with the two we have noticed. He says: 'The utilitarian doctrine is, that happiness is desirable, and the only thing desirable, as an end'.[8] But we already have from the second chapter that 'By happiness is intended pleasure, and the absence of pain'.[9]

Let us complete our survey of alternative versions of the predicate of the principle. Those already given establish the relevance of the two extended discussions, in Chapter I and in Chapter IV, of the justification of action by appeal to ends. In these passages we can observe the interchanging of 'ultimate ends' and 'things which are in themselves good' and 'good . . . as an end;'[10] and again of 'ultimate end' with 'an end of conduct', 'desirable as an end', 'a good', and 'intrinsically a good.'[11] In addition to these introductions of the notion of a good, the opening paragraph of the essay says that the question concerning the *summum bonum* is the same as that concerning the foundation of morality. But since the idea of the highest or supreme good seems more complex than those of a thing good in itself, or an ultimate or intrinsic good, and since the idea is not invoked except in this historical reference, we can ignore it. We can also discount apparently careless uses of 'an end' and 'a good' in contexts which require 'an ultimate end' and 'a thing good in itself'. Boiling down the remainder to singular predicative expressions without specifications of uniqueness, we arrive finally at the following list of expressions which Mill seems prepared to use indifferently in formulating the Principle of Utility:

> desirable as an end
> ultimate end of action
> good as an end
> in itself good
> intrinsically a good

A corresponding list for the subject term of the principle need not for any practical purpose extend beyond the formulations we have:

> pleasure and freedom from pain
> an existence exempt as far as possible from pain, and as rich as possible in
>   enjoyment, both in point of quantity and quality
> happiness

By taking something referred to in the second list, and saying of it, with appropriate adjustments, that it is the only thing which answers to some description from the first list, we can construct fifteen versions of the Principle of Utility. I think it is clear that Mill would regard these fifteen versions as equivalent.

To select the best formulation, we need to weigh both text and argument. Occurrence in the main announcements, and aptness for a place in Mill's background theory of practical reasoning, both seem to me to favour the same choice. Reasons of the latter kind, drawn from the background theory, will have to wait for the next two sections. But in the meantime I adopt the following version:

> *The Principle of Utility:* Happiness is the only thing desirable as an end.

The difficulty of making this choice, and of abandoning the alternatives to it, measures the superficial dimension of the indeterminacy which

I claim to infect the Principle of Utility. As we go on now to consider some points about practical reasoning, we will encounter the problem about self and others which I alluded to above. That problem gives rise to doubt whether any or all of the fifteen versions could be adequate to express the whole of the Principle of Utility and sets a more serious limit to the determinacy with which we can identify it.

2. The General Theory of Practical Reason

Chapters I and IV of *Utilitarianism* are both devoted to questions about the foundation or final justification of practical principles. They are preoccupied with the same subject as the final chapter of the *System of logic*, 'Of the logic of practice, or art; including morality and policy'. That chapter in turn, which refers to an 'ultimate principle of Teleology', acquired in later editions a footnote referring us to *Utilitarianism* for 'an express discussion and vindication of this principle'.[12] Mill's ethical writing is difficult to follow because it constantly draws upon his abstract theory of practical reasoning, and because it treats that idiosyncratic and controversial theory as perfectly obvious. Mill appears to assume that no-one will question it, or will object to relying on it in the identification and derivation of practical principles. It would be too large an undertaking to state and explore the theory in its own right. But unless we look at some features of it we will not be able to describe the role of the Principle of Utility, and this we need to do. For it is a particular role which Mill wants his principle to fill (and which I doubt that any principle could fill) that places his formulations under strain, and accounts for the second kind of indeterminacy in what the Principle of Utility is. In this section I will look at the general theory, and in the next, at the implications for the Principle of Utility.

Mill is explicit that he offers a single general account of practical reasoning, and applies it to morality as a special case. This general account is his account of art as opposed to science. The dichotomy between science and art he presents with extreme simplicity, indeed crudity, in both the essay 'On the definition of political economy . . .'[13] and the *Logic*. In the *Logic* he introduces morality as

> an enquiry the results of which do not express themselves in the indicative, but in the imperative mood, or in periphrases equivalent to it; what is called the knowledge of duties; practical ethics, or morality.
>
> Now, the imperative mood is the characteristic of art, as distinguished from science. Whatever speaks in rules, or precepts, not in asser-

tions respecting matters of fact, is art: and ethics, or morality, is properly a portion of the art corresponding to the sciences of human nature and society.

The method, therefore, of Ethics, can be no other than that of Art, or Practice, in general. . . .[14]

Having arrived at the notion of the Art of Life, to which all other arts are subordinate, since its principles determine the desirability of the special aim of any particular art, he shows what significance he assigns to this master art by the following comment:

Every art is thus a joint result of laws of nature disclosed by science, and of the general principles of what has been called Teleology, or the Doctrine of Ends; which, borrowing the language of the German metaphysicians, may also be termed, not improperly, the principles of Practical Reason.[15]

I am not aware that Mill anywhere shows doubt whether principles can be exclusively, exhaustively, and neatly divided into two logical types. He shows some doubt, as well he might, about the appropriateness of the indicative-imperative criterion. Where the account in 'On the definition of political economy . . .'[16] says roundly 'The language of art is, Do this; Avoid that', the *Logic* account (above) allows *periphrases* of the imperative mood, and these turn out to include saying that something is 'desirable', and that it 'ought to be' or 'should be'.[17] He cannot avoid shipwreck on the hard fact that these important examples of imperatives are actually indicatives; his appeal to a grammatical criterion will not bear examination. But his confidence in the dichotomy, and in the general lines of his account of art, seems unshaken.

Given that Mill's account of morality is an application of his account of art, the next point to grasp is that his account of art, as the last quotation implies, is thoroughly teleological. He not only starts with the concept of an end, he tries in effect to forestall the possibility of an alternative analysis. That is to say, he conceives of art, which in his terms includes the whole of practice and of the exercise of practical reason, as a matter of having an end and seeking the means to achieve that end. This conception, however, is not offered as an alternative to an analysis of art in terms of rules, precepts, imperatives, and the like; it does not treat rule-following, and doing the right thing, as rival conceptions to that of pursuing an end. The teleological conception rather swallows them whole and incorporates them in its notion of the rational pursuit of an end. This is the point Mill is making with particular application to ethics, in the well-known passage in the second paragraph of *Utilitarianism:*

> All action is for the sake of some end, and rules of action, it seems natural to suppose, must take their whole character and colour from the end to which they are subservient. When we engage in a pursuit, a clear and precise conception of what we are pursuing would seem to be the first thing we need, instead of the last we are to look forward to. A test of right and wrong must be the means, one would think, of ascertaining what is right or wrong, and not a consequence of having already ascertained it.

This passage is remarkable for presupposing the same kind of view as it asserts. The first sentence presupposes that rules of action are subservient to an end, and the transition of thought from the second to the third presupposes that a test of right and wrong is provided by a conception of what we are pursuing. The obsessive parentheses of the form 'one would think', which might indicate qualification or doubt, seem better diagnosed as the impatience of a writer who finds a teleological theory of practical reason utterly truistic.

3. Self and Others

Let us now consider the implications of Mill's general theory of practical reasoning for his conception of the Principle of Utility. Mill regards the principles of practical reasoning as constituting Teleology, or the Doctrine of Ends, and the role to which he assigns the Principle of Utility is that of the supreme principle of Teleology. The art of life has a single ultimate end, and the desirability of all other ends is to be determined by their subservience to it. The principle which sets out this end therefore has an extraordinary burden to bear. To appreciate the problem of finding any principle which could fill this role, let us look at possible applications of an analysis of practical reasoning in terms of ends and means, moving from the least to the most ambitious applications that might be attempted.

The most straightforward case is the satisfaction of a particular desire. The end is given by whatever the desire happens to be for, and deliberation is concerned with the means of achieving it. To add one dimension of complexity, we can consider purely technical reasoning, in the sense of the hypothetical application of the same schema, taking the end as a supposition, and reaching conclusions about what one will have reason to do if one has that end. From this level it is a considerable step to the individual's pursuit of his own over-all, long-run interest. But those at least who think in terms of the maximization of utility are ready with some account of an end which can plausibly be offered as the single end being pursued. Even though competing desires, over a period of time, have somehow to be harmonized, a quantitative conception of satisfaction seems to make intelligible the individual's pursuit of his own happiness as an end.

Furthermore, we can get beyond the individual's pursuit of happiness to a reasonable account of social action directed to shared ends. Joint deliberation, as in a representative assembly, on the legislation needed to secure public order, can be analysed quite directly by the same schema as an individual's pursuit of an end he desires. As long as we abstract from the problems of ultimate divergence among the values of different individuals, the analysis may be simpler than that of an individual's pursuit of his interest.

Morality, however, on many philosophical conceptions of it, presents special difficulty for a means-end analysis. On many conceptions, the principles and rules of morality are categorical in the sense of having an authority independent of what the agent desires; and they generate considerations capable of overriding practical reasons of any other kind. In particular, morality attaches importance impartially to the interests of all concerned, and commits the rational agent to practical judgments which potentially may require the sacrifice of his own interest. Of these points, the categorical status of moral considerations is perhaps the most controversial, and Mill can hardly accept it. But even Mill is Kantian enough to believe that morality and prudence may conflict and to regard moral reasons as overriding prudential reasons. He explicitly admits the possibility, in the imperfect state of the world, that a person 'can best serve the happiness of others by the absolute sacrifice of his own', an exhorts utilitarians that they should 'never cease to claim the morality of self-devotion as a possession which belongs by as good a right to them, as either to the Stoic or the Transcendentalist. The utilitarian morality does recognise in human beings the power of sacrificing their own greatest good for the good of others'.[18] The problem for any means-end analysis of practical reasoning is to specify the end to which moral principles are subservient, and to give an account of the relation between that end and the agent's own happiness which will accommodate the rationality of his sacrificing his own interest. Mill has also made an explicit commitment to exhibit both of these ends as subservient to a single end.

It is interesting that when Sidgwick set out to sift Mill's ethics the main problem he uncovered, and failed to solve, was the relation between interest and duty. In the preface to the Sixth Edition of *Methods of Ethics*,[19] he tells how he was led under Butler's influence to accept a "Dualism of the Practical Reason,"[20] and in the concluding section of the book itself, he is still left in the position that, unless we can prove or postulate a connection of virtue and self-interest, we are forced 'to admit an ultimate and fundamental contradiction in our apparent intuitions of what is Reasonable in conduct . . .'.[21] The response of Sidgwick's I think shows a better grasp of Mill's problem than of Mill's attempt at solution, but it attests to the difficulty of what Mill needs to do.

It might seem natural for Mill to take an essentially Humean position. On such a view the end of moral action is given by the fundamental moral sentiment, which we could call, in Hume's phrase,[22] 'a feeling for the happiness of mankind, and a resentment of their misery'. If this sentiment is thought of as simply another desire, the account of morality as the pursuit of an end is actually simpler than the account of prudence, which must deal with conflicts among a variety of desires. In a sense, therefore, a Humean sentiment theory can deal with moral reasoning by regressing to a level of analysis adequate for the satisfaction of simple desires. But there is a cost to be paid, which falls on the analysis of moral reasons. Where prudential and moral considerations do conflict, the moral ones are entered along with those arising from any other particular desire into the inclusive weighing which constitutes prudential reasoning, and by hypothesis they are there sometimes outweighed. Moral conduct then becomes actually irrational. It becomes an amiable lapse from the behaviour of the perfectly rational agent, who will remain true to his own interest. A version of this conclusion is implicit in Hume's own position, but he is protected from embarrassment by his systematic denial that any intelligible question can arise about the rationality of conduct.

Mill evidently wants to move in the opposite direction, and to save the rationality of both prudence an morality by dissolving both in a higher, more abstractly conceived pursuit of an end. Plato is to swallow both Hume and Kant whole. The rationality of Practice, or Art, requires a single ultimate end. In the face of the diverse desires of the individual, and of the diversity of individuals, practical reason requires, of course, the subordination of particular desires to interest; but it also requires the subordination of the agent's interest, and of his concern for the interests of others, to a single more inclusive pursuit.

The principle by which Mill seeks to define this pursuit, namely the Principle of Utility, is stated as the principle that happiness is the only thing desirable as an end. On the face of it, reading these words in the most straightforward way, the principle seems to embody a plausible 'utilitarian' conception of the good life. It sounds like a theory of individual interest, appropriately addressed to an agent considering conduct from his own point of view. As a result it sounds in principle inadequate to adjudicate the conflict of interest and duty. The trick is turned by the parenthetical but momentous insertion of the words 'whether we are considering our own good or that of others'.

How are we to make sense of the claim of indifference, or interchangeability, implied in this phrase? What if our own good, and that of others, should diverge? Of course, we could fall back on interpreting the parenthesis in the following way. When considering one's own good, one's own pleasure and the absence of pain for oneself are the only things to be taken as ultimate ends; and when considering the good of others, their pleasure and the absence of pain for them are the only things to be taken as ultimate ends. On this reading, the second part would be a mere application of the first, since the first part applies to anyone's good. But then the question would be, how does the agent come to be considering the good of others, and when he sees wherein it lies, what weight should he attach to that consideration in deciding how to act? As we have seen, Mill could not be saying that the agent will consider the good of others, perhaps at the cost of his rationality, when he happens to be moved by moral sentiment, and that when so moved he will be well advised to promote their pleasure and the absence of their pain. The Principle of Utility is not a piece of technical advice, telling us how to pursue the good of others (namely, by promoting their pleasure and so on) if we happen to think that desirable. The principle tells us that that is desirable, in itself, just as our own happiness is desirable, in itself; and it requires us impartially to consider the good of all.

It is tempting then to say that for Mill the Principle of Utility is a moral principle after all, disguised by its language as a principle about the good for any individual. It actually establishes an end of action which entails impartial regard for the pleasures and pains of all, and whose application may well cancel the pursuit of one's own interest, the pursuit of any aesthetic ideal, and any other pursuit whatever. If it differs from a straight announcement, in the best intuitionist or Kantian style, of a single duty of benevolence, it seems to do so only through being couched in the blandly reasonable terms, Platonic or Aristotelian, of what is or is not desirable in itself. On this interpretation, the determination of the agent's interest provides only one body of data to be fed into the general summation of desirabilities required by the principle, whose whole business is the final moral adjudication of action, all things considered.

But this is not what Mill says. He says that this same Principle of Utility governs prudence. When the agent is considering his own interest, it is the Principle of Utility in accordance with which he is promoting his own happiness, meaning pleasure and the absence of pain. Then, when the agent considers his moral situation, the same principle continues to direct him to promote happiness, only the incidence of pleasure and pain is more widely surveyed, so as to take in the pleasures and pains of others on exactly the same terms. The transition, in this sense, from self to others is smoothed out to the point of invisibility, by the idea that pleasure and the absence of pain, regardless of whose, are in themselves simply desirable, and therefore ends of (anyone's) rational action.

The abstractness of this conception evoked a protest from one of Mill's earliest and most acute critics, John Grote.

> The utilitarian half assumption (I call it *half* assumption, because the language of utilitarians about it seems sometimes studiously confused) is that the desire of happiness in *general,* the charmingness of the idea, independent of the thought of the enjoyment of it, is the starting-point, and then from this we proceed, for enjoyment, to assign so much to ourselves, so much to others.[23]

If I follow Grote's argument in the surrounding passages, he claims at least that this is not a realistic analysis of the structure of any familiar prudential or moral reasoning. Further, I take him to claim that if we were to set out a pure principle about the desirability of happiness as the beginning of a reconstruction of moral reasoning, the principle would be acceptable enough but would say nothing on all the essential questions of what distribution of happiness is morally called for. He even speaks of such a doctrine as 'the utilitarianism which is common to all moral philosophy',[24] and he calls it a doctrine about the end of all reasonable action. But he insists that the doctrine is quite indeterminate as to whose happiness morality requires us to promote. Mill's stipulation of impartiality is an independent doctrine, implausible in itself but adopted as the most colourless principle which will yield definite moral conclusions at all.

In the light of such a criticism, we can set out a dilemma which confronts Mill on our interpretation of his formulations of the Principle of Utility. Being completely inclusive, the principle must transcend the distinction between specifically moral injunctions and specifically prudential injunctions. Yet at the same time it must, in conjunction with empirical premises alone, have enough content to determine all the subordinate ends of action and thereby to determine both what is in the agent's interest and what moral demands arise from the interests of others. The demand for that inclusiveness to which Mill is committed might be met by an interpretation, for example, which said merely that any reason for any action must somehow make some reference to the promotion of happiness for someone. The demand for content might be met by an interpretation which reverted to desirability from the agent's point of view or by one which went on to specify the moral weighing of the claims of individuals. But it is difficult to see how both demands can be met at once. But until we see how Mill thought they could be, it is difficult to decide what Mill meant. This is what I referred to as the deeper source of indeterminacy in what the Principle of Utility is.

The difficulties I have raised fall short of proving that Mill's enterprise cannot succeed. One way to carry the investigation further, if there were room in this article to do so, would be to invoke the analysis offered by Thomas Nagel in *The possibility of altruism*.[25] In the terms which Nagel defines there,[26] I think it is natural and proper to take the principle that happiness is the only thing desirable as an end as being a *subjective* principle. For it implies only, in my view, that a particular person, P, will have certain reasons for action if the action conduces to the happiness of P. It does not seem to me by itself to generate the moral demands which the happiness of P no doubt can lay upon the conduct of other agents. But if Nagel could convince me, as the argument of his book fails to do, that in order for this principle to give P acceptable prudential reasons it must rest on an *objective* principle, and that ultimately all good reasons for action must rest on objective principles, then I think he would have gone a long way toward vindicating Mill. That each person's happiness is a good to that person would have been shown to imply that the general happiness was a good to each person. But I continue to find such conclusions not merely unsupported but also unclear.

It remains only to comment that the discussion of these two sections confirms my choice among the fifteen versions of Mill's principle, and in particular supports 'happiness' over 'pleasure and the absence of pain' or the longer form of the latter. If Mill were to become convinced that happiness was quite distinct from pleasure and the absence of pain, which ought he to regard as belonging to the essence of his principle? This would be necessarily, in part, a question of the relative merits of the doctrines thus forced into distinction, and in part a question of the propriety of giving the name 'Principle of Utility' to a doctrine he preferred or to a doctrine he rejected. I believe that Mill's essential concern was with the rationality of prudential reasoning and its relation to the rationality of moral reasoning. He took the hedonistic theory he inherited, which was one attempt at a theory of practical reasoning, and developed it. In fact he took it to the brink of abandoning all reference to pleasure and pain in favour of a theory of informed preference and its relation to desirability as an end. His drift toward something like modern decision theory was strong, and I think his analysis of morality pivots on the general conception of the individual's rational pursuit of his interest rather than on a hedonistic theory of that pursuit. Consequently, if we formulate the Principle of Utility in terms of happiness, however happiness is to be conceived, we secure to the principle that structurally fundamental role in Mill's theory which he intended it to have.

To sum up: It seems to me that the Principle of Utility should certainly be formulated as the principle that happiness is the only thing desirable as an end. The problem is that Mill evidently conceives *desirability as an end* in such a way that it generates reasons for action for all agents at once who can promote the end. Until this conception is clear, it is not clear what the Principle of Utility is.*

References

Brown, D. G., 'Mill on liberty and morality', *Philosophical review* LXXXI (1972), 133–158.

Dryer, D. P., 'Mill's utilitarianism', an introductory essay in: John Stuart Mill, *Essays on ethics, religion and society,* ed. J. M. Robson, *Collected works of John Stuart Mill,* Vol. X, Toronto, University of Toronto Press, 1969.

Grote, John, *An examination of the utilitarian philosophy,* ed. J. B. Mayor, Cambridge, Deighton Bell and Co., 1870.

Hume, David, *An enquiry concerning the principles of morals,* London, 1751.

Mill, J. S., 'On the definition of political economy; and on the method of philosophical investigation in that science': 1836. Reprinted in *Essays on some unsettled questions of political economy,* 1844, as Essay V, with altered title. Page references to: *Essays on economics and society,* ed. J. M. Robson, *Collected works of John Stuart Mill,* Vol. IV, Toronto, University of Toronto Press, 1967.

Mill, J. S., *A system of logic ratiocinative and inductive:* First edition 1843. Page references to: Eighth edition, in two volumes, London, Longmans, Green, Reader, and Dyer, 1872.

Mill, J. S. *Utilitarianism:* 1861. Page references are double. The first is to: *Essays on ethics, religion and society,* ed. J. M. Robson, *Collected works of John Stuart Mill,* Vol. X, Toronto, University of Toronto Press, 1969. The second is to the Everyman edition: J. S. Mill, *Utilitarianism, Liberty and Representative government,* London, Everyman, 1910.

Nagel, Thomas, *The possibility of altruism,* Oxford, Clarendon Press, 1970.

Ryan, Alan, 'John Stuart Mill's art of living', *The Listener,* 21 October, 1965, 620–622.

Ryan, Alan, *John Stuart Mill,* New York, Pantheon, 1970.

Sidgwick, Henry, *The methods of ethics,* Sixth Edition, London, Macmillan, 1901. (First Edition 1874).

NOTES

★ I am grateful for criticisms of an earlier draft to J. Dybikowski and Elbridge Rand. I also profited from unpublished work of Alister Browne, especially with respect to the relations among Mill's formulations.

1. D. G. Brown, "Mill on liberty and morality," *Philosophical review* LXXXI (1972), 133–158.

2. Alan Ryan, "John Stuart Mill's art of living," *The Listener,* 21 October, 1965, 620–622. Alan Ryan, *John Stuart Mill* (New York: Pantheon, 1970).

3. D. P. Dryer, "Mill's utilitarianism," an introductory essay in John Stuart Mill, *Essays on ethics, religion and society,* edited by J. M. Robson, *Collected works of John Stuart Mill,* Vol. X (Toronto: University of Toronto Press, 1969).

4. J. S. Mill, *Utiliatarianism* (1861). Page references are double. The first is to: *Essays on ethics, religion and society,* edited by J. M. Robson, *Collected works of John Stuart Mill,* Vol. X (Toronto: University of Toronto Press, 1969). The second is to the Everyman edition: J. S. Mill, *Utilitarianism, Liberty and Representative government* (London: Everyman, 1910).

5. Mill (1861), p. 210; p. 6.

6. Mill (1861), p. 207; p. 3.

7. Mill (1861), p. 214; p. 11.

8. Mill (1861), p. 234; p. 32.

9. Mill (1861), p. 210; p. 6.

10. Mill (1861), p. 207–208; p. 4.

11. Mill (1861), pp. 234, 237, 239; pp. 32–33, 36, 38.

12. J. S. Mill, *A system of logic ratiocinative and inductive:* First edition 1843. Page references to: Eighth edition, in two volumes (London: Longmans, Green, Reader, and Dyer, 1872). See section VI, XII, 7.

13. J. S. Mill, "On the definition of political economy; and on the method of philosophical investigation in that science": 1836, p. 312. Reprinted in *Essays on some unsettled questions of political economy,* 1844, as Essay V, with altered title. Page references are to *Essays on economics and society,* edited by J. M. Robson, *Collected works of John Stuart Mill,* Vol. IV (Toronto: University of Toronto Press, 1967).

14. Mill (1843), VI, XII, 1.

15. Mill (1843), VI, XII, 6.

16. Mill (1836), p. 312.

17. Mill (1843), VI, XII, 6.

18. Mill (1861), pp. 217–218; p. 15.

19. Henry Sidgwick, *The methods of ethics,* Sixth Edition (London: Macmillan, 1901 [First edition 1874]), pp. xvi, xviii, xix.

20. Sidgwick, p. xix.

21. Sidgwick, p. 506.

22. David Hume, *An enquiry concerning the principles of morals* (London, 1751), App. 1, third paragraph.

23. John Grote, *An examination of the utilitarian philosophy,* edited by J. B. Mayor (Cambridge: Deighton Bell and Co., 1870), p. 98.

24. Grote, pp. 79–84, 93.

25. Thomas Nagel, *The possibility of altruism* (Oxford: Clarendon Press, 1970).

26. Nagel, p. 90ff.

· 3 ·

MILL'S ACT-UTILITARIANISM

D. G. Brown

Several commentators have been assembling the materials to show that Mill's utilitarianism, however exactly it should be stated, is at any rate of the "act-" kind rather than the "rule-" kind. But we now have available a statement by Mill himself which can suitably close this note and I hope the whole controversy.*

The textual claims put forward by Urmson,[1] tending to show that Mill was in some sense a rule-utilitarian, have been answered in various places, for example by Mandelbaum.[2] Perhaps the evidence on Urmson's side has not been thoroughly sifted, but I shall not try to complete the task of showing how slight that evidence is. In any case, the more decisive considerations so far presented come from Mill's positive account of the status of moral rules or principles. Mandelbaum pointed out[3] that the *Logic* account of moral reasoning should govern the interpretation of *Utilitarianism*. John M. Baker[4] has set out the most important relevant parts of that account in an elegant short note. The gist of Baker's interpretation is that moral rules (or "principles", "maxims", "laws", and so on), like other precepts of art, rest on middle principles or intermediate generalizations of science, in this case on casual laws from those parts of the deductive sciences of human nature and society which deal with the consequences of actions for happiness. Accordingly, to find Mill's views on how we should form and modify moral precepts, what we should do about conflicts among them, and how we should regard their relevance to particular actions, we can consult the substantial discussion of such questions in his account of art or practice in general. One satisfying feature of the interpretation arrived at in this way is that it rejects both the alternatives usually offered to Mill. It quite excludes the idea that Mill regarded moral rules as either "practice rules" in the sense of Rawls[5] or "instrumental rules in force" in the sense of Diggs.[6] On the other hand, it shows that it is thoroughly misleading to say that he regarded moral rules as merely "rules of thumb".

25

Baker's account enables us to meet the main challenge for an act–utilitarian reading of Mill, which is to explain why, in the assessment of actions as right or wrong, Mill so continually assigns such importance to the question of an action's conformity to secondary principles or moral rules. The account shares with a "rule-of-thumb" interpretation the basic claim that reference to secondary principles is relevant because of their bearing on the consequences of the particular act. But it has the advantage of invoking Mill's high estimate of the scientific status of secondary principles. In particular Mill is entitled to argue that the tendency of a particular act literally is a causal tendency, statable in an empirical law, but easily masked by conflicting tendencies. It becomes especially relevant to consider the consequences of people's generally doing the same, but the relevance of this is determined not by moral principle but by the conditions for establishing causal judgments.

This much we might have arrived at on the basis of evidence long familiar. For example, in "Dr. Whewell on Moral Philosophy" Mill writes:

> If the effect of a "solitary act upon the whole scheme of human action and habit" is small, the addition which the accompanying pleasure makes to the general mass of human happiness is small likewise. So small, in the great majority of cases, are both, that we have no scales to weigh them against each other, taken singly. We must look at them multiplied, and in large masses. The portion of the tendencies of an action which belong to it not individually, but as a violation of a general rule, are as certain and as calculable as any other consequences; only they must be examined not in the individual case, but in classes of cases.[7]

In the illustrations which follow these remarks, Mill seems not to have achieved the full clarity of the position of, say, Lyons,[8] and shows some tendency to slide from a pure causal argument against the breach of a rule towards an argument making essential use of fairness. In my view this casts only a light shadow of doubt over the claim that consistently and throughout his life Mill's official position was that the rightness and wrongness of an action depended on the consequences of the particular action.

To dispel such shadows we have needed a more direct and unequivocal statement from Mill than anyone has yet seemed able to find. Hence the value of Mill's letter of April 14 1872 to John Venn, published apparently for the first time in the *Later Letters*.[9] I think the following two sentences from the letter entitle Mill to the last word on the subject.

> I agree with you that the right way of testing actions by their consequences, is to test them by the natural consequences of the particular

action, and not by those which would follow if every one did the same. But, for the most part, the consideration of what would happen if every one did the same, is the only means we have of discovering the tendency of the act in the particular case.

REFERENCES

Baker, John M., "*Utilitarianism* and Secondary Principles", *Philosophical Quarterly*, 21 (1971), 69–71.

Diggs, B. J., "Rules and Utilitarianism", *American Philosophical Quarterly*, 1 (1964), 32–44.

Lyons, David, *Forms and Limits of Utilitarianism* (Oxford, 1965).

Mandelbaum, Maurice, "Two Moot Issues in Mill's *Utilitarianism*", in J. B. Schneewind, ed., *Mill: A collection of critical essays* (New York, 1968).

Mill, John Stuart, "Dr. Whewell on Moral Philosophy", *Westminster Review*, 1852. Page references to *Essays on Ethics, Religion and Society*, ed. J. M. Robson, *Collected Works of John Stuart Mill*, Vol. X (Toronto, 1969).

Mill, John Stuart, *Later Letters of John Stuart Mill 1849–1873*, ed. Francis E. Mineka and Dwight N. Lindley, Vol. IV, *Collected Works*, Vol. XVII (Toronto, 1972).

Rawls, John, "Two Concepts of Rules", *Philosophical Review*, 64 (1955), 3–32.

Urmson, J. O., "The Interpretation of the Moral Philosophy of J. S. Mill", *Philosophical Quarterly* 3 (1953), 33–9.

NOTES

* I am grateful for criticisms of the first draft of this note by Jonathan Bennett and R. I. Sikora.

1. J. O. Urmson, "The Interpretation of the Moral Philosophy of J. S. Mill," *Philosophical Quarterly*, 3 (1953), 33–39.

2. Maurice Mandelbaum, "Two Moot Issues in Mill's *Utilitarianism*," in J. B. Schneewind, ed., *Mill: A collection of critical essays* (New York, 1968).

3. Ibid., pp. 214–221.

4. John M. Baker, "*Utilitarianism* and Secondary Principles," *Philosophical Quarterly*, 21 (1971), 69–71.

5. John Rawls, "Two Concepts of Rules," *Philosophical Review*, 64 (1955), 3–32.

6. B. J. Diggs, "Rules and Utilitarianism," *American Philosophical Quarterly* 1 (1964), 32–44. Citation from Section 1.0; see section 2.0.

7. John Stuart Mill, "Dr. Whewell on Moral Philosophy," *Westminster Review,* 1852. Page references to *Essays on Ethics, Religion and Society,* edited by J. M. Robson, *Collected Works of John Stuart Mill,* Vol. X (Toronto, 1969), p. 181.

8. David Lyons, *Forms and Limits of Utilitarianism* (Oxford, 1965).

9. John Stuart Mill, *Later Letters of John Stuart Mill 1849–1873,* edited by Francis E. Mineka and Dwight N. Lindley, Vol. IV, *Collected Works,* Vol. XVII (Toronto, 1972) Letters 1717A, p. 1881.

· 4 ·

HUMAN RIGHTS AND THE GENERAL WELFARE

David Lyons

Our Constitution tells us that it aims "to form a more perfect union, establish justice, insure domestic tranquility, provide for the common defense, promote the general welfare, and secure the blessings of liberty to ourselves and our posterity." But these grand words must to some extent be discounted. Because of the "three-fifths rule,"[1] which tacitly condoned human slavery, for example, the original Constitution fell short of promising liberty and justice for *all*. At best, the document seems to represent a compromise. But with what? Consider the other aims mentioned: a more perfect union, domestic tranquility, the common defense—these might easily be viewed as either means to, or else included under an enlarged conception of, the general welfare, and it might be thought that this last-mentioned standard is what the Constitution was truly designed to serve—the general welfare, at the expense, if necessary, of those "inalienable rights" and that universal equality which the Declaration of Independence had earlier maintained governments are supposed to serve. At least in that early, critical period of the republic, it might have been argued that the interests of the nation as a whole could be served only through sacrificing the interests of some, even if those interests—in life, liberty, and the pursuit of happiness—amount to basic rights. The Bill of Rights, after all, had to be added to the original document to secure some of the rights of concern to the drafters of the Declaration of Independence. The general idea behind this interpretation cannot lightly be dismissed; at any rate, critics of utilitarianism have often objected that the general welfare standard condones immoral inequalities, injustice, and exploitation, because the interests of a community as a whole might sometimes most efficiently be served by benefiting some individuals at the expense of others. One might be tempted, therefore, to identify the Declaration of Independence with the doctrine of human rights and the Constitution with a commitment to the general

29

welfare, and then conceive of the differences between these documents as transcending their distinct functions and representing a fundamental conflict between commitment to the general welfare and the principles of rights and justice.

These issues need examination now, not just because this nation's Bicentennial obliges us to acknowledge its original ideologies. Thanks to a convergence of political and philosophical developments—including movements to secure equal rights at home and a less barbaric policy abroad, and the somewhat connected resuscitation of political and legal theory—substantive questions of public policy are being discussed more fully today than they have been for many years. Nevertheless, the philosophical attitudes expressed sometimes threaten to become, in their way, just as trite and unreflective as the average politician's Bicentennial claptrap. It is very widely assumed that the general welfare standard, or more specifically utilitarianism, is essentially defective; but the grounds on which this conclusion is reached are often so slender as to make it seem like dogma, not a proper philosophic judgment. Our professional obligations make it incumbent on us, I believe, to challenge such dogmas.

I wish to explore the connections between human rights and the general welfare (where I assume that commitment to the general welfare standard does not entail commitment to full-blown utilitarianism, which regards all other standards as either derivative or else invalid). These matters were not pursued very deeply in the eighteenth century, so my historical references, indeed the basis for my suggestions on behalf of the general welfare, go back only half way, to John Stuart Mill (who was, fittingly, a champion of rights and liberty as well as of the general welfare). Mill's contributions to this area have been neglected and so, I believe, somewhat misunderstood. I hope to throw some light on Mill while seeking a better grasp upon the principles that our republic in its infancy endorsed.

Rights as well as justice have been problems for utilitarians. Aside from Mill, only Bentham gave much thought to rights, and Bentham thought enforcement was essential. He could conceive of rights within an institution but not of rights one might invoke when designing or criticizing institutions. He thus rejected what we call "moral" rights. Recent views of utilitarianism seem to imply that this neglect of rights is theoretically unavoidable. Critics and partisans alike generally suppose that a commitment to the general welfare means that rights are not to count in our deliberations except as conduct affecting them also affects the general welfare, and critics contend that this fails to take rights seriously.[2] Rights are supposed to make a difference to our calculations, which they fail to do if we hold—as utilitarians are supposed to maintain—that rights may be infringed if that is necessary to bring about the smallest increase in the general welfare. Perhaps there are no rights that may absolutely never be overridden; some rights, at least, may be infringed in order to prevent calamities, for example; but infringement of a right should always count against a policy, a law, or a course of action, even when considerations of the general welfare argue for infringement. And it is not necessarily the case that infringement of a right always detracts significantly from the general welfare. For such reasons, commitment to the general welfare standard seems to conflict with genuine acknowledgment of rights; utilitarianism seems positively to abhor them. In this paper I shall sketch how Mill challenges such a conclusion.

One strategy of response could be built upon the idea of "rule-utilitarianism." In this century, utilitarianism was initially understood, by Moore and others, as requiring one always to promote the general welfare in the most efficient and productive manner possible, any failure to do so being judged as wrong, the breach of one's sole "moral obligation." Faced with objections that this "act-utilitarianism" neglects ordinary moral obligations, which do not require one to "maximize utility" but indeed require contrary conduct, revisionists constructed new kinds of "utilitarian" principles. They required adherence to useful rules and excluded case-by-case appeal to the general welfare, hoping that these requirements would match the assumed obligations while still being based upon the general welfare. In the present context, one might extend this rebuttal by supposing that some useful rules would also confer rights, infringement of which would generally be prohibited, and infringement of which would never be warranted by direct appeal to the general welfare. Something like this is in fact suggested by Mill.

Mill's system does, in part, resemble a kind of rule utilitarianism, with the distinct advantage over recent theories that it explicitly acknowledges rights as well as obligations. It has a further, more general advantage. Recent rule-utilitarian theories seem either to have been concocted to avoid objections to act utilitarianism or else to offer an alternative but equally narrow interpretation of the general welfare standard. Both "act" and "rule" versions of utilitarianism seem arbitrarily to restrict the application of the general welfare standard to just one category of things—acts, say, or rules—among the many to which it might reasonably be applied. In contrast, Mill's endorsement of the general welfare standard leaves him free to judge all things by that measure. But he supplements it with analyses of moral judgments which commit him to acknowledging both moral rights and obligations.

For simplicity's sake, let us postpone examination of Mill's theory of rights and consider first his more famous (and initially simpler) principle of personal liberty.³ Mill says that the only reasons we should entertain in support of coercive social interference is the prevention of harm to people other than the agent whose freedom may be limited. For example, we should not try to force a person to serve his own happiness or prevent a person from harming himself. In effect, Mill says that we should *not* apply the general welfare standard directly to such intervention. But how could Mill say this—without forsaking his commitment to the general welfare standard? Mill recognizes that his principle of liberty is not entailed by his "general happiness principle" taken by itself. The latter commits him in principle to approving paternalistic intervention that would serve the general welfare. And so Mill *argues* for his principle of liberty. But wouldn't such a principle be emptied of all practical significance by the tacit qualifications that are inevitably imposed by Mill's commitment to the general welfare?

These questions arise when we assume that Mill's commitment to the general welfare standard amounts to the idea that one is always morally bound to serve the general welfare in the most efficient and productive manner possible. His principle of liberty is then conceived of as a "summary rule," a rough guide to action that is meant to insure the closest approximation to the requirements laid down by his principle of utility. This is, I think, mistaken on several counts.

Let me suggest, first, that Mill be understood as reasoning along the following lines. The general welfare will best be served in the long run if we restrict social interference, by both legal and informal means, to the prevention of social harm. Experience shows that less limited intervention is very largely, and unavoidably, counterproductive. Even when we try our best to prevent people from harming themselves, for example, we are in all probability bound to fail. Before embarking on such intervention we are unable to distinguish the productive from the counterproductive efforts. We are able to do that later; but later is always too late. Since the stakes are high for those we coerce, and nonexistent for us, we *ought to make it a matter of principle* never to entertain reasons for interfering save the prevention of harm to others. The general welfare would best be served in the long run by our following such an inflexible rule.

Now this seems to me a perfectly intelligible position, and one even an act–utilitarian might consistently adopt. One need not reject the general welfare standard—as a basis, or even the sole basis, for evaluating things—in order to accept such a principle of liberty. Some possible objections ought however to be noted, though they cannot adequately be considered here. First, it may be said that this could not be a complete account of our objections to paternalism and other forms of social interference (so far as we object to them) because our convictions about the sanctity of liberty are much stronger than our warranted confidence in the factual assumptions required by Mill's argument. This seems to me, however, to prove nothing without independent validations of those judgments. Our moral convictions need justification; they are not self-certifying. If we are uncertain about the relevant facts, then we should retain at least an open mind about the relations between liberty and the general welfare.

Second, the argument attributed to Mill suggests that the general welfare will best be served only if we are something other than utilitarians, for it tells us *not* to apply the general welfare standard. The argument thus seems self-defeating for a utilitarian. But, while this problem might arise for utilitarianism in some other contexts, I do not think it need worry Mill right here. I might make it a matter of principle to avoid certain situations that I know will lead to choices that are self-destructive, though they will not seem such to me at the time. This is compatible with my continuing to appreciate my reasons for that policy. Mill's argument is similar. Indeed, one would expect the Mill of *On Liberty* to insist that we remind ourselves of the rationales for our rules and principles if we do not wish them to become ineffective dogmas. This presumably advises us to keep in mind the utilitarian foundation for the principle of liberty.

Third, it may be said that Mill's principle is too rigid and inflexible, that the general welfare would in fact be served better by a more complex principle, which incorporates some exceptions. It may be argued, for example, that paternalistic legislation within certain clearly defined limits should be tolerated.[4] But this is a point that Mill might easily accept—provided that any proposed qualifications on the principle of liberty would not lead to such abuse as to be counterproductive.

It should be clear, now, that the principle of liberty is no "summary rule," of the sort associated with act-utilitarianism; nor is it one of those ideal rules of obligation obtained by applying some modern rule-utilitarian formula. It results from a direct application of the general welfare standard to the question, What sorts of reasons would it serve the general welfare for us to entertain when framing social rules?

Mill is not obliged to be either a rule utilitarian or an act-utilitarian because he does not conceive of the general welfare standard in so limited a way. His principle concerns ends, specifically happiness, and provides the basis for evaluating other things in relation to that end. It does not concern acts or rules as such. It says nothing about right or wrong, duty or obligation. And it does not require one, in moral terms, to maximize the general welfare.

These points are indicated in Mill's "proof" of the principle of utility (where one would expect him to be careful at least in his formulation of his principle, even if his argument fails). In a typical passage Mill says: "The utilitarian doctrine is that happiness is desirable, and the only thing desirable, as an end; all other things being only desirable as means to that end" (chap. IV, par. 2).[5] At the end of the main part of his "proof" Mill says: "If so, happiness is the sole end of human action, and the promotion of it the test by which to judge of all human conduct; from whence it necessarily follows that it must be the criterion of morality, since a part is included in the whole" (chap. IV, par. 8). The relationship between moral judgments and the general welfare standard is then explained more fully by Mill in the next and longest chapter of *Utilitarianism,* which is devoted to the topic of rights and justice.[6]

Mill maintains that judgments about the justice of acts are a specific form of moral appraisal: acts can be wrong without being unjust. To call an act unjust is to imply that it violates another's right, which is not true of all wrong acts. In a perfectly parallel manner, Mill maintains that moral judgments (about right and wrong, duty and obligation) are a proper subclass of act appraisals in general: acts can be negatively appraised—as inexpedient, undesirable, or regrettable, for example—without being regarded as immoral or wrong. To call an act wrong is to imply that "punishment" for it (loosely speaking) would be justified (chap. V, paras. 13–15).

Mill's distinction between immorality and mere "inexpediency" indicates that he is no act-utilitarian and also that his general welfare standard does not lay down moral requirements. There must be some basis within Mill's system for appraising acts negatively even when they are not to be counted as wrong. This is either the general welfare standard or some other. But the general welfare standard is quite clearly Mill's basic, most comprehensive criterion. It therefore seems reasonable to infer that Mill would wish to rank acts according to their instrumental value (their promotion of the general welfare), *preferring* those that rank highest in a set of alternatives, without implying that a merely "inexpedient" act is wrong because it falls below the top of such a ranking and thus fails to serve the general welfare in the most productive and efficient manner possible.

According to Mill, to show that an act is wrong, and not merely inexpedient, one must go further and show that sanctions against it would be justified. For Mill says that to judge an act wrong is to judge that "punishment" of it would be fitting or justified.[7] The "punishment" or sanctions Mill has in mind include not just legal penalties but also public condemnation (both can be classified as "external sanctions") as well as guilt feelings or pangs of conscience (the "internal sanction").[8]

Now, Mill presents this as a conceptual point, independent of his commitment to the general welfare; but it has a bearing on our understanding of that standard. Mill distinguishes between general negative appraisals of the "inexpediency" of acts and moral judgments specifically condemning them as wrong. I have suggested that the criterion of "inexpediency" for Mill is an act's failure to promote the general welfare to the maximum degree possible. If so, this cannot be Mill's criterion of wrongness, for from the fact that an act is inexpedient in this sense it does not follow that sanctions against it could be justified. For sanctions have costs of the sort that a utilitarian always counts, and these costs attach to the distinct acts connected with sanctions. The justification of such acts presumably turns somehow upon *their* relation to the general welfare, not upon (or not alone upon) the relation of the act that is to be sanctioned to the general welfare. On Mill's view, therefore, the general welfare standard *can* be applied directly to acts, but then it simply determines their expediency (and enables one to rank them accordingly). However, this is not, according to Mill, a moral judgment, and it has no direct moral implications.[9]

Mill also seems to hold that a wrong act is the breach of a moral obligation, at least in the absence of some overriding obligation.[10] But what differentiates morality from mere expediency, as we have seen, is the justification of sanctions. Mill appears to regard the internal sanction as basic. His formulations imply that public disapproval may be justified even when legal sanctions are not, and that pangs of conscience may be warranted when no external sanctions can be justified. Mill suggests that greater costs and risks attach to social sanctions (which is plausible so long as conscience is not excessively demanding). It may also be observed that the justification of external sanctions involves an extra step, since they require distinct acts by other persons, while guilt feelings are triggered more or less automatically. Errors of judgment aside, to justify the operation of self-reproach in particular cases one must justify no more than the internalization of certain values. But to justify external sanctions one must also justify distinct acts by other persons, based on their corresponding values—acts ranging from expressions of disapproval to legal punishment. In Mill's view, then, to argue that an act is wrong is basically to argue that guilt feelings for it would be warranted. Other sanctions may be justified as well, depending on the stakes involved and on the circumstances.

Following Bentham, Mill clearly thinks of sanctions operating not just after an act, as responses to a wrong already done, but also beforehand, in order to discourage such conduct.[11] This conception presupposes that sanctions are attached to general rules, which serve as guides to conduct, and has its more natural application to rules of the social variety, to which external sanctions are also attached. We can combine this with the previous point as follows. Internal sanctions require that the corresponding values be "internalized," thoroughly accepted by the individual. For external sanctions to be justified they must work efficiently, and this requires that the corresponding values be shared widely, within, say, a given community; which amounts to the existence of a common moral code. A reconstruction of Mill's account of moral judgments, then, would go something like this. To argue for a moral obligation is to argue for the widespread internalization (within a community) of a value relevant to conduct; to show that an act is wrong is to show that it breaches such a rule, in the absence of an overriding obligation.

Mill thus suggests a fairly sophisticated version of what would now be called "rule-utilitarianism"—except, of course, that he does not limit the general welfare standard to rules of conduct, any more than he limits it to acts. Following Bentham's conception of social rules and his theory of their justification, Mill also takes into account the costs of sanctions—the social price of regulating conduct—which most recent rule utilitarians have ignored.[12] Mill departs from Bentham on two important and related points. First, Mill acknowledges the internal sanction, conscience and guilt feelings, which Bentham had neglected, but which Mill thinks is fundamental to the idea of morality. Second, while Bentham analyzed the idea of obligation in terms of actual coercion or institutionally authorized coercion—which might not be justified—Mill analyzes obligation in terms of sanctions that could be justified. That is a much more plausible and promising conception than Bentham's.

I do not mean that Mill's account of moral judgments is adequate as it stands. For example, while Mill seems right in emphasizing the connections between judgments of one's own immoral conduct and guilt feelings, he seems to put the cart before the horse. For we usually think of determining whether guilt feelings would be justified by asking, first, whether one has acted immorally, while Mill finds out whether a given act is wrong by first calculating whether internal sanctions for such an act are justified. Perhaps Mill's analysis of moral judgments is misguided. But his general approach to these matters is instructive.

Since Mill's theory of obligation does not seem inconsistent with his general welfare standard, it seems to show that an advocate of the general welfare standard can take moral obligations seriously. For, on Mill's view, obligations alone determine whether an act is wrong; they alone lay down moral requirements. Even if the general welfare would be served by breaching an obligation, it does not follow, on Mill's account, that one would be morally justified in breaching it.

We are now in a position to consider Mill's account of rights. In distinguishing justice from morality in general, Mill says that obligations of justice in particular, but not all moral obligations, correspond with moral rights. An unjust act is the violation of another's right; but an act can be wrong without being unjust—without violating any person's right. Mill believes that we can act wrongly by failing to be generous or charitable or beneficent, and he treats the corresponding "virtues" as imposing "obligations"; but these do not correspond with anyone's rights. "No one has a moral right to our generosity or beneficence because we are not morally bound to practice those virtues towards any given individual" (chap. V, par. 15).

Though not all obligations involve corresponding rights, Mill seems to hold that rights entail corresponding obligations. Consequently, it seems reasonable to interpret his explicit analysis of moral rights in terms of moral obligations. This analysis is presented as follows:

> When we call anything a person's right, we mean that he has a valid claim upon society to protect him in the possession of it, either by the force of law or by that of education and opinion. If he has what we consider a sufficient claim, on whatever account, to have something guaranteed him by society, we say he has a right to it [chap. V, par. 24].

After some elaboration Mill restates the point, and then goes one step further:

> To have a right, then, is, I conceive, to have something that society ought to defend me in the possession of. If the objector goes on to ask why it ought, I can give him no other reason than general utility [chap. V, par. 25].

Mill first analyzes ascriptions of rights; his analysis refers to arguments with conclusions of a certain type. After completing this account, Mill resumes his advocacy of utilitarianism; he indicates that, on his view, such arguments are sound if, and only if, they turn entirely upon the general welfare.

Mill holds that someone has a right when he ought to be treated in a certain way, which serves (or refrains from undermining) some interest of his. Combining this with Mill's theory of obligation, we get the view that someone has a moral right when another person or persons are under a beneficial moral obligation towards him;[13] or, in other words, when there are sufficient grounds for the widespread internalization of a value that requires corresponding ways of acting towards him.

Mill's approach seems to me significant. Someone who rejected the general welfare standard could consistently accept Mill's analysis of rights (or something like it) and use a different basis for validating the relevant claims. This is because his analysis of rights, like his analysis of moral obligations, is independent of the general welfare standard.

Now, if something like Mill's approach is correct, then we can say the following. If one's principles actually support the relevant sort of claim, then one is committed to the corresponding rights. Mill believes that some such claims are validated by the general welfare standard—that is, that it would serve the general welfare to protect individuals in certain ways—so he believes himself committed to moral rights. Mill's principle of liberty can be construed as a defense of some such rights, and its defense as an argument for—among other things—constitutional protections for them. Since Mill's belief is plausible, it is plausible to suppose that a utilitarian such as Mill—indeed, anyone who accepts the general welfare as a standard for evaluation—is committed to certain categories of rights. And it is vital to observe that this conclusion flows, not from a concocted version of "utilitarianism" designed to yield conclusions that external critics demanded, but from a reasonable interpretation of the general welfare standard coupled with a plausible analysis of rights.

Moreover, since Mill is not committed morally to maximizing welfare—to regarding the failure to so act as wrong—he is not committed to infringing rights whenever it would serve the general welfare in the smallest way to do so. Quite the contrary, since such an act would breach a moral obligation that Mill recognizes, and obligations may be breached only when other obligations override them. In this sense, Mill shows that a proponent of the general welfare standard—even a utilitarian—can take rights seriously.

Mill's account of rights is superior to Bentham's in ways that follow from the differences in their conceptions of obligation. Bentham also held that to have a right is to be someone who is supposed to benefit from another's obligation. But, as I have noted, Bentham analyzed obligation in terms of actual or authorized coercion, which might not be justified. This led to his notorious rejection of unenforced rights, including the rights that we invoke to argue for changes in the social order (as was done most famously in our Declaration of Independence and the French Declaration of the Rights of Man, both of which Bentham consequently criticized). Mill, however, is free to recognize such rights, which would be clearly in the spirit of his discussion.

It may also be noted that defects in Mill's account of obligation do not necessarily transfer to his account of rights. It is possible to understand both Bentham and Mill as embracing the idea that rights are to be understood in terms of beneficial obligations, and to interpret this in terms of an *adequate* account of obligation (whatever that may be). One could, of course, go further and say that the implications of the general welfare standard concerning moral rights cannot be fully understood without applying it to an adequate account of rights. Failing that, Mill has at least given us some reason to believe that utilitarians need not ignore or reject rights.

Let us now look at the specific commitments that Mill thinks utilitarians have towards moral rights. He holds that rules conferring rights take precedence over those that merely impose useful obligations, because they "concern the essentials of human well-being more nearly, and are therefore of more absolute obligation, than any other rules for the guidance of life" (chap. V, par. 32). In particular:

> The moral rules which forbid mankind to hurt one another (in which we must never forget to include wrongful interference with each other's freedom) are more vital to human well-being than any maxims, however important, which only point out the best mode of managing some department of human affairs [chap. V, par. 33].

According to Mill, our most important rights are to freedom of action and security of person; these concern our most vital interests, which must be respected or served if a minimally acceptable condition of life, in any setting, is to be possible. That position, I have tried to show, is not inconsistent with utilitarianism, and may in fact be part of a reasonably developed utilitarian theory. (Other rights concern, for example, specific debts or obligations that are due one and matters of desert.)

Mill's underlying reasoning may be understood as follows. An act is not wrong just because it fails to serve the general welfare to the maximum degree possible. This is because an act's being wrong involves the justification of sanctions, and sanctions (including internal sanctions) have unavoidable costs. The stakes must therefore be high enough so that the benefits to be derived from the redirection of behavior resulting from the existence of the sanctions (including the internalization of the corresponding values) exceed the costs entailed. But this applies to all moral obligations, including those "imperfect" obligations of benevolence which merely require generally helpful, charitable, or compassionate patterns of behavior. The obligations of justice are more demanding, and have greater costs attached, because they are "perfect." In the first place this means that they require one to behave towards certain other individuals in more or less determinate ways—that is, to serve or respect certain interests of theirs—on each and every occasion for so acting. In the second place this means that people are entitled to act in ways connected with their having rights: to demand respect for them, to challenge those who threaten to infringe them, to be indignant and perhaps noisy or uncooperative when their rights are violated or threatened, and so on. The obligations of justice are more demanding on the agent, since they do not leave one nearly as much choice as other moral obligations; they also involve greater liability to internal and external sanctions, as well as to demands by other persons upon one's conduct. This means that on a utilitarian reckoning they have special costs, which must be outweighed by the benefits they bring. The stakes must therefore be higher than for other moral obligations. Thus the interests that they are designed to serve must be more important. Rules concerning them will therefore generally take precedence over other moral rules. Such rights are not "inviolable," but their infringement will not easily be justified.

We can now make some further observations about the general nature of the rights that may be endorsed by the general welfare standard. In the first place, they may be characterized as morally fundamental, since they are grounded on a *non*moral standard and are not derived from some more fundamental moral principle.[14] In the second place, if Mill is correct about the importance to anyone of certain interests (such as personal liberty and security), regardless of particular social settings,[15] some of the rights endorsed by the general welfare standard could reasonably be characterized as "universal human" rights. Mill therefore gives us reason to believe, not only that the general welfare standard would not be hostile to such rights, but that it is positively committed to them—that is, to the sorts of rights associated with the Declaration of Independence. If so, the general welfare standard cannot be blamed for any corresponding injustices that are condoned by arguments invoking the general welfare; for such arguments would simply be mistaken.

I do not wish to imply, however, that Mill's suggestions should be accepted without much more severe scrutiny. I merely wish to emphasize that the matter seems far from settled against the general welfare standard.

One final comment in defense of arguments for rights from the general welfare standard. These rights are grounded upon nonmoral values. This will seem unsatisfactory to someone who thinks that some basic rights, or the principles that proclaim them, are "self-evident," as the Declaration of Independence declares. Now, I am not sure what "self-evidence" amounts to, but I know of no account that makes it plausible to suppose that moral principles can somehow stand on their own feet, without any need for, or even possibility of, supporting argument. So I cannot see this as a serious objection to Mill.

A somewhat related and more familiar objection to Mill's manner of defending rights is to note that it relies upon the facts—not just too heavily, but at all. It is sometimes suggested, for example, that the general welfare standard must be rejected or severely limited because it is *logically* compatible with unjust arrangements. From any reasonable definition of human slavery, for example, it would not follow that such an institution could never satisfy the general welfare standard. It is therefore *logically possible* that enslaving some would sometimes serve the general welfare better than would any of the available alternatives. This objection does not rest on factual assumptions, and a utilitarian who tried to answer it by citing the *actual* disutility of human slavery would be accused of missing its point. Facts are simply irrelevant, for "basic" moral principles are involved.

A utilitarian might answer as follows. If moral principles independent of utilitarianism are assumed, the idea that the general welfare standard is valid is tacitly rejected at the outset; but that simply begs the question. At this point, any friend of the general welfare standard (even one who accepts other basic principles as well) might join in the rebuttal: Why should we assume that the principles of rights and justice are independent of the general welfare standard? Let us see the arguments for them, so that we can determine whether they are not actually grounded on and limited by considerations of utility.

Moreover, if facts cannot be called upon to help us interpret the general welfare standard, they must not be assumed by any objections to it. But it is difficult to see how facts can be excluded both from arguments for moral principles and from their applications. If moral principles are not regarded as self-evident, then they must be defended in some manner. The only plausible arguments that I know of in defense of moral principles— such as Rawls'—make extensive use of facts.[16] Moreover, most general principles require considerable information for their application to the varied circumstances of human life.[17] Someone who believes that facts are thus relevant to morality cannot reasonably object to the general welfare standard on the grounds of its unavoidable consideration of the facts. Until we have established principles of rights and justice on nonutilitarian grounds and also have shown that utilitarian arguments for them are ineffective, we must consider what proponents of the general welfare standard might have to say about such matters.

NOTES

This essay was originally presented as the Special Bicentennial Invited Address to the Pacific Division A.P.A. Meetings in Berkeley, 25 March 1976. I am grateful to Sharon Hill for her comments on that occasion.

1. In Article I, section 2—just after the Preamble.

2. See, for example, Ronald Dworkin, "Taking Rights Seriously," *New York Review of Books,* 18 December 1970; reprinted in A.W.B. Simpson, ed., *Oxford Essays in Jurisprudence, Second Series* (Oxford: Clarendon Press, 1973).

3. Mill's essay *On Liberty* appears consistent with his essay on *Utilitarianism* (written soon after) on all points relevant to the interpretation I am offering here. My interpretation of *On Liberty* does not so much ignore as render it unnecessary to hypothesize nonutilitarian tendencies in Mill's argument; for an alternative account, see Gerald Dworkin, "Paternalism," in Richard A. Wasserstrom, ed., *Morality and the Law* (Belmont, Calif.: Wadsworth, 1971), section V.

4. For some suggestions along these lines, see Gerald Dworkin, "Paternalism," section VI; and, on speech, see Joel Feinberg, "Limits to the Free Expression of Opinion," in Joel Feinberg and Hyman Gross, eds., *Philosophy of Law* (Encino, Calif.: Dickenson, 1975).

5. All references in the text hereafter will cite chapters and paragraphs of *Utilitarianism.*

6. I discuss this matter more fully in, "Mill's Theory of Morality," *Nous* 10 (1976): 101–120.

7. For simplicity's sake, I shall understand Mill to mean "justified" or "warranted."

8. Mill uses the terminology of "sanctions" in chapter III of *Utilitarianism.*

9. The act-utilitarian reading of Mill is most strongly suggested in *Utiltiarianism,* chapter II, paragraph 2. But, as D.G. Brown has noted, the passage is ambiguous; see his paper, "What is Mill's Principle of Utility?" *Canadian Journal of Philosophy* 3 (1973): 1–12.

10. This paragraph has been revised in response to a very helpful comment by a reader for *Philosophy & Public Affairs,* for which I am grateful. Note, now, that Mill does not differentiate in *Utilitarianism* between duties and obligations. He may link both too closely with wrong actions, but he does not hold that an act is wrong if it simply breaches a moral obligation. This is because he recognizes that obligations can conflict. And when they do, rules or obligations are ranked by reference to the general welfare standard. Mill does not indicate that acts are so evaluated directly, even when obligations conflict; see the last paragraph of chapter II, as well as chapter V.

11. Since Mill criticized Bentham's views extensively, but had only praise for Bentham's theory of punishment, I assume that Mill follows Bentham on all relevant points except where the evidence and the requirements of a coherent theory indicate the contrary.

12. An exception is Richard Brandt; see especially his "A Utilitarian Theory of Excuses," *Philosophical Review* 68 (1969): 337–361.

13. For a fuller discussion of this sort of theory, see my "Rights, Claimants, and Beneficiaries," *American Philosophical Quarterly* 6 (1969): 173–185.

14. In this respect they are just like the basic rights endorsed by John Rawls in *A Theory of Justice* (Cambridge, Mass.: Harvard University Press, 1971). Rawls'

argument invokes self-interest, not the general interest, but on the view we have been considering the latter is no more a "moral" standard than the former.

15. It is interesting to note that Rawls endorses such a notion with his use of "primary goods."

16. A good example is Rawls' argument for his principles, which makes much more extravagant use of fact than Mill's.

17. This is true, not just of Rawls' principles, but, I think, of all principles of similar scope.

· 5 ·

John Stuart Mill on Justice and Fairness

F. R. Berger

The main difficulty utilitarians have faced is the problem of reconciling the dictates of utility with what seem clearly to be moral duties, but based on considerations of justice. John Stuart Mill addressed this problem in his essay, *Utilitarianism,* and the result has not served to silence the critics of utilitarianism on this score. In part, this is due to the fact that Mill's position in the chapter on justice is not entirely clear, nor is it entirely convincing where it is clear. Still, I do not think Mill's views on justice have been given their due.[1] In this essay, I shall try to show that Mill anticipated recently defended principles that rely on appeal to a notion of fairness or fair play, and that these can be given a utilitarian foundation.

Utilitarianism, it has been argued, is committed to aggregating utilities, hence, is committed in theory to preferring greater to lesser distributions of utilities even when the lesser is fairer. Moreover, it is held that by its commitment to the maximization of utility, it permits the sacrifice of some for the greater good of others, permits punishing the innocent, and sanctions "free-loading" on cooperative schemes, in violation of a duty of "fair play." It is this last claim on which I shall concentrate. A so-called "duty of fair play" has come to play an important role in contemporary moral philosophy. I shall try to show that Mill was committed to recognizing some such principle, that it was an important consequence of his theory of justice, and that it played an important role in his moral theory. This will, I think, elucidate how a utilitarian approach to these issues is possible.

Probably the earliest statement of a duty of fairness to be found in the contemporary debate was formulated by H. L. A. Hart, in his well-known article, "Are There Any Natural Rights?": "when a number of persons conduct any joint enterprise according to rules and thus restrict their liberty, those who have submitted to these restrictions when required have a right to a similar submission from those who have benefited by their sub-

45

mission . . . the moral obligation to obey the rules in such circumstances is *due to* the cooperating members of the society, and they have the correlative moral right to obedience."[2]

A further formulation, which clearly was influenced by Hart's, has been given by John Rawls in his contemporary classic, *A Theory of Justice*: "The main idea is that when a number of persons engage in a mutually advantageous cooperative venture according to rules, and thus restrict their liberty in ways necessary to yield advantages for all, those who have submitted to these restrictions have a right to a similar acquiescence on the part of those who have benefited from their submission. We are not to gain from the cooperative labors of others without doing our fair share."[3]

There is considerable disagreement over the conditions necessary for such a duty to hold, and over what acts we are obligated to perform by considerations of fair play, and some critics deny there is any general duty of this sort. Among those who do recognize some such principle, however, there are some who believe its acceptance is incompatible with utilitarianism since complying with a duty of fairness need not thereby maximize utility. Utilitarianism is sometimes rejected as a moral theory for this reason. I want to show that Mill was committed to such a principle, based on a utilitarian conception of justice.

1. RIGHTS AND JUSTICE

The concept of a right played an important role in Mill's moral theory. This may come as a surprise in a utilitarian theorist since many critics have thought that there can be no place for rights in a theory that judges the morality of an act by its consequences. The assertion that someone has a right implies nothing, in and of itself, about the consequences of acting in any way.

But Mill divided duties into two classes: duties of perfect and imperfect obligation. Duties of perfect obligation are specified by certain moral rules—the rules of justice. What is distinctive about the rules of justice is that they impose duties toward "assignable" individuals, who, correlatively, have rights to the others' performances or forebearances. The duty to keep a contract is owed *to* the other contractor, who has a right to the performance promised. In the case of duties of imperfect obligation, there are no specifiable persons who can claim a right to a performance. There is a duty to be generous and give charity, but there are no specifiable persons on whom we must bestow charity, i.e., who can claim a right to our largess. "Justice," according to Mill, "implies something which it is not only right to do, and wrong not to do, but which some individual person can claim from us as his moral right."[4]

In Mill's view, moral judgments express certain sentiments—approval, disapproval, resentment, indignation—and, in the case of judgments of right and wrong—praise and blame. Indeed, he held that what is distinctive about judgments of duty, obligation, right and wrong (he did not systematically distinguish among these) is that they all imply that punishment, if only in the form of a blaming conscience, is appropriate for conduct which violates the duty:

> We do not call anything wrong, unless we mean to imply that a person ought to be punished in some way or other for doing it; if not by law, by the opinion of his fellow creatures; and if not by opinion, by the reproaches of his own conscience. . . . It is a part of the notion of Duty in every one of its forms, that a person may rightfully be compelled to fulfill it. Duty is a thing which may be *exacted* from a person, as one exacts a debt. Unless we think that it might be exacted from him, we do not call it his duty.[5]

It was Mill's view that the duties of justice are concerned with protecting certain interests of persons—those which they have in common, the violation of which they desire not be repeated. When harms are done persons, this calls forth resentment or indignation; these feelings are "moralized," i.e., become moral feelings if aroused by a concern for those interests "common to all mankind." Thus, Mill summarized his analysis of the idea of justice as follows:

> To recapitulate: the idea of justice supposes two things; a rule of conduct, and a sentiment which sanctions the rule. The first must be supposed common to all mankind, and intended for their good. The other (the sentiment) is a desire that punishment may be suffered by those who infringe the rule. There is involved, in addition, the conception of some definite person who suffers by the infringement; whose rights (to use the expression appropriated to the case) are violated by it. And the sentiment of justice appears to me to be, the animal desire to repel or retaliate a hurt or damage to oneself, or to those with whom one sympathizes, widened so as to include all persons, by the human capacity of enlarged sympathy, and the human conception of intelligent self-interest. From the latter elements, the feeling derives its morality; from the former, its peculiar impressiveness, and energy of self-assertion.[6]

In the paragraph which follows this quotation, Mill explained the "elements" of the idea of a right which is violated as: a hurt to an assignable person or persons, and the demand for punishment. Mill held that having a right entails having something that society ought to protect:

> When we call anything a person's right, we mean that he has a valid claim on society to protect him in the possession of it, either by the force of law, or by that of education and opinion. If he has what we consider a sufficient claim, on whatever account, to have something guaranteed to him by society, we say that he has a right to it. If we desire to prove that anything does not belong to him by right, we think this done as soon as it is admitted that society ought not to take measures for securing it to him, but should leave it to chance, or to his own exertions.[7]

Now there is no argument given by Mill which connects the analysis of the ideas of justice and rights with the claim that having a right implies something society should protect. On the one hand, he seems to view the claim as following from the analysis of the idea of justice; on the other hand, he seems to have drawn the claim (as in the above quotation) as a conclusion of an appeal to an ordinary language type argument about the necessary and sufficient conditions for asserting that someone has a right.

From the text, and other writings of Mill, his reasoning seems to have been somewhat as follows. Duties of justice involve interests which are common. A harm to such interests thus threatens harm to others. Therefore, socially concerned persons will react to such conduct. (We do have social feelings, he held, as a natural product of our development as human beings.) The natural reactions to harms are feelings of resentment, indignation, and a desire for revenge and retaliation. In a footnote he added when editing his father's *Analysis of the Phenomena of the Human Mind,* he wrote that "our earliest experience gives us the feeling . . . that the most direct and efficacious protection is retaliation."[8] He goes on to say that we naturally desire that our social institutions provide this for us. This feeling is not, by itself, a moral feeling. As previously explained, our feelings are made moral by their conformity with the general good, "just persons resenting a hurt to society, though not otherwise a hurt to themselves, and not resenting a hurt to themselves, however painful, unless it be of a kind which society has a common interest with them in the repression of."[9] Since everyone has an interest in reacting to and suppressing such conduct, the desire that society punish the transgression is a moral sentiment. The judgment that society should punish such conduct would be a true moral judgment if common social interests would indeed be furthered. Otherwise, the desire for social punishment, and the corresponding moral judgment, would not be justified. It would follow that someone has a right if, and only if, society should provide him protection from certain conduct by means of punishment.

It remained for Mill to explain how the duties of justice come to have such great weight and be regarded as so stringent. He explained this by holding that the recognition and enforcement of rights protect interests all people have, and especially the strong interest in security. Beneficial conduct by others can often be foregone, or at any rate, we are not so dependent on it as we are on others abstaining from harming us:

> security no human being can possibly do without; on it we depend for all our immunity from evil, and for the whole value of all and every good, beyond the passing moment. . . . Now this most indispensable of all necessaries, after physical nutriment, cannot be had, unless the machinery for providing it is kept unintermittedly in active play. Our notion, therefore, of the claim we have on our fellow-creatures to join in making safe for us the very groundwork of our existence, gathers feelings round it so much more intense than those concerned in any more common cases of utility, that the difference in degree (as is often the case in psychology) becomes a real difference in kind.[10]

It is because of the great importance to us of the guarantees of justice that the dictates of justice are so stringent. Indeed, in his discussion, the duties of justice come close to swallowing up all of morality, as he contrasts the stringency of these duties with "ordinary expediency and inexpediency." His analysis of right and wrong and the connection with punishment, may not be fully consistent with his earlier statements about duties of imperfect obligation.[11] And, it may conflict with his discussions of morality in other works. Duties of imperfect obligation require *beneficial* acts, and are nevertheless duties. In his essay, "Auguste Comte and Positivism," he recognized the category of acts we now call "supererogatory," and argued that there are some acts we are not bound to perform, but which, if performed "are fit objects of moral praise."[12] Moreover, he argued that sanctions—the tools for the enforcement of duty—are properly applied not only to conduct which is harmful, but also to enforce promises, and "inasmuch as every one, who avails himself of the advantages of society, leads others to expect from him all such positive good offices and disinterested services as the moral improvement attained by mankind has rendered customary, he deserves moral blame if, without just cause, he disappoints that expectation."[13] Beneficial acts which have not become customary, though meritorious, are not obligatory.

It may be, of course, that failures to perform these beneficial acts *do* harm people *via* the disappointment of expectation, and, no doubt, Mill thought of this as the disutility in them which justifies punishment, and labeling them as "wrong." But then, these acts threaten common interests which generally deserve protection, and therefore they violate our rights. Such acts would violate duties of justice. It is hard to know how duties of imperfect obligation fit into this, as there need be no particular act which is expected. Moreover, there is no extended argument in his discussion why uncommon virtue should not be enforced. He held that supererogatory acts gain part of their value from being spontaneously performed and this is inconsistent with requiring them. Perhaps he thought that if beneficial acts have become expected, they cannot be so spontaneous and do not reflect so clearly a superior character. At this stage, they are perceived as related to patterns of reciprocity in social life, which are important for promoting a well-developed social character, and thus the general welfare.[14] Also, helping others can interfere with their plans for running their lives, or not accord with their own judgment of what they want, and may conflict with one's own legitimate needs, wants, or duties. So, perhaps these considerations led him to think that acts which are common and beneficial may usefully be required, while uncommon virtue is best left spontaneous. It would still be unclear how imperfect obligations are to be explicated.

However duties of imperfect obligation are to be treated, it is clear that Mill thought that sometimes the failure to perform a beneficial act *is* a kind of harm *via* the disappointment of expectation, from which we can expect society to protect us. He held that disappointment of expectation "constitutes the principal criminality of two such highly immoral acts as breach of friendship and a breach of promise."[15] He held this sort of hurt is of an extreme kind: "Few hurts which human beings can sustain are greater, and none wound more, than when that on which they habitually and with full assurance relied, fails them in the hour of need; and few wrongs are greater than this mere withholding of good; none excite more resentment, either in the person suffering, or in a sympathizing spectator."[16]

These are debatable claims. Surely not every breach of promise, not even wrongful ones, disappoint expectations in this way. Nor do all cases involving serious disappointment of expectation involve the commission of moral wrongs. Mill himself implied as much in denying society's right to interfere with the freedom of conduct which only *indirectly* harms others, though expectations may be seriously disappointed. How *can* a utilitarian consistently hold to the stringency of duties of justice, while basing his argument on the need for security? I believe an important part of the answer consists in stressing the role of moral rules in moral reasoning, and in reasoning about justice, in particular.

2. RULES AND JUSTICE

There are at least two models of utilitarian moral reasoning that give a significant role to moral rules. On standard rule-utilitarian models, the principle of utility is a test of rules, not of particular acts. Once it is determined what rules are justified, to ask if a particular act is right is to ask if it is sanctioned by the rules or not. A version of a rule-utilitarian position has been attributed to Mill by J.O. Urmson and others.[17] If such an attribution is correct, then clearly the account of rights and justice we attribute to Mill must stress the role of rules in actual moral reasoning.

The alternative sort of model holds that the rightness or wrongness of an act is determined by the consequences of the particular act. Traditionally, Mill has been interpreted as holding such a theory. It would be out of place to argue the correct interpretation of Mill here, especially as I believe there is not conclusive evidence either way. I shall try to develop Mill's views on justice as part of a kind of act-utilitarian theory for the following reasons: (1) Professor David Lyons has already given an account that places Mill's theory of justice in the context of a moral theory that derives moral obligations from moral rules.[18] (2) It will thus be useful to see if a plausible theory of justice can be developed in Mill's terms on the basis of an act-utilitarian theory. This is especially important since it has seemed to many critics an impossible task, and the chief impetus to the development of rule-based theories has been the alleged incapacity of the traditional theories to account for justice and fairness. (3) I believe the weight of evidence from Mill's writings, though not conclusive, favors the claim that he held something very like the act-utilitarian view I shall outline.[19]

According to this view, the rightness or wrongness of an act is determined by its contribution to happiness.[20] From the point of view of the *theory*, the test of the morality of an act is to trace out its consequences. In practice, however, we can only rarely judge these accurately. The consequences of acts are especially hard to judge in cases where: (a) the act is related to other acts, e.g., as part of a general practice of truth-telling, or in a cooperative enterprise; (b) where the act may produce effects on one's character and dispositions, or on those of others; and (c) it is important that regularity of conduct is maintained, e.g., in situations such as cooperation where trust and confidence are important, or in a legal system, where security depends on uniform rule observance. These considerations suggest that in practical situations one would determine what to do, and evaluate the conduct of others, primarily by appeal to rules (and, perhaps, other considerations such as that a given act is inconsistent with a desirable state of character). The *immediate* test of acts would be rules. In saying this, two things are implied: (a) one will, in practice, base conduct on rules, and (b) it is possible that one will sometimes do something that is, in fact, wrong, i.e., that does not produce the best consequences. The adoption of rules for practice is a kind of strategy for maximizing the doing of right acts. One adopts rules to test one's acts because so doing is more likely to produce good results than trying directly in every case to do so.[21] Two further points of importance need to be made: (c) the theory does not sanction *knowingly* doing what will detract from utility; if one knows for sure that disobedience of the rule will be productive of greater good, then that is what is sanctioned; but (d) in cases where there is good reason for thinking the rule relates to a class of cases where one *cannot* be sure, and what is at stake if one miscalculates is of very great utility, it can sanction *strict* obedience to rule. At the extreme, this theory could consistently (though perhaps not plausibly) hold that we can *never* be sure enough to justify disobedience of useful rules, and hence insist on the practical application of rules to determine our obligations in all cases.[22] Essential to this theory is the view that there is a difference between a *criterion* of right and wrong, and a *procedure* for deciding what to do.[23] The former can guide the latter, but, under the conditions of life, cannot in practice *be* the rule which directs our behavior. Mill did argue that the attempt to guide one's conduct in each case by the calculation of consequences will *not* result in conduct which meets the criterion of utility.[24]

This last point is of great importance, as some critics of utilitarianism hold that if one bases his or her conduct on rules (or acts out of inculcated, "fixed" states of character), maximizing utility has been given up and act-utilitarianism has been abandoned.[25] This criticism is mistaken. Alternative criteria of behavior are adopted or inculcated as a means of maximizing the doing of right acts as judged by the act–utilitarian standard. An analogy may clarify the point. Bowlers often use lane markings to aim at. Some bowlers try to avoid looking at the pins themselves and concentrate solely on hitting the lane markings several feet in front of them. Though they are aiming directly at the markings, they have not given up trying to knock down the pins. Conscious adoption of the policy *is* a way of maximizing hitting the pins *by virtue* of its entailing *not* aiming at the pins. It is true that the analogy, and the "strategy" conception outlined, do not describe or fully explain character-related actions, such as might be based on friendship for example, or gratitude, which are not "adopted" or dictated by a "strategy." Mill did not sufficiently discuss these. It is not obvious, however, that acts undertaken *as* acts of friendship, or displays of gratitude, cannot be *justified* ultimately by their contribution to utility.[26]

As we saw in the last section, Mill held that the idea of justice makes reference to a rule of conduct, and he said that "justice is a name for certain classes of moral rules." The connection between rights, rules, justice, and happiness is brought out more clearly in a letter Mill wrote to George Grote:

> human happiness, even one's own, is in general more successfully pursued by acting on general rules, than by measuring the consequences of each act; and this is still more the case with the general happiness, since any other plan would not only leave everybody uncertain what to expect, but would involve perpetual quarrelling: and hence general rules must be laid down for people's conduct to one another, or in other words, rights and obligations must, as you say, be recognised; and people must, on the one hand, not be required to sacrifice even their own less good to another's greater, where no general rule has given the other a right to the sacrifice; while when a right *has* been recognised, they must, in most cases, yield to that right even at the sacrifice, in the particular case, of their own greater good to another's less. These rights and obligations are (it is of course implied) reciprocal. And thus what each person is held to do for the sake of others is more or less definite, corresponding to the less perfect knowledge he can have of their interests, taken individually; and he is free to employ the indefinite residue of his exertions in benefitting the one person of whom he has the principal charge, and whose wants he has the means of learning the most completely.[27]

Several points of importance are made in the paragraph: general rules are needed to most successfully achieve happiness, and this is due, in part, to difficulties of knowledge and the need for regularity of conduct; the rules set out reciprocal rights and obligations; the rights must, "in most cases," be respected. Thus, for the most part, in determining what one should do, one would base his or her action on the rights that bear on the case, as defined by rules of justice. Rights should play an important role in ordinary reasoning about morality.

It is extremely important to stress the conceptual connection between rights and rules. Act-utilitarian theories have been thought to be inconsistent with recognition of rights. There are at least two grounds for such doubts. On the one hand, it would seem that the act-utilitarian must make the existence of a right depend on the consequences of acts in the particular case. This is not how right claims are supported. Second, the act-utilitarian appears committed to overriding a right whenever it is perceived that greater utility will thereby be produced, even if the gain is quite small. Rights, however, cannot be overridden in this way if they are to be taken seriously. Mill's theory, even on the act-utilitarian interpretation I have attributed to him, has neither of these untoward consequences. While there are places in *Utilitarianism* where Mill gives the impression that determining whether someone has a right is merely a matter of the utilities of the particular case, the letter to Grote makes clear that this was not his view. The very point of recognizing rights would be defeated, since the device of rights is meant to forestall calculation in each case and to avoid the uncertainties that would result. To show that someone has a right, it is sufficient to show that there is (or, perhaps, ought to be) a moral rule which gives rise to that right.[28] Thus, the possession of a right (either recognized or claimed) is not a matter of the utilities of the particular case. It is a matter of the "secondary" rules that are applicable.

Similarly, since rights are designed to enhance security, and to assure uniformity in our conduct toward one another, appeal to small increments to utility in particular cases would be ruled out. This is especially so when one considers the liability to error in calculation which creates the need of rules in the first place. As I shall stress later, the rules of justice create a *system* of rights and duties that provide security, in part, by virtue of the regularity the system introduces. Part of the utility of the system would be compromised if a right can be so readily overthrown.

I do not mean to suggest that Mill's theory of rights is without its problems. For one thing, it is somewhat unclear what Mill's intention was in presenting the theory. At the very least, he wanted to explain how a utilitarian could recognize, and give great stringency to, rules of justice. But did he think that thereby he was giving an account of the ordinary notion of a right?[29] At any rate, aside from marking the distinction between legal and moral rights, there is no attempt in *Utilitarianism* to account for the various uses of the language of rights. Second, Mill made no attempt to distinguish different *kinds* of rights and the sorts of arguments relevant to reasoning about them. To cite just one example, there is little in his account that could shed light on the concept of a "basic" right, as opposed to rights which it is useful to have, but which are not fundamental to social or political life. Yet, his theory of human happiness appears to be pregnant with the possibility of such a distinction. Finally, the theory may be defective on its own terms in that it seems to sanction, *at least in principle,* sacrificing individuals' rights in order to maximize utility.[30] These issues are beyond the scope of this paper and cannot be answered, in my opinion without a rather complete account of Mill's theory of value.[31] I think I can show, however, that by stressing points Mill did recognize, it is possible to give a utilitarian justification for recognizing some form of a duty of fairness in cooperative ventures. Such a duty entails that each participant has a right to the performances of the others.

3. Fairness and Cooperation

In the last section, I called attention to the fact that the recognition of rights and reciprocal duties creates a *system* that contributes to security. This is so for two reasons that Mill cited. First, the rules of justice themselves forbid us to harm one another, and they engage societal protection from harm through social enforcement. Second, by virtue of producing regularity of behavior, by virtue of the connectedness of acts *as part of a system,* we know better what to expect of one another, and mutual trust is facilitated. We can plan our lives more readily without fear of harm to ourselves, and with greater assurance of the security of our belongings and arrangements. Thus, a system of rights, "kept unintermittedly in active play," provides the "machinery" whereby security is maintained.

This second point shows that the recognition of rights crates a new range of interests, deriving from the existence of the system itself. Everyone who shares in the system has an interest in maintaining it. We can call these "systemic" interests. One consequence of the creation of the system of rights is that almost all violations of rights have some disutility. By reintroducing the uncertainties associated with departure from the rules, a violation of a right is a form of harm in and of itself, merely *as* a violation of a right. This, of course, strengthens the utilitarian ground for taking rights seriously.

A bit of reflection will show that there are also what may be called "antecedent" or "underlying" systemic interests. Given the uncertainties of constant calculation, we all have an interest in the establishment of enforced rules. Acting on calculation in a particular case always has the disutility of not being system-related. Prior to the establishment of the "rule of the road," for example, driving on the left is no more (nor less) dangerous than driving on the right. But *both* pose dangers to others by virtue of not being system-related. Once a "rule of the road" is established, then one mode of driving becomes generally safer than the other, and safer than both were before.[32]

The sorts of interests I have labeled "systemic" are important for a utilitarian treatment of cooperation. Cooperation is engaged in because there is some state of affairs which is wanted but which it is perceived can only be achieved (or can be achieved best) if most persons involved engage in coordinated effort. Either they do the same kind of thing, or undertake interrelated roles with corresponding duties. Cooperation, then, serves an underlying systemic interest. Moreover, failure to comply, by upsetting trust, disappointing expectations, giving evidence of an uncooperative character, or, even, by raising the mere possibility of doing these, poses a threat to that interest.

Mill was aware of such interests, and he recognized that cooperation is needed to serve those interests. Moreover, he was aware that cooperation is "unstable" to the extent that some in the group fail to comply. Indeed, he held that the law may properly be used to guarantee sufficient compliance in certain cases. In an important section of his *Principles of Political Economy,* he called attention to cases in which law is needed "not to overrule the judgment of individuals respecting their own interest, but to give effect to that judgment."[33] As an example, he supposed that workers in a factory could receive as high, or nearly as high, wages, cutting back to nine hours a day from ten. If an individual cut back alone, he would either lose his job or would sacrifice a part of his wages.[34] He cannot safely set the example unless he is convinced the others will follow suit. Nor is it likely that a voluntary agreement among them which is unenforced in a rigorous way will bring about the desired cooperation. "For however beneficial the observance of the regulation might be to the class collectively, the immediate interest of every individual would lie in violating it."[35] Ideally, of course, it would be desirable if the nine hour day were the general rule, while those who wished to work extra time would be free to do so. It is not likely this could be maintained, however. The workers might, then, be better off with an enforced law which guarantees that each may safely work the shorter hours.

He also held that the government may rightfully regulate the acquisition of land. He argued that even if it is in the general and individual interest for persons not to occupy more than they can cultivate, "it can never be the interest of an individual to exercise this forebearance, unless he is assured that others will do so too."[36]

Thus, the need for systematizing behavior generates a need for cooperation, and that, in turn, creates a need for an enforceable rule that sets out a duty of compliance. A similar discussion is found in *On Liberty,* in the section in which Mill discussed "Sabbatarian legislation." He there recognized that where there is a cooperative practice enforced by law, it is "grounded in the direct interest which others have in each individual's observance of the practice."[37] The interest referred to here is clearly what I have called a systemic interest.

If we combine this analysis of cooperation with Mill's theory of rights, we get the beginnings of a theory of fairness. As we have seen, cooperation springs from and generates systemic interests for the participants. There are times when those interests ought to be protected by means of a socially enforced rule. These are precisely the conditions under which Mill's analysis of rights commits him to holding that each cooperator has a right to the performances of the others. The interest which is systematically protected is the interest each has in the others' performances. The correlative duty has all the features of a duty of fairness.

Now, Mill did not systematically employ his theory of rights, or the language of rights, in discussing issues of cooperation. Nor did he utilize the theory explicitly in *On Liberty*. However, many otherwise questionable parts of that work can be more readily explained, using that language and his theory. To cite just one example, Mill held in *On Liberty* that a person may be compelled not only to refrain from harming others, but may also be compelled to perform "positive" acts which benefit others, such as giving evidence in court, and to "bear his fair share in the common defense, or in any other joint work necessary to the interest of the society of which he enjoys the protection."[38] Moreover, he held that individuals may rightly be compelled to aid others, e.g., to save someone's life, or protect defenseless persons against harm. These are actions, he contended, which a person has a duty to perform, hence, there is a *prima facie* case that society can compel their performance. He added that we can harm others by "inaction" as well as through action.

These claims by Mill have been called into question by several commentators.[39] I shall concentrate on the "joint work" necessary to achieve social interests, as it is such situations which are the focus of this paper. Professor D.G. Brown, in an important commentary on Mill, has challenged Mill's position:

> That the individual is necessarily injuring others by not bearing his share of protecting them from injury is a relatively arguable if dubious claim. But that he is necessarily injuring them by not bearing his share in any joint work necessary to the interest of the society seems to be a much stronger claim and an indefensible one. There can be no guarantee that joint works necessary to the interest of society will not include institutional care for the mentally defective, urban redevelopment, or foreign aid to countries whose economic condition might otherwise lead to war. I cannot see how refusal to co-operate in such efforts toward alleviation of existing problems could be shown to constitute causing harm to others.[40]

Further, in a more recent paper, he has argued that there are "two branches of distinct and assignable obligation" for Mill.[41] There are duties toward the public and duties toward particular individuals. Only in the latter case does failure to fulfill the duty violate a duty to an assignable individual, and hence a duty of justice. Such a breach of duty violates public rights, not those of individuals.

Part of Brown's argument involves textual analysis which it is beyond this paper to explore. Moreover, I have conceded that Mill did not consistently apply the language of the theory of rights in *Utilitarianism* in the essay on liberty. Though *On Liberty* was published earlier, the essays are from the same period in his thought, so it is not implausible that they should be interconnected in doctrine. More importantly, I believe I can show how the treatment of cooperation I have outlined would explain Mill's claims in *On Liberty*.

Where there are public goods pursued through cooperation, the participants have two sorts of interest at stake. First, is their interest in the goods produced through cooperation. In addition, each individual has systemic interests which concern the cooperative scheme itself; in the cases Brown cites, this is, minimally, the taxing framework. The failure to conform to the requirements of cooperation does harm others by posing a danger to the systemic interests they have.[42] Moreover, by posing that danger, Mill held that it makes it more to the interest of the others to violate the requirements. As this, in turn, endangers the continuance of the benefits of the scheme, the original non-compliance poses a danger to the ultimate goods. Thus, it endangers both kinds of interests of all the others, and in this way harms them.[43] As I argued earlier, these claims can be rephrased in terms of Mill's theory of rights. Since the cooperators have interests which it is useful to society to protect *as a matter of enforced rule,* it would follow that each has a right to the others' performances.

Now, it is true that the correlative duties in these situations can be described as "duties to the public." But, there is no reason to suppose a category of "public rights" is thereby created which is not fully explained by Mill's notion of a duty to "assignable" persons. The duty *is* public *by virtue of* being owed to *each* person. Virtually all the rules of justice mentioned by Mill in *Utilitarianism* ("in which we must never forget to include wrongful interference with each other's freedom")[44] are duties toward everyone. The only contrast Mill makes there is with duties *no* particular person can claim is owed him or her.

My main objectives have been to give an account of Mill's theory which, at the same time, would shed light on how an act-utilitarian can account for duties of justice and fairness. There has been nothing definitive in either attempt, even if I have been successful. There are many aspects of Mill's theory I do not understand, or with respect to which Mill (so far as I know) said nothing. And, though I have tried to present Mill's theory in a way that makes it plausible, I have not tried to defend it. Of great importance would be the questions of *what* principles of justice he could recognize. This is not a difficulty, however, because Mill was silent on the subject. In various places are to be found defenses by Mill of a number of principles of distributive justice, in particular. As an example, in the *Principles of Political Economy,* he defended *as* a principle of justice, a principle of "Equality of Taxation," which requires "apportioning the contribution of each person towards the expenses of government, so that he shall feel neither more nor less inconvenience from his share of the payment than every other person experiences from his."[45] The problem is that Mill wrote on these subjects in a number of places, and an extended study is required to trace out the principles he defended, or to which he was committed.

In addition, we still do not know what form of a principle of fairness he would accept. There is some evidence (primarily from the examples he discussed in *Principles of Political Economy* and *On Liberty*) that he would have insisted that such a principle applies only when individuals have voluntarily undertaken cooperation.[46] But, we cannot say for sure. Nor have I attempted to discuss the special role that some writers attribute to intentions and motives in arguments about fairness.[47] In any event, my own study of Mill convinces me that we cannot argue for specific principles he would accept without reference to his complex conception of human happiness, and his emphasis on certain things as essential to human well-being. For example, he held that the "sense of dignity" is found in all of us, and he wrote that "no one could without voluntary degradation admit that he ought to be counted for nothing."[48] Such statements tantalizingly suggest the principle of treating individuals as having worth in themselves, as a requisite of the happiness of a human being. He also maintained that we are social beings who require the development of our social feelings in order to attain the highest states of well-being.[49] Among the social feelings are sympathy and "the desire to be in unity with our fellow creatures."[50] In the proper development of a society, he held, we would come not to desire that which could not be shared with others.[51] Though there is reason to think he would, and did, qualify these claims, it is evidence that he was committed to a strong principle of equality, and that he would favor strong principles of cooperation which forbid exploiting cooperative schemes in ways not open to the others without their consent. This is not because he was not utilitarian, but because he had an enlarged conception of what has value for human beings, and the role that cooperation itself has aside from its further products, in human happiness. But the task of assaying these issues must be left for another time.

NOTES

1. The chief exception is the work of Professor David Lyons. I refer below to several papers of his that lead up to his treatment of Mill on justice. He has very kindly allowed me to read several papers he has written on Mill's theory of justice, not yet published; and he has given me helpful comments on an earlier version of this paper, for which I am grateful. Also, a part of this paper was developed in a personal exchange of views with Professor Gertrude Ezorsky, to whom I am also grateful.

2. H.L.A. Hart, "Are There Any Natural Rights?" *The Philosophical Review,* 64 (1955), 185.

3. John Rawls, *A Theory of Justice* (Cambridge, Mass.: Harvard University, 1971), 112. Later in the book, Rawls elaborates important qualifications, and distinguishes the principle of fairness from a "natural" duty to support and further just institutions (pp. 333–355). I shall not be concerned with these finer points.

4. J.S. Mill, *Utilitarianism,* Vol. X of *Collected Works,* ed. J.M. Robson (Toronto: Toronto University Press, 1969), 247. (Hereafter, the *Collected Works* will be abbreviated by "CW".)

5. *Ibid.,* 246. Mill's analysis of the nature of a moral judgment raises some problems of interpretation. On the one hand, he may be interpreted as holding that a speaker expresses a moral judgment only if he or she asserts that someone ought to do something (or has a duty, etc.) *and* has a moral sentiment that is expressed. On the other hand, he can be taken to hold that a moral judgment *asserts* that the speaker has a moral sentiment. This is, roughly, the distinction between a non-cognitivist and subjectivist interpretation of moral language. He may also have accepted both analyses. The relevant discussions in addition to those already cited are in: "Letter to William George Ward," *The Later Letters,* ed. Francis E. Mineka and Dwight N. Lindley, II, 649, Vol. XV of *CW;* and *A System of Logic,* ed. J.M. Robson, 949, Vol. XIII of *CW.*

6. *CW,* X, 249–50.

7. *Ibid.,* 250.

8. James Mill, *Analysis of the Phenomena of the Human Mind,* ed. John Stuart Mill (London: Longmans Green Reader and Dyer, 1869), II, 325.

9. *CW,* X, 249.

10. *Ibid.,* 251.

11. In an introductory essay in Volume X of *CW,* D.P. Dryer contends that though Mill had taken the notion of duty "in every one of its forms" to imply that the person having it may be compelled to fulfill it, he later exempted duties of imperfect obligation from this connection. (*CW,* X, xcix–c.) If "compelled to" can mean "may be subject to moral reproach for violating," as Mill sometimes did mean, then Dryer's claim is not clearly true. There is some reason to think, however, that Mill would have limited the "enforcement" of imperfect duties to reproach, recrimination, entreaty, etc., in which case there would be a significant difference in the mode of enforcement to which the two sorts of duty are liable;

for, violations of duties of perfect obligation may properly call forth the infliction of harm, limitations on liberty, social ostracism, etc., as well as reproach.

12. *CW*, X, 338.

13. *Ibid.*

14. *Ibid.*, 231–33.

15. *CW*, X, 256. This is almost certainly an incorrect analysis of the morality involved in breach of friendship. It is not merely that expectations are disappointed, but that our *friend* has done this. I have discussed some of the features of the morality of interpersonal relations, and the possibility of a utilitarian account of them, in my essay "Gratitude," *Ethics*, 85 (1975), 298–309. Though Mill himself did not take up these issues at any length, he did complain that Bentham's limited view of human nature disabled him from shedding light on the morality of such interpersonal relations as "the sexual relations, or those of family in general, or any other social and sympathetic connexions of an intimate kind." (*CW*, X, 98.)

16. *CW*, X, 256. David Lyons has suggested that here Mill emphasizes not merely the disappointment of expectation, but also habitual reliance. This suggests that it is expectations on which we base important features of our lives which deserve protection, as this reliance generates needs of important kinds which carry the "wound" beyond mere disappointment. At the least, such considerations would be a basis for distinguishing the different *degrees* of wrongness of various promise and friendship breaches.

17. J.O. Urmson, "The Interpretation of the Moral Philosophy of J.S. Mill," *The Philosophical Quarterly*, 3 (1953), 33 9. I believe the most plausible version of a rule-related view attributed to Mill is that of David Lyons, "Mill's Theory of Morality," *Nous*, 10 (1976), 101–20. Lyons contends that the principle of utility is not itself a moral rule, and does not lay down moral obligations. Rather, Mill analyzed the concept of moral duty as applying to acts which may justifiably be required by a coercive rule, though coercion may take only the form of guilt feelings at the thought of doing the act. On this view, our obligations derive wholly from the rules. The principle of utility specifies an *end* to be achieved—happiness; and Mill's theory is that happiness is attained by means of the adoption of morality, which is a set of rules laying down rights and duties. I shall claim this fits his analysis of justice, but not a morality as a whole.

18. David Lyons, "Human Rights and the General Welfare," *Philosophy & Public Affairs*, 6 (1977–8), 113–29.

19. I shall cite just a small part of the evidence—some passages which are not well known. When commenting on Bentham, he wrote: "Insofar as Bentham's adoption of the principle of utility induced him to fix upon the consequences of actions as the consideration determining their morality, so far he was indisputably in the right path." (*CW*, X, 111.) In a review he wrote with George Grote, he wrote: "To admit the balance of consequences as a test of right and wrong, necessarily implies the possibility of exceptions to any derivative rule of morality which may be deduced from that test. . . . Philosophy commands that in dealing with any particular case, the whole of the circumstances, without exception, should be taken

into view . . . and if a man wilfully overlooks the latter [the special circumstances of the case], when they are pregnant with mischievous consequences, he cannot discharge himself from moral responsibility by pleading that he had the general rule in his favor." (*CW,* XIX, 638, 640.) This would seem to imply that in the exceptional cases, we act *wrongly* if we adhere to the rule. The rule-related theory of obligations that Lyons attributes to Mill also permits violations in these cases. However, Lyons' Mill would be forced to justify such violations on non-moral grounds, overriding morality itself by utility. I believe the above statement of Mill's (joined in by Grote), rejects this view. Aside from the further evidence in *Utilitarianism* that is well-known, there is additional support in his "Carlyle's *French Revolution,*" in *Mill's Essays on Literature and Society,* ed. with an intro. J.B. Schneewind (New York: The Macmillan Company, 1965), 201–02; and, several years after the publication of *Utilitarianism,* in "Thornton on Labour and Its Claims," *CW,* V, 659.

20. I have not attempted a precise formulation as this would raise interpretive difficulties beyond my present concerns. Mill did not think *every* act is of moral significance, though most contemporary versions of act-utilitarianism have this consequence. In particular, he appears to have held (in common with his father), that self-regarding conduct does not raise issues of right and wrong. The theory of morality I want to attribute to Mill is act-utilitarian in the sense that it holds that within the class of acts which are morally assessable, rightness or wrongness is a function of an act's consequences.

21. Contrary to some interpreters who hold that John Austin's theory is ambiguous between an act- or rule-utilitarian interpretation, the theory I have sketched seems to me quite clearly to be Austin's. Austin defined the tendency of an act to be "the sum of its probable consequences," and the *test* of the tendency to consist in asking what would happen if it were generally done. (John Austin, *The Province of Jurisprudence Determined and The Uses of the Study of Jurisprudence,* intro. H.L.A. Hart [London: Weidenfeld and Nicolson, 1954], 38.) Calculation in every case is not needed because rules are available, moreover, "the *true* result would be expressed by that rule, whilst the process would probably be faulty if it were done on the spur of the occasion." (*Ibid.,* 49.) Nonetheless, he contended, there will be special cases in which we must calculate specific consequences "to the best of our knowledge and ability." (*Ibid.,* 53.)

In a letter responding to the logician, John Venn, John Stuart Mill also endorsed the role of rules as a test of the probable consequences: "I agree with you that the right way of testing actions by their consequences, is to test them by the natural consequences of the particular action, and not by those which would follow if every one did the same. But, for the most part, the consideration of what would happen if everyone did the same, is the only means we have of discovering the tendency of the act in the particular case." (*The Later Letters, CW,* XVIII, 1881.)

More recently, R.M. Hare has outlined an act-utilitarian theory that has many of the features of the theory I attribute to Mill. See, R.M. Hare, "Principles," *Proceedings of the Aristotelian Society,* 73 (1972–73), 1–18.

22. I do not believe this was Mill's view. Alan Ryan, however, has held that Mill

was not entirely consistent on this point; he claims that Mill's essay, "Whewell on Moral Philosophy" bears the stricter interpretation. (Alan Ryan, *J.S. Mill* [London: Routledge & Kegan Paul, 1974], 122.) The essay on Whewell is in *CW,* X, 165–201.

23. The importance of making this distinction is argued for carefully by R. Eugene Bales. See, "Act-Utilitarianism: Account of Right-Making Characteristics or Decision-Making Procedure?" *American Philosophical Quarterly,* 8 (1971), 257–65. Though Bales seems unaware of it, the classical utilitarians appear to have recognized the distinction in at least embryonic form.

24. *CW,* X, 111.

25. E.g., D.H. Hodgson, *Consequences of Utilitarianism* (Oxford: Clarendon Press, 1967), 48.

26. See, footnote 15, above. The role of strategies with respect to various principles of justice is explored at some length in the pioneering work of Professor Torstein Eckhoff. See, *Justice: Its Determinants in Social Interaction* (Rotterdam: Rotterdam University Press, 1974).

27. *The Later Letters, CW,* XV, 762. The quotation lends some support to David Lyons' rule-related interpretation of Mill's moral theory. It is, however, consistent also with my interpretation, especially in light of the qualifying clauses "in most cases" and "generally." Also, the utilities cited seem to follow from recognized rules, not merely ideal ones.

28. It should be noted that Mill almost never made it clear when he was referring to recognized rules, ideal-if-conformed-with rules, ideal-if-adopted rules, etc. It may well be that he thought it is some sort of ideal rule to which appeal is properly made, however, since he also believed that existing social rules tend to embody the results of utilitarian calculation, these can provide a criterion of action, as approximations to the ideal rules. David Lyons may have something like this in mind; see, "Mill's Theory of Morality," p. 116.

29. There is some reason to think he was not attempting an account and reconciliation of the ordinary notion of a right with his own. He discussed rights in his essay on Austin, in which he stressed that a right is intended for the benefit of the right-holder. In a much earlier essay he took up the ordinary concept of a right in some detail, in the course of a review of a book by a George Cornewall Lewis. He distinguished several senses of a right in ordinary usage, and made some points that may not be entirely consistent with the theory in *Utilitarianism.* In particular, he held that there is a difference between having a right and having a right to enforce the right. ("Austin on Jurisprudence," *Dissertations and Discussions* [London: Longmans, Green, Reader, and Dyer] III, 206–74; and "Use and Abuse of Political Terms," *CW,* XVIII, 10.) This latter distinction has come to have some importance in contemporary political philosophy. It is stressed in Robert Nozick, *Anarchy, State, and Utopia* (New York: Basic Books, Inc., 1974), 91ff. Mill's comments, however, suggest that it is only a weak kind of right—one which implies only the absence of a duty on the actor's part—to which this distinction applies. See, also, *A System of Logic, CW,* VIII, 818.

30. It is of interest to note that the theory Lyons attributes to Mill has a similar result, in that he holds that for Mill, appeal to utility itself is open when rights conflict. However, his Mill seems to have to justify overriding rights in these cases on non-moral grounds. See, e.g., "Mill's Theory of Morality," 113–14.

31. I have outlined the most important parts of that theory in my essay "Mill's Concept of Happiness," *Interpretation,* to appear.

32. Though the point is a bit sophistical, we can claim that Mill could consistently make the point that society can interfere only with harmful conduct *(On Liberty)* and still institute a "rule of the road." The antecedently harmful conduct is unsystematic or unregulated behavior.

33. *Principles of Political Economy,* Vol. III of *CW,* 956.

34. I presume that Mill supposed the employer would want to pay reduced wages.

35. *Principles of Political Economy,* 957.

36. *Ibid.,* 959. He went so far as to hold that the criminal law as a whole is based primarily on the consideration that each complying citizen is given some guarantee that his or her restriction of behavior will not be a sacrifice to those who do not comply. A similar view of the law is given in H.L.A. Hart, *The Concept of Law* (Oxford: Clarendon Press, 1961), 193.

37. *On Liberty,* Vol. XVIII of *CW,* 289.

38. *Ibid.,* 225.

39. E.g., H.J. McCloesky, *John Stuart Mill: A Critical Study* (London: Macmillan, 1971), 107–08; and D.G. Brown, "Mill on Liberty and Morality," *The Philosophical Review,* 81 (1972), 145–46.

40. Brown, *ibid.,* 146.

41. D.G. Brown, "Mill on Harm to Others' Interest," *Political Studies,* 26 (1978), pp. 395–9.

42. In discussing the sentiments expressed in a moral judgment, Mill indicated that they are a response to "hurts, which wound us *through,* or in common with, society at large." (*CW,* X, 249. Italics added.)

43. These may still appear to be weak claims, easily overridden. Mill, however, seems not to have thought so. In the letter to John Venn, cited in note 21, he held that the mischievous tendency of an act which violates a rule is shown by considering its effect on the security provided by the rule: "And that this mischievous tendency overbalances (unless in very extreme cases) the private good obtained by the breach of a moral rule, is obvious if we take into consideration the importance, to the general good, of the feeling of security, or certainty; which is impaired, not only by every known actual violation of good rules, but by the belief that such violations ever occur." (*The Later Letters,* XVII, 1881–82.)

44. *CW,* X, 255.

45. *Principles of Political Economy,* 807.

46. Some of the problems to be faced in framing an acceptable principle are canvassed in David Lyons, *Forms and Limits of Utilitarianism* (Oxford: Clarendon Press, 1965), 161–77. There is some further evidence that Mill would have re-

stricted the punishable duty to cases where voluntary entrance into the scheme had been procured. In "Thornton on Labour and Its Claims," he considered the case of the propriety of labor unions forcing workers to pay dues, go on strike, etc. He argued that the law ought not to permit forcing workers to do these things, though some will benefit from the sacrifices of the others. Still, the others may properly feel and express "genuine moral disapprobation." (*CW*, V, 659–60.) The discussion has some further importance in that it implies a difference in kind between "social pressure" that takes the form of the expression of disapprobation, and that which consists in inflicting further harms or disadvantages. What is left unclear is whether the non-complying workers *do* have a duty to comply, but that only the weaker enforcement is appropriate.

47. Lyons, *Forms and Limits of Utilitarianism*, 175–77. The problem is especially complicated in Mill's case, as he held that an act consists of an intention and a physical movement. Where there are different intentions, there are, presumably, different acts. See, especially, *A System of Logic*, Vol. VII of *CW*, 55; and *On Liberty*, *CW*, XVIII, 219–20.

48. *The Later Letters*, *CW*, XV, 600.

49. "Remarks on Bentham's Philosophy," *CW*, X, 15.

50. *Utilitarianism*, *CW*, X, 232.

51. *Ibid.* This point is reiterated in "Auguste Comte and Positivism," *CW*, X, 339.

What's the Use of Going to School? The Problem of Education in Utilitarianism and Rights Theories

Amy Gutmann

Education seems to present special difficulties for all liberal theories.[1] Utilitarians and those whom I shall call 'rights theorists', i.e. those who give priority to the equal right of all to civil and political freedom, agree on one point about the education of children: at least in principle they both are committed to providing an education that is neutral among substantive conceptions of the good life.[2] Yet we probably will never be able to educate children without prejudicing their future choice of particular ways of life. One might argue, therefore, that education creates the same problem for any form of liberalism. That argument is incorrect. Although rights theorists also must take consequences into account, they can provide a more consistently liberal solution to the problem of education for several reasons, which I shall summarise here and elaborate below. Freedom provides a better standard than happiness by which to determine what and how to teach children. In addition, one can derive some essential features of a liberal educational programme from the standard of freedom that cannot be derived from that of happiness. That educational programme will be neutral towards many, though not all, ways of life and concrete enough to guide educators. In addition, unlike utilitarianism, rights theorists can respond cogently to the conservative claim that education must perpetuate particular societal values and prepare children for necessary social functions.

1. Education for Happiness

Utilitarians pay a high price for assuming that happiness must be subjectively defined by each individual, an assumption that frees them of the need to defend an objective conception of the good. How is society to prepare children for the pursuit of their own, self-defined happiness? Children cannot themselves determine the particular ends of education, nor is maximising their present happiness a reasonable utilitarian standard for education, if only because the rest of their life is likely to be much longer than their childhood. Yet what will make children happy in the future is largely indeterminate. To make matters more complicated still, education itself significantly shapes how children will define their happiness once they become adults. To guide the education of children, utilitarians need to find a standard that is not tied to a particular conception of the good life and that is not derived from the circular argument that if they become happy adults their prior education must have been good. Thus, the major problems that utilitarians face in determining the purpose of educational institutions are prior to the problem of aggregating happiness, for which utilitarians have been amply criticised by rights theorists.[3] These problems can be best illustrated by looking more closely at the foundations of Benthamite utilitarianism and at Bentham's specific recommendations for educating children.

Benthamite utilitarianism takes the preferences of individuals as a given and regards attempts to maximise satisfaction of those preferences as 'good'. 'Pushpin is as good as poetry', so long as the satisfaction a person derives from each is equal and each contributes equally to the happiness of others. As J. J. C. Smart points out, the latter condition will almost certainly mean in practice that poetry will be a better activity than pushpin, because poetry will add to the happiness of others more than pushpin will.[4] Even critics of utilitarianism recognise that happiness, broadly interpreted, is a minimally controversial good in that it accommodates almost all conceptions of the good life.[5] Very few people want to lead an *un*happy or *un*satisfying life.[6] Utilitarianism maintains a neutral position among conceptions of the good life, asking people only to recognise the equal claims of all others to lead a happy life as they define it.

Of course, that request may entail a sizable amount of self-sacrifice since, at least in theory, the greatest happiness principle can override one person's claim to happiness by its recognition of the validity of many claims with which it comes in conflict. However, rights theories must also have to establish some priority in such cases. The neutrality principle, combined with the Benthamite view that happiness is a subjectively defined state, requires that every person's capacity for happiness be considered equal. This equality assumption and the law of diminishing marginal utility all but guarantee that utilitarianism will demand no greater sacrifice of individuals for the general good than will most rights theories, which also make provisions for overriding an individual's right in extreme situations.[7]

Utilitarians must reject a few common solutions to the problem of education. They cannot avoid the task of specifying standards that ought to guide the education of children simply by allocating decision-making authority to some paternalistic agent. According to utilitarian reasoning, neither parents nor the state have a natural right to determine the education of children. Children are neither the property of their parents nor mere creatures of the state.[8] Utilitarians are correct on this score: even if we must ultimately allocate rights of control over education, the exercise of those rights ought to be contingent upon the fulfilment of duties to educate properly. Therefore, the definition of educational standards should be prior to the allocation of paternalistic authority.[9]

A strict utilitarian must also reject John Stuart Mill's suggestion that education be guided by the perfectionist ideal of maximising development of the particular capacities of each individual. Mill claims that what constitutes maximum development of character is decided by reference to happiness as the standard, and that therefore perfectionism (as he understands it) is consistently utilitarian. Mill provides two standards by which he claims perfectionism is rendered compatible with happiness. Both are inadequate. His first standard of happiness—'the comparatively humble sense of pleasure and freedom from pain'—does not necessarily lead to a perfectionist ideal: playing pushpin is probably more pleasurable, at least in the comparatively humble sense of the word, than writing poetry. And his second—that life which 'human beings with highly developed faculties can care to have'—is extremely problematic from a utilitarian or any other liberal perspective, because it smuggles in a particular conception of the good life under the guise of a universally acceptable choice criterion of pleasure.[10] So, although perfectionism would save utilitarianism from the problem of finding some standard of happiness external to children's preferences, it would do so only by sacrificing utilitarianism's neutrality with regard to conceptions of the good life.

Utilitarians could dodge the problem entirely by educating children so as to maximise the happiness of adults. Since the future preferences of children are unknown while those of adults are known and relatively stable over time, this might be a 'safe' utilitarian strategy. But it is also an intuitively unappealing course, which would again raise in the educational context the general aggregation problem of utilitarianism. The intuitively plausible rationale for discounting the present preferences of children is to help them realise greater happiness in the future, not to sacrifice their happiness entirely to that of their elders. What if 'educating' children to be garbage collectors would maximise the happiness of adults? Although children seem to wallow in dirt (as Fourier noted), no sane utilitarian has ever advocated such a policy, which could hardly be called educational. Even on utilitarian standards, it would be shortsighted to educate children for the happiness of adults. Since children will outlive adults, their education then will cease to have any point.

Education, according to James Mill, ought to render each individual's mind, 'as much as possible, an instrument of happiness, *first* to himself, and next to other beings'.[11] Utilitarians cannot consistently claim that education ought first be concerned with a child's own happiness because such an education is a child's right or because that is the intrinsic nature of the educational good. But they can plausibly claim that most *educated* persons will be better judges and hence better 'instruments' of their own happiness than they will be of others' happiness. The classic utilitarian plan for education, *Chrestomathia,* therefore focusses upon education as a means of rendering each child's mind an instrument of his or her own happiness. (Bentham argued that girls as well as boys be admitted to Chrestomathia.) As the neologism implies, education ought to 'conduce to useful learning'.[12]

Useful for what? Happiness is surely too indefinite an end (as utilitarians themselves admit) to guide an educational programme. Bentham therefore listed secondary ends, which he assumed were constitutive of every child's future happiness. Education ought to supply children with the means to (1) avoiding 'inordinate sensuality (and its mischievous consequences)', (2) securing profit-yielding employment, (3) securing admission into 'good company' from which the previous advantage could also be obtained, (4) avoiding ennui and the 'pain of mental vacuity', and (5) gaining a 'proportionable share of general respect'.[13]

Surveying Bentham's list, we discover that each secondary end is problematic. Either it is not clearly derivable from happiness as an ultimate end, not sufficiently neutral among conceptions of the good life, or as indeterminate an educational goal as happiness itself.

If *inordinate* sensuality is defined as the amount that proves counterproductive to the pursuit of long-term happiness, then utilitarians can of course consistently teach children to control their inordinate sensual desires. Otherwise, the goal of avoiding sensuality is not clearly consistent with utilitarian principles. One suspects that Bentham has conveniently yielded to prevailing moral opinion that sensuality is a bad thing.

Securing profit-yielding employment and admission into good company is no more consistent with the greatest happiness principle. Surely, many types of employment that are not often profit-yielding—artistic vocations, for example—can be pleasure yielding, perhaps even more so than jobs in business. But if a child has no independent source of income, then income-producing employment is likely to be essential to living a minimally happy life. Once one accepts the prevailing economic reality—that only independently wealthy children can afford to be educated to pursue non-income producing vocations—then Bentham's educational goal seems to follow. Similarly, if admission into good company provides a ticket to gainful employment, then from a utilitarian perspective an education that enables children to enter into good company may be sufficiently neutral among conceptions of the good life.

Yet the results of this reasoning are incongruous with liberalism. A theory that on principle is neutral among a wide range of ways of life turns out to be partial to those particular ways that happen to produce steady income and social approval. Furthermore, those people who will determine that partiality will not be the same people who will be subject to its consequences. Utilitarianism thus appears to be in this sense illiberal and to have conservative consequences when applied to education: children are to be educated so that they can fit into society as it exists. Whether this is a fatal criticism of utilitarianism from a liberal perspective will depend upon whether any liberal theory can better cope with this educational dilemma.

The goals of avoiding ennui and gaining the respect of others are sufficiently neutral among conceptions of the good life and can be derived from the summa bonum of happiness.[14] However, neither is more determinate than happiness. Indeed, it would be hard to conceive of a more nebulous educational goal than avoiding the 'pain of mental vacuity'.

2. EDUCATION FOR FREEDOM

Rights theorists face a problem analogous to that of utilitarians, since children cannot plausibly be granted freedoms equal to those of adults and education necessitates a curtailment of freedom. As Russell noted in a lecture on J. S. Mill, 'There is one sphere in which the advocate of liberty is confronted with peculiar difficulties: I mean the sphere of education.'[15] Does freedom provide a better standard than happiness by which to determine what and how to teach children? Can one derive from the standard of freedom an educational programme that remains neutral among conceptions of the good life?

Some of Bentham's secondary goals for education are more compatible with an education designed to prepare children for freedom than with one designed for happiness. By preparing every child through education for profit-yielding employment, we are providing children with the background conditions for free choice in a society that attaches a price to most valued goods. And if admission to good company facilitates access to many valued goods, then education directed at securing such access will also increase a child's future freedom. In fact, these secondary goals seem more reasonably connected to the end of future freedom than to that of future happiness. By all accounts, children of the Old Order Amish who are denied secondary schooling by their parents, and are therefore trained for only a very narrow range of vocations, grow up to be as happy as, and probably more secure than, their more educated peers.[16] But, by their parents' own admission and intent, their lesser education makes them less free to choose among ways of life. Utilitarians have traditionally denied that 'he that increaseth knowledge increaseth sorrow', but they have offered little or no specific evidence to support their counterclaim that the question of whether people should have more or less education 'is merely the question, whether they should have more or less of misery, when happiness might be given in its stead'.[17] A consistent utilitarian could, of course, deny the need for education in cases like those of the Amish. But it is hard to find a consistent utilitarian because most are unwilling to abandon their commitment to educating children in order to pursue the goal of maximising happiness.[18]

But suppose utilitarians did remain faithful to the principle of happiness, and in the case of the Amish children defer to their parents' opposition to secondary education. Utilitarians will then face the problem of neutrality. Amish children did not themselves choose to pursue the traditional Amish way of life; their parents have no right to determine how their children will live when they grow up. Then, why should utilitarians defer to the preferences of the adult Amish in denying an education to their children? Once having been raised in an Amish family, Amish children may well be happier, and thus be better off by utilitarian standards, without any secondary education. Therefore utilitarians seem bound to defer to the wishes of Amish parents. Yet in so doing, they forsake any commitment to educating children for their own choice among ways of life.

So the problem of neutrality now reappears on another level. Amish parents raise their children so as to prevent them from finding happiness outside of the Amish way of life. If happiness is subjectively determined, utilitarians committed to maximising social happiness cannot be content to permit any group to shelter their children from influences that permit a wide range of choice among ways of life that might lead to happiness. Yet so long as all forms of education predispose children toward certain ways of finding happiness and away from others, utilitarians must choose the forms that are most likely to produce happy people. The more serious problem specific to utilitarianism is that it lacks any means of comparing the level of satisfaction gained from radically different ways of life.

John Stuart Mill's choice criterion of pleasure can be viewed as an attempt to solve this problem of incommensurability, but it begs the issue from a utilitarian perspective.[19] Socrates cannot possibly know what it is like to be as happy as a fool. And once we are educated and exposed to worldly influences, we are effectively deprived of the possibility of experiencing the satisfactions of the Amish way of life. That we then choose not to become Amish is immaterial to the question of which is a better way of life on utilitarian grounds.

Dewey's educational criterion shares the same problem as Mill's choice criterion of pleasure. A utilitarian cannot recommend as the standard for what 'the community [must] want for all of its children' what 'the best and wisest parent wants for his own child'.[20] Only actual preferences or actual satisfactions can count on utilitarian grounds. Dewey's standard appears equally suspect on grounds of free choice. A liberal cannot assume that the best education is that which a particular group of people want to provide for their children. At the very least, liberals must provide criteria for what a good education is or else tell us why a particular group has the right to determine educational standards for the whole community

3. THE SOCIAL BOUNDARIES OF FREEDOM

The issue of education puts the conflict between utilitarians and rights theorists in a different light than it is usually seen. Defenses of education in both schools of thought are consequentialist; neither invokes the claim that compulsory education is a good in itself or that the pursuit of knowledge can be justified by its own internally generated principles.[21] But the nature of the consequentialist reasoning differs significantly. Utilitarians must judge the subjective outcome of being educated relative to that of remaining uneducated. Rights theorists need only determine whether education expands or contracts the opportunities children will have for rational choice in the future. This objective criterion is easier to apply in practice because it does not depend upon a difficult counter-factual assessment of future states of mind: how much happier or sadder would they have been were they uneducated? Nor does it succumb to the circularity of Mill's choice criterion of pleasure.

But the task of rights theorists still is not easy. They have to determine how to select among the possible courses of education that which will maximally expand each child's future civil and political freedom. An education directed at maximising future choice cannot be neutral among all ways of life. Even if Bentham's curriculum was unduly restrictive (he opposed teaching music in schools because it would make too much noise),[22] there is no way of educating children to choose impartially between becoming a farmer in an Amish community and becoming a jazz musician. Any curriculum that is secular and imparts scientific knowledge will make the choice of some religious ways of life much more difficult than would a religious education. In addition, the methods of teaching—reliance upon competition or cooperation, upon rewards or punishment—also predispose children towards particular private and political choices in the future.

Education for freedom, then, must operate within some boundaries in any case. The question becomes: which boundaries are most justifiable? Freedom itself seems to provide a standard if one counts the possibilities left open by each educational programme and chooses the one that leaves open the most (reasonable) options. But notice that this standard depends on the nature of the society to which it is applied. What one counts as reasonable options will be determined in part by the social context within which children will have to make their future choices. Were we living in seventeenth-century America, a religious education would provide children with more opportunities for choice among ways of life than would a secular education. An education that employs cooperative methods of learning would prepare children for more occupations in Maoist China than would the competitive educational methods used in most schools in the United States. Interpreted in this way, the freedom standard also has a conservative bias: it permits partiality—reflected both in educational content and methods—towards those conceptions of the good life that are most commonly pursued and that are income-producing within any given society.[23] Once again, this non-neutrality cannot itself be justified by reference to the choices children have made or will make, once educated, to pursue these established ways of life.

We might ask, therefore, whether a more conservative theory provides a better prescription for the content of education. Unlike utilitarians and rights theorists, Durkheim explicitly defends the idea that education should have a conservative function. He criticises both the utilitarian view that education ought to be a means toward individual happiness and the idea (which he gathers from Kant) that education ought to be a means towards individual perfection. Because happiness is a subjective state, Durkheim argues, it leaves the end of education to individual fancy and hence undetermined. Perfectionism ignores the demands that the division of labour places upon modern education for specialised training. More generally, Durkheim maintains that the educational philosophies of political theorists are all misguided: 'they assume that there is an ideal, perfect education, which applies to all men indiscriminately; and it is this education universal and unique, that the theorist tries to define'. In place of an ideal education, Durkheim argues for an education that is the product of the common life of a society and therefore expresses the educational needs of that society. 'Of what use is it to imagine a kind of education that would be fatal for the society that put it into practice?'[24]

Even if an education 'fatal for the society that put it into practice' is an idle—and perhaps dangerous—fancy, Durkheim's recommendation does not immediately follow. Why should education perpetuate the particular roles demanded by the collective life of each particular society? Durkheim himself makes the transition from 'is' to 'ought' without explicit argument. He seems to assume that because education serves this integrative function in most societies, it ought to do so. But there is something to be said for Durkheim's conclusion. In advanced industrial societies, educational institutions are well-equipped to perpetuate common and unifying beliefs. Aside from the family, schools and television are the only institutions that come into prolonged contact with the younger generation of citizens. As long as family life is to remain a private realm—valued in part for its diversity and immunity from intervention—then schools and television are the only plausible socialising institutions that can be effectively regulated (even if not fully controlled) by a liberal or illiberal state. This functional importance does not of course justify a conservative use of education, but it does suggest that if a society's values are worth preserving the educational system may be an essential instrument.

Must rights theorists oppose this socialising function of schools as a form of tyranny of the majority over the individual? Durkheim denies that socialisation (through education) is tyranny. Education gives children what is uniquely human and moral: control over their inclinations, a socially determined morality and a language that enables them to communicate that morality to their peers. Socialisation into a liberal democratic society entails more than mere discipline and the acquisition of language. The state also has a legitimate interest in educating children to respect reason, science, and the 'ideas and sentiments which are at the base of democratic morality'.[25] Now, one might dispute the importance of the particular objects of respect that Durkheim has chosen (e.g. respect for science), but the challenge that his argument poses for liberalism would remain the same. At least in its early stages, education is not primarily a liberating institution but a constraining one; the constraints are justified by the needs of society for cohesion; and children are 'humanized' (which for Durkheim means socialised) by those constraints. According to Durkheim, this same rationale of social cohesion also accounts for specialisation of education at higher levels, because 'without a certain diversity all cooperation would be impossible; education assures the persistence of this necessary diversity by being itself diversified and specialised'.[26] Insofar as children themselves are the beneficiaries, rights theorists must also embrace the socialising function of schools.

But Durkheim's challenge to liberalism is only partially successful. Rights theories can account for the constraints education places upon the thoughts of children and for the fact that those constraints are—and ought to be—relative to the society in which children are raised. Rights theorists must also justify those constraints by taking into account the interests of children in becoming social beings and, more specifically, in becoming citizens of the society in which they are born. But for rights theorists, social cohesion is a virtue only in a society in which membership is a benefit, rather than a burden, i.e. in a society in which children will become citizens with the full range of civil and political liberties, and not be mere subjects of the state. Even if elementary education must discipline children, the ultimate purpose of education on a rights theory will be to equip every child with the intellectual means to choose a way of life compatible with the equal freedom of others.

Social cohesion is a prerequisite for this freedom, but such cohesion can be achieved through many different educational and non-educational methods, some of which are inimical to freedom. Rights theorists must choose those methods that are most consistent with maximising the future freedom of children. Durkheim and rights theorists converge in their reasoning so long as the state provides the context within which individual freedom is best protected.[27] But they part company in their understanding of how diversity should be accomplished within a democratic state. If social cohesion and economic welfare are the only rationales for educational specialisation, then tracking children into particular specialised vocational programmes would be justified so long as the number of children in each track was sufficient to meet future social needs and the tracks were divided according to ability. Rights theory, however, also demands that education provide (as far as possible given the diversity of natural talents) an equal educational opportunity for every child. This demand is based upon the value of maximising each child's freedom to choose a way of life consistent with the like freedom of all others.[28] The requirements of the division of labour, therefore, are only to be met by specialised education after children are given sufficient opportunity to discover how they wish to specialise within the range of options that their natural capacities permit.

Were the only justifiable function of education from the standpoint of freedom to maximise choice among readily available ways of life, then rights theory would rest upon a conservative educational foundation very similar to that which Durkheim recommends and upon which (I have argued) Benthamite utilitarianism must rest. But there is a justifiable and essential function of education that goes beyond preparing children for becoming law-abiding citizens, for pursuing happiness or for choosing vocations. Education ought also to provide children with the ability to conceive of and evaluate ways of life, and the political systems appropriate to them, other than those found within their own society or within any existing society. This educational goal is often based upon the view that knowledge should be pursued for its own sake, that is, for the sake of developing the intellect and its logical and imaginative capacities. Our lives are in fact often altered by knowledge of ways of life and types of polities not readily available for us to choose. We may become more critical of political participation and representation in our own society with the knowledge of how much more extensive political participation would be in Rousseau's ideal society. Utilitarians could teach *The Social Contract* as a means of convincing children that Rousseau's theory is utopian or as a means of introducing children to impractical literature that might occupy their leisure time as adults. But neither rationale is very compelling. Knowledge of Rousseau and of Greek literature is surely not necessary to ensure social cohesion and is very unlikely to make children happier or more satisfied with their lives or even more productive and hence more useful to people in the future. However, education in literature, history, anthropology, and political philosophy (for example) does provide a type of freedom—freedom to think beyond the established forms of private and political life. Such knowledge is necessary in order both to appreciate fully and to criticise the political systems and the choice among ways of life we have inherited. One might therefore conclude that this knowledge is a prerequisite for being a good democratic citizen, but this is not the sort of knowledge upon which any existing democratic government is likely to depend for its (mere) survival.

4. THE CONTENT OF EDUCATION: VOCATIONAL OR THEORETICAL?

Utilitarianism is commonly recommended over rights theories on the grounds that it supplies one standard, the common currency of happiness, by which all goods can be ranked.[29] By contrast, rights theorists lack a single standard and therefore must devise priority rules for ranking freedoms and goods that come into conflict with each other. This necessity arises once again in the case of education. Educating children to be capable of finding profit-yielding employment in their society places very different demands upon schooling than does the goal of educating children to think beyond the established forms of life and thereby freeing them 'from the tyranny of the present'.[30] The advocate of liberty can embrace both goals in his theory. But, without some priority rule, the theory will be inadequate to determining educational practice in a non-ideal society. The imperfections in our economic and political institutions as well as scarcity of time and resources demand that we choose between an education instrumental to finding employment and what is commonly called a liberal education.[31]

The job of equipping children for profit-yielding employment seems to place very specific demands upon schools: that they teach technical skills to future technicians, secretarial skills to future secretaries, teaching skills to future teachers, etc. But even Bentham did not give priority to teaching more practical subjects because they prepared people for specific occupations, but because he believed that applied sciences (for example) were easier to learn than pure science. Only if one believed that children were destined for particular vocations and that educators could discern their pre-destinations would the goal of vocational training be this simple to implement educationally. Otherwise, elementary, secondary and perhaps even higher education must be broad enough to allow children themselves to determine their future vocational plans. If equality of opportunity includes the right to choose and not only the right to be selected on grounds of merit, then even the liberal goal of vocational preparation demands an education sufficiently extensive to expose children to many types of intellectual skills, or skills and knowledge general enough to be useful in many professions.

At the elementary school level, however, the requirements of vocational training probably do not conflict with the requirements of a 'liberal education': the three 'Rs' are no doubt a prerequisite to all desirable vocations and not only to understanding *Macbeth* and *The Origin of Species*. But as children graduate to higher levels, the requirements of a vocational and a liberal education are likely to diverge more. A curriculum designed to sharpen the critical and imaginative capacities of the mind will place more emphasis on literature and political philosophy than one designed to prepare students for choosing among available careers, given the job structure of our society.

The criterion of neutrality itself does not help us choose between a more theoretical and more applied curriculum. Neither is neutral among ways of life. A more theoretical curriculum is more likely to encourage children to seek intellectual vocations, while a more practical curriculum will discourage children from pursuing the life of the mind. Ideally, we would want schooling equally to serve the functions of expanding the intellectual imagination and of preparing all children for a socially useful and desirable profession, at least until children reach the age when they can choose a vocation or a form of education for themselves. But in the practice of our non-ideal society, most children will not be exposed to enough education to accomplish both tasks before they reach the age of consent. So, rights theorists face a common liberal dilemma of having to choose between two incomplete and not totally compatible goods.

The resolution of this dilemma, if there is one, does not depend upon a determination of which function is more important: expanding the minds or the job opportunities of children. Arguments claiming saliency for the life of the mind cannot succeed on liberal grounds. And a rights theorist cannot accept Durkheim's claim that, beyond teaching the basic principles upon which social unity depends, teaching specialised job-related skills is the most important role of schooling. Specialisation may be necessary for the survival of industrial societies, but it does not follow that it is therefore a more important function of education in a liberal society than a broader, more general education. But if we cannot rank the two educational goals by their intrinsic importance, we must be able to decide which educational end schools can most effectively serve and which end is less likely to be better served by another social institution.

Although Americans have had a tendency to view education as a panacea for all social ills, surely we should not be surprised to discover that schooling in itself is not an effective means to equalising economic opportunity. No kind of education—vocational or liberal—can overcome the effects of intentional discrimination on racial or class grounds. That there is as much inequality among adults with the same level of schooling as there is among the general population could be attributable to discrimination, to the ineffectiveness of our present methods (or content) of education, or to the unmeasured, or unmeasurable, difference in talents and skills among those with the same amount of schooling.[32]

However, even if schools by themselves cannot equalise economic opportunity, they still may have a necessary role in achieving such a desirable egalitarian purpose. Perhaps more vocational education for less-advantaged children would provide them with more job opportunities than they now have. But when we argue for equalising economic opportunity, we are not arguing simply that all children should be prepared for *some* job, but that all should be given an education that prepares them for choosing a satisfying job that is not wasteful of their talents. This is one reason why even if a highly-specialised education is a pre-condition for certain occupations, it should be chosen by, rather than imposed upon, children. But this criterion of choice suggests that a highly-specialised education ought only to follow a more general education since children of five and ten are very different in their capacity to choose than adolescents of sixteen or young people of twenty. At least, this should be the case unless something is *very* wrong with education, from a liberal point of view. Accepting this premise, we will begin education by teaching those arts, skills and knowledge most essential to all future choice; reading, writing and arithmetic are most clearly among such arts. Later, we will give students greater, and increasingly greater, freedom to determine their own programmes of education because they become better equipped to make choices as they mature, and also because they need exercise in making choice. This line of argument suggests that specialised, vocational education may have a place in liberal schooling, but that it must follow a broader, less specialised education and must be the object of genuine choice by students capable of choice, and not a substitute for a broader education or part of a mandated curriculum.

Suppose that specialised, vocational education could be effective in equalising economic opportunity. In general, schools are likely to be less efficient (and probably also less successful, once we take problems of motivation into account) providers of such education than are employers who use on-the-job training. Educators themselves know very little about the details of non-academic jobs, and on-the-job success depends upon attendance to those details. Now more than ever, vocational education within schools is bound to lag behind job specifications, as the demands of the division of labour change in ways unforeseeable by educational institutions. Educators are unlikely to be aware of the different skills that are required for what are nominally the same jobs, another fact which suggests that vocational schooling will be less effective and less efficient than on-the-job training.

I have granted that even the best education of which we are capable will not be neutral towards all conceptions of the good life. Yet the neutrality ideal still requires that liberals seek to provide an education that maximises choice among ways of life. This ideal demands recognition of the fact that more ways of life are possible than now are pursued and that collective action is often necessary to actualise some possible—but unrealised—ways of life. Collective action is greatly facilitated if people are aware of remote as well as actual possibilities, as they are more likely to be if they are taught anthropology, history, philosophy and literature, and if they are capable of thinking abstractly about polities, economies and other social institutions.[33]

There is also another positive, more political reason to choose a theoretical above a vocational education. The legitimacy (as distinguished from the justice) of liberal democracies is generally based upon a theory of the consent of citizens to democratic rule. Yet most citizens of liberal democracies have no real choice but to obey the government of the society in which they were born, raised and educated. Although they have no real option to leave, they might at least not be required to accept their state uncritically. That option is a real one only if they are intellectually exposed to alternative political systems and ways of life more common within other political systems. Schools are uniquely equipped to supply children with the knowledge and intellectual skills necessary to appreciate alternative political philosophies and ways of life.[34] An education designed to facilitate this exposure will be closer to a traditional liberal education than to a vocational education, although a liberal can reject the metaphysical baggage that supported the classical idea of a liberal education: that the mind can come 'to know the essential nature of things and can apprehend what is ultimately real and immutable' and that the attainment of knowledge therefore is in itself the realisation of the good life.[35]

The advocate of liberty, like the utilitarian, supports a liberal education for consequentialist reasons: it is useful in preparing children to choose among—or at least to evaluate—alternative ways of private and political life. But since the advocate of liberty is committed to providing equal educational opportunity for all children rather than to maximising the total store of freedom, he need not compare how much freedom could be gained by suppressing the education opportunities of one group to increase the opportunities of another. The consequentialism of rights theorists therefore has form and content that are both distinct from that of utilitarians. The right to education can be constrained only by another child's equal right, and educational rights must be justified by reference to future freedom, not happiness.

Liberals can accept Durkheim's claim that the content of education ought to be determined by the social context within which schools operate. The educational requirements for maximising the future freedom of children surely will vary with societies. A liberal education suitable to contemporary social conditions will not replicate a classical liberal education in which the study of Greek and Latin were primary requirements. But education ought not to serve only to maintain the present state of social and political organisation. If the present state of social and political organisation can survive an education that develops critical intellectual faculties, then education will serve an integrative as well as a critical function. If not, then a liberal education will serve to prepare children 'for a possibly improved condition of man in the future'.[36] Whether any existing society is capable of fully providing this sort of liberal education is another question. I have tried here to demonstrate that unlike utilitarians, rights theorists can consistently advocate the use of schools in a liberal democratic society as critical, rather than simply as conserving, social institutions.[37]

NOTES

1. For the definition of liberalism upon which this essay relies, see Ronald Dworkin, 'Liberalism', in *Public and Private Morality*, edited by Stuart Hampshire (Cambridge: Cambridge University Press, 1978), p. 127.

2. For recent examples of rights theories, see John Rawls, *A Theory of Justice* (Cambridge, Mass.: Harvard University Press, 1971); Dworkin, 'Liberalism'; Charles Fried, *Right and Wrong* (Cambridge, Mass.: Harvard University Press, 1978); and Alan Donagan, *The Theory of Morality* (Chicago: University of Chicago Press, 1977). Nozick's theory in R. Nozick, *Anarchy, State, and Utopia* (New York: Basic Books, 1974) is also a rights theory, but it is hard to imagine how a state based only upon the right not to be interfered with can provide for the education of children.

3. For criticisms of the aggregative aspect of utilitarianism, see Rawls, *A Theory of Justice*, pp. 187–92; B.A.O. Williams, 'A Critique of Utilitarianism', in J.J.C. Smart and B.A.O. Williams, *Utilitarianism: For and Against* (Cambridge: Cambridge University Press, 1973), pp. 82–118, 135–50; and Ronald Dworkin, *Taking Rights Seriously* (Cambridge, Mass.: Harvard University Press, 1977), pp. 231–8, 272–8.

4. See J.J.C. Smart in *Utilitariansm: For and Against*, p. 24.

5. See, for example, B.A.O. Williams, *Morality: An Introduction to Ethics* (New York: Harper & Row, 1972), p. 91.

6. This assessment of utilitarianism is independent of one's understanding of the meaning of happiness so long as happiness is understood as a subjectively-defined state of individuals. The same problems arise whether happiness is what individuals deliberately approve or what gives them pleasure.

7. For a recent description of the convergence of consequentialist and rights theories, see B. Barry, 'And Who Is My Neighbor?', *Yale Law Journal* 88 (1979), pp. 629–35.

8. Compare Fried, *Right and Wrong*, p. 152. See also Justice McReynold's decision in *Pierce v. Society of Sisters*, 268 U.S. 535.

9. I make a more thorough argument for this position in Amy Gutmann, 'Children, Paternalism and Education: A Liberal Argument', *Philosophy & Public Affairs* 9 (1980), pp. 338–58.

10. See John Stuart Mill, *Philosophy of Scientific Method*, edited by E. Nagel (New York: Hafner, 1950), p. 358.

11. W.H. Burston, ed., *James Mill on Education* (Cambridge: Cambridge University Press, 1969), p. 41. Emphasis added.

12. See Jeremy Bentham, *Chrestomathia*, in *The Works of Jeremy Bentham*, edited by John Bowring (Edinburgh: William Tait, 1843), Vol. 8, p. 8.

13. *Ibid.*, pp. 8–10.

14. One could specify some plausible conditions of achieving *self*-respect through education such that they conflict with other ways of educating children to find happiness. If certain methods of education undermine self-respect by subjecting children to unquestionable and inaccessible authority and by continually rank-

ing children in a hierarchy of intellectual merit, then this secondary goal is not as innocuous as Bentham's educational plan suggests. In fact, the monotorial method of education endorsed by Bentham and the panopticonal design of Chrestomathia (wherein the schoolmaster could observe all classes without being seen) might be challenged on these non-utilitarian grounds—even if a Chrestomathic education would produce the happiest of people. 'Call them soldiers, call them monks, call them machines, so long as they be [or, in the case of education, become] happy ones, I shall not care' is not a response open to anyone who takes self-respect to be a demanding criterion of distributive justice, and its development a goal of education.

15. Bertrand Russell, *John Stuart Mill* (Oxford: Oxford University Press, 1955), p. 56.

16. See J.A. Hostetler and G.E. Huntington, *Children in Amish Society: Socialisation and Community Education* (New York: Holt, Rinehart and Winston, 1971); Donald A. Erickson, 'Showdown at an Amish Schoolhouse: A Description and Analysis of the Iowa Controversy', in *Public Controls for Nonpublic Schools*, edited by Donald A. Erickson (Chicago: University of Chicago Press, 1969), pp. 15–59.

17. James Mill in *James Mill on Education*, p. 105.

18. Those who do defend the position of the Amish parents do so on grounds of religious freedom. See Justice Burger's opinion for the majority in *State of Wisconsin v. Yoder* 406 U.S. 205. I have examined and criticized this position in 'Children, Paternalism and Education; A Liberal Argument'.

19. See John Stuart Mill, *Utilitarianism* (London: Collins, 1962), Ch. 2, para. 6.

20. John Dewey, *The School and Society* (Chicago: University of Chicago Press, 1943), p. 7.

21. Compare P.H. Hirst, 'Liberal Education and the Nature of Knowledge', in *Education and the Development of Reason*, edited by R.F. Dearden, P.H. Hirst and R.S. Peters (London: Routledge & Kegan Paul, 1972), pp. 391–414.

22. See *Chrestomathia*, p. 40.

23. I mean 'conservative' in the strict sense of that which is intended to preserve the values of any society, even one that is liberal or Marxist.

24. Emile Durkheim, *Education and Sociology*, translated by Sherwood Fox (New York: The Free Press, 1956), p. 64.

25. *Ibid.*, p. 81.

26. *Ibid.*, p. 70. More accurately, without a certain diversity, *some* important kinds of cooperation would be impossible.

27. This means, however, that outside of the context of a liberal state, the positions of Durkheim and of rights theorists will conflict.

28. See, e.g., Rawls, *A Theory of Justice*, pp. 101, 107.

29. For a critique of this characteristic of utilitarianism, see Williams, *Morality: An Introduction to Ethics*, pp. 92 ff.

30. See Neil Postman, *Teaching as a Conserving Activity* (New York: Delacorte Press, 1979), p. 37.

31. Alternatively, one might call the latter a 'general' education. See the report of the Harvard Committee, *General Education in a Free Society*, Cambridge, Mass., 1945, and Hirst, 'Liberal Education and the Nature of Knowledge'.

32. See Christopher Jencks (with M. Smith; H. Acland; M.-J. Bane; D. Cohen; H. Gintis; B. Heyns; S. Michelson), *Inequality: A Reassessment of the Effect of Family and Schooling in America* (New York: Basic Books, 1972), p. 218; and Otis Dudley Duncan, 'Discrimination Against Negroes', *Annals of the American Academy of Political and Social Science* 371 (1967), pp. 85–103.

33. I am grateful to Stanley Kelley, Jr., for bringing this argument and the argument on pp. 79–80 to my attention.

34. Of course, this is not to say that American and British schools have yet to succeed in achieving this goal, but their failure can more plausibly be attributed to lack of will, rather than to lack of power. Even radical critics acknowledge the unique capacity of schools to expose students to critical political philosophies and alternative ways of life. See, e.g., Samuel Bowles and Herbert Gintis, *Schooling in Capitalist America* (New York: Basic Books, 1977), pp. 5, 270 ff. See also M. Kent Jennings, 'Comment on Richard Merelman's "Democratic Politics and the Culture of American Education"', *American Political Science Review* 74 (1980), p. 336; Herbert H. Hyman, Charles R. Wright and John Shelton Reed, *The Enduring Effect of Education* (Chicago: University of Chicago Press, 1975); and Herbert H. Hyman and Charles R. Wright, *Education's Lasting Influence on Values* (Chicago: University of Chicago Press, 1979).

35. Hirst, 'Liberal Education and the Nature of Knowledge', p. 392.

36. Immanuel Kant, *Pädogogik* (1803), translated as *On Education* (Ann Arbor, Mich.: 1960), p. 14.

37. I am indebted to Michael W. Doyle, Stanley Kelley, Jr., and Dennis Thompson for many helpful comments on an earlier draft.

· 7 ·

MILL'S "PROOF" OF THE PRINCIPLE OF UTILITY

Henry R. West

U tilitarianism, in every one of its forms or formulations, requires a theory for the evaluation of consequences. Whether the units of behavior
being judged are acts, rules, practices, attitudes, or institutions, to judge
them by their utility, that is, by their contribution to good or bad ends,
requires a theory of what count as good or bad ends. In the philosophies of
the classical utilitarians, Jeremy Bentham and John Stuart Mill, some variety
of hedonism served this purpose. Mill calls this

> the theory of life on which this theory of morality is grounded—namely
> that pleasure, and freedom from pain, are the only things desirable as
> ends; and that all desirable things (which are as numerous in the utilitar-
> ian as in any other scheme) are desirable either for the pleasure inherent
> in themselves, or as means to the promotion of pleasure and the preven-
> tion of pain.[1]

In Chapter IV of his essay entitled *Utilitarianism*, Mill addresses himself
to the question of what sort of proof this principle is susceptible. The
twelve paragraphs of the chapter present an argument which, if successful,
is one of the most important arguments in all of moral philosophy, for,
although Mill says questions of ultimate ends are not amenable to "direct
proof," he believes that considerations may be presented capable of determining the intellect to give its assent to the doctrine.[2]
Unfortunately, few commentators on Mill have had their intellects
convinced, and perhaps even fewer have agreed on the correct interpretation of the argument. J. B. Schneewind says of it:

> A greater mare's nest has seldom been constructed. It is now generally
> agreed that Mill is not, in this chapter, betraying his own belief that proof
> of a first moral principle is impossible, but there is not a general agree-

ment as to what he is doing. In the last fifteen years there have been more essays dealing with the topic of "Mill's Proof" than with any other single topic in the history of ethical thought.[3]

Mill does say of the Utilitarian formula of ultimate ends that it is impossible to give a proof in the "ordinary or popular meaning of the term," but he continues,

> We are not, however, to infer that its acceptance or rejection must depend on blind impulse or arbitrary choice. . . . The subject is within the cognizance of the rational faculty, and neither does that faculty deal with it solely in the way of intuition. Considerations may be presented capable of determining the intellect either to give or withhold its assent to the doctrine, and this is the equivalent of proof.[4]

Furthermore, at the end of Chapter IV, he says that if the doctrine he has argued for is true, "the principle of utility *is proved.*"[5]

Given the claim, that he has proved his principle or presented something equivalent to proof, I think it is worthwhile to lay out the structure of the argument in deductive form. In that way we can determine the nature of the premises he introduces, locate the gaps that prevent it from being a valid deduction, and see if plausible assumptions can be formulated or interpretations offered that will support the premises and bridge the gaps. I shall present what I believe to be a reasonable interpretation of what Mill had in mind, and I shall claim that the assumptions necessary to make the argument sound are—though controversial—at least plausible.

The conclusion he is seeking is stated in Paragraph 2: "The utilitarian doctrine is that happiness is desirable, and the only thing desirable, as an end, all other things being only desirable as a means to that end." The connection between this idea and morality is mentioned at the end of Paragraph 9, where he says that the promotion of happiness is the test by which to judge all human conduct, "from whence it necessarily follows that it must be the criterion of morality, since a part is included in the whole." Mill has a complex view of the way the ultimate standard of the promotion of happiness is to be applied in morality, and morality is only one of the "three departments" of what he calls the "Art of Life." These general teleological views on testing conduct, and the place of morality within this teleological framework, are found elsewhere in the essay and in the *Logic*.[6] They are not part of this "proof," and I shall not be discussing them in this paper. I shall be examining only how he gets to the conclusion that happiness is desirable and the only thing desirable as an end.

The structure of the argument is very simple. In Paragraph 3 he argues that happiness is desirable. In the remainder of the chapter he argues that happiness is the only thing desirable. The outline of the argument can be given in Mill's own words:

> (1) "The sole evidence it is possible to produce that anything is desirable is that people do actually desire it." (Paragraph 3)
> (2) "Each person, so far as he believes it to be attainable, desires his own happiness." (Paragraph 3)
> (Therefore,)
> (3) "Happiness is a good." (Paragraph 3)

He substitutes the expression "is a good" for the expression "is desirable," but I presume that this is only for stylistic reasons. I think he would regard his use of these two as interchangeable in this context.[7]

The argument to show that happiness is the only thing desirable is likewise based on the evidence of actual desire:

> (4) "Human nature is so constituted as to desire nothing which is not either a part of happiness or a means of happiness." (Paragraph 9, but argued throughout Paragraphs 5–10)
> (Therefore,)
> (5) "Nothing is a good to human beings but in so far as it is either pleasurable or a means of attaining pleasure or averting pain." (Paragraph 11)

Here his use of "pleasure" and "pleasurable" instead of "happiness" is merely stylistic. Throughout the essay he says that by happiness he means pleasure and freedom from pain.

This is the simple outline of the argument. It is complicated by the fact that each individual's desire is for *his own* happiness, whereas the utilitarian doctrine that Mill is seeking to establish is that the *general* happiness is the foundation of morality.[8] In Paragraph 3, this distinction is explicit. Having said that each person desires his own happiness, Mill says we have all the proof it is possible to require

> that happiness is a good, that each person's happiness is a good to that person, and the general happiness, therefore, a good to the aggregate of all persons.

These propositions we may state as separate theses:

> (3A) "Each person's happiness is a good to that person."

(Therefore,)

(3B) "The general happiness [is] a good to the aggregate of all persons."

The distinction also can be introduced into the second part of the argument. Without doubt the psychological premise (4) means:

(4') Each person desires nothing which is not either a part of his happiness or a means of his happiness.[9]

And parallel to (3A) and (3B) the distinction between each person and the aggregate of all persons can be introduced. This would give:

(5A) Nothing is a good to each person but insofar as it is either a part of his happiness or a means of his happiness.
(Therefore,)
(5B) Nothing is a good to the aggregate of all persons but insofar as it is either a part of the general happiness or a means of the general happiness.

From (3B) and (5B), we can then deduce an interpretation of the "utilitarian doctrine," as follows:

(6) "[The general] happiness [or a part of the general happiness] is desirable, and the only thing desirable, as an end, all other things being only desirable as means to that end." (Paragraph 2)

Examining the argument, it can be seen that (1) is a methodological premise; (2) and (4) are factual psychological premises; (3) or (3A) and (5) or (5A) are supported by (2) and (4), respectively. (3B) and (5B) putatively follow from (3A) and (5A), respectively. The premise (2) is probably non-controversial. The controversial premises are (1) and (4), and the controversial steps are from the fact of happiness being desired to its being normatively desirable, and from each person's happiness being desirable to that person to the conclusion that the general happiness is desirable to the aggregate of all people. There seem, then, to be three central issues: (A) Mill's methodology, which is to argue for what is desirable on the evidence of what is in fact desired; (B) his psychological hedonism, that each person desires his own happiness as an end and nothing as an end which is not a part of his happiness; and (C) the argument that if each person's happiness is a good and inclusive of the only good for him, as an end, the general happiness is a good, and encompasses the only good, as an end, to the aggregate of all persons. I shall take these issues up in turn.

A. Desire as Evidence of Desirable

I think it is hardly necessary to point out that Mill did not say that "desirable" or "the good" *means* "desired," as Moore says he does.[10] He is not committing a naturalistic or definist fallacy.[11] Mill is quite explicit in demarcating factual and normative propositions.[12]

I also think it is not likely he was misled by the similarity of the verbal endings of "visible" and "audible" into thinking that "desirable" means "able to be desired."[13] The significance of the analogy with visible and audible is announced in the first paragraph of the chapter: The first premises of our knowledge do not admit of proof by reasoning, but are subject to a direct appeal to the senses; he suggests that the first premises of conduct are subject to a direct appeal to our desiring faculty. It does not follow that he regards what is desirable as a "permanent possibility of desire." That would be to regard it as a matter of fact. The analogy is that as judgments of existence are based on the evidence of the senses and corrected by further evidence of the senses, so judgments of what is desirable are based on what is desired and corrected by further evidence of what is desired. The only evidence on which a recommendation of an end of conduct can be based is what is found appealing to the desiring faculty.

Mill also supports his appeal to desire by what is a pragmatic argument:

> If the end which the utilitarian doctrine proposes to itself were not, in theory and in practice, acknowledged to be an end, nothing could ever convince any person that it was so.[14]

Nothing about the logic of recommending an end of conduct prevents any end whatsoever from being recommended, but only one based on actual desires will be convincing. This is one respect in which the "proof" is not a proof in the ordinary sense. There is no necessity about accepting desire as the sole evidence for desirability. It is logically possible that ends of conduct that are not in fact desired be recommended without contradiction. The force of the appeal to what is desired is only to convince, not logically to rule out all other possibilities.

The import of premise (1), however, is primarily negative. It denies the existence of an intellectual intuition of the normative ends of conduct. The faculty to which Mill appeals is one that takes "cognizance" of practical ends, but by way of feeling or "sensibility" rather than intellect or moral sense. He is denying that we intuit what is intrinsically a good in some directly cognitive way.

The only way to argue a negative claim such as this conclusively would be to take each putative intuition and examine it critically to try to show that it can be reduced to desire or else to absurdity. I can obviously not do this to defend Mill's proof. I can only state that I find unconvincing all claims to intuit values, independent of desires (or likes and dislikes); so I find his skeptical starting point a plausible one. However, the desires we do have provide practical ends that will be pursued unless frustrated by the pursuit of the ends of other desires. This provides an arena in which practical reason can seek to bring order out of disorder by analyzing desires to determine which, if any, are illusory; which, if any, are fundamental; what, if anything, is the common object of them all. It is this last question that Mill's psychological hedonism claims to answer.

B. Psychological Hedonism

Mill's argument for (4) has two parts. One is in Paragraph 11, which classifies as mere habit those ends of conduct that are sought neither as means to happiness nor as a part of happiness. He claims that they have become ends of conduct:

> Will is the child of desire, and passes out of the domination of its parent only to come under that of habit. That which is the result of habit affords no presumption of being intrinsically good.[15]

That argument leaves him with everything that affords any presumption of being intrinsically good an object of conscious desire. I think it is unnecessary to accept Mill's Associationist accounts of all habitual conduct or his account of all nondeliberative nondesiring willed behavior as habit. It is enough if actions that are not the result of deliberation and conscious desire afford no presumption that their ends help to identify for us what is desirable. Evolutionary ethicists, natural law theorists, and many others would perhaps deny this, but I find it a plausible skepticism.

The other part of his argument is to claim that every object of conscious desire is associated with pleasure or the absence of pain, either as a means or an end. Many desires are acquired, such as the desire for virtue or for the possession of money, and have come to be desired through the mechanism of their association with pleasure or the absence of pain. Whether acquired or not, the ultimate ends of the desires can be regarded as experiences or states of affairs with a pleasure component: They are pleasures or "parts of happiness." Although they may fall under various other descriptions, it is the fact that they are ingredients of happiness that provides a common denominator and a unified account of desire.

If Mill is correct that there is a pleasure component to the ultimate end of every desire, and if no other common denominator provides a unified account of desire, then Mill has a persuasive claim that it is the pleasure component (i.e., being part of happiness) that is the element in all objects of desire that makes them desirable as ends, which recommends them to the intellect as the basis for action and which can provide for critical assessment in case of conflict between desires.

It is tempting to read into Mill the claim that it is the agreeable quality of the state of consciousness desired that is the real object of desire. Just as the sense-data theorist claims that one sees only sense data, although it is palpable that he sees things that, in common languages, are decidedly distinguished from sense data (i.e., from whatever common language words are sense data words—"sights," "sounds," "appearances," or whatever), so Mill might be thought to hold that one desires only the pleasure component of desired experiences, although it is palpable that people "do desire things, which, in common language, are decidedly distinguished from happiness."[16] I think this is impossible to reconcile with Mill's talk of the objects of desire as being "music," "health," "virtue," "power," "fame," "possession of money," not just the agreeable feeling attending these. Furthermore, he does not need to make such a strong claim. He only needs to claim that, as a psychological fact, music, health, etc., would not be desired if no pleasure or freedom from pain or past association with these were connected with music, health, etc. Desire is evidence of desirability, but it does not confer desirability. This is obvious in the case of things desired as means. On reflection, it is obvious in the case of things desired as ends. The possession of money is desired by the miser. This desire does not make the possession of money a normative object of action for a reasonable person. The evidence furnished by desire must be analyzed; it is only by analysis of the fact that the miser desires the possession of money as part of his happiness—that he would be made happy by its possession—that the evidence of desire fits into a comprehensive theory. It is this comprehensive theory that identifies the pleasure inherent in desirable things as what makes them desirable. The pleasure inherent in them does not itself have to be discriminated as the *object* of desire.

Some commentators also have thought that Mill reduces the relation between desire and pleasures to a trivial one in the passage where he says that:

> desiring a thing and finding it pleasant, aversion to it and thinking of it as painful, are phenomena entirely inseparable, or rather two parts of the same phenomenon—in strictness of language, two different modes of naming the same psychological fact; that to think of an object as desirable (unless for the sake of its consequences), and to think of it as pleasant, are one and the same thing; and that to desire anything, except in proportion as the idea of it is pleasant, is a physical and metaphysical impossibility.[17]

This statement is certainly puzzling to the twentieth-century reader, but in context Mill is asking the reader to engage in "practiced self-consciousness and self-observation." If the terms were reducible to one another independent of observation, it is hard to see why he would invite one to attempt what appears to be an empirical discovery. A clue to interpretation is that "metaphysical" means approximately "psychological" for him.[18] In his notes on his father's *Analysis of the Phenomena of the Human Mind*, Mill takes issue with his father's statement, "The term 'Idea of a pleasure' expresses precisely the same thing as the term Desire. It does so by the very import of the words."[19] J. S. Mill says that desire:

> is more than the idea of pleasure desired, being, in truth, the initiatory state of Will. In what we call Desire there is, I think, always included a positive stimulation to action.[20]

According to J. S. Mill, then, a distinction is to be made between desiring a thing and thinking of it as pleasant. Desire is psychologically more complex and conceivably could have an object not thought of as pleasurable. It is obvious that it may have a more inclusive object, as is the case in desiring the means to an end when the means are unpleasant. In any case the question is a psychological, not a linguistic one.

Mill's substantive claim is that desire and pleasure (or the avoidance of pain) are psychologically inseparable. If this is true, two things follow: First, (4) is established—each person desires nothing that is not either a part of his happiness or a means of his happiness; second, since attainment of pleasure and avoidance of pain are the common denominators of desire, the evidence of desire supports the theory that it is the pleasure and pain aspects of the objects of desire and aversion that make them desirable and undesirable and that should serve as the criteria of good and bad consequences in a normative theory of conduct.

An adequate defense of Mill's position would require a more thorough analysis of desire and of pleasure and pain, happiness and unhappiness. I believe, however, that the interpretation given above shows that the position does not completely lack plausibility and that it might be supported by such a refined analysis.

C. From Each Person's Happiness to the General Happiness

If the intellect is convinced that the person's happiness is a good and the sole good to that person, does it follow that it will be convinced that the general happiness is a good and the sole good to the aggregate of all persons? Mill presumably thinks this is obvious, simply asserting it without argument. He apparently thinks he has practically established (3B) when he has established (3A), and (5B) when he has established (5A). I think Mill has been misinterpreted in this argument because commentators have thought his conclusion to be a much stronger claim than it is. He is making a very weak claim, which is seen when we notice what he means by "the general happiness."

According to Mill "the general happiness" is a mere sum of instances of individual happiness. Just as personal happiness is not a "collective something" but simply a sum of pleasures,[21] so we can take Mill as holding that the general happiness is simply a sum of individual pleasures. There are still two ways of understanding the argument. One is that "to that person" represents the point of view of the agent when he is making prudential decisions; "to the aggregate" represents the point of view of the benevolent man when he is acting morally. Some things can be said in support of this interpretation, but I do not think that it is the correct one. I think rather that he believes that his analysis of desire shows that happiness is the *kind* of thing that constitutes intrinsic welfare, wherever it occurs. All instances of happiness will be parts of the personal welfare of someone, that is, "a good *to someone*," but being instances of happiness, they have a common denominator that makes them the same kind of thing wherever they occur—whether in different experiences of a given individual or in the experiences of different individuals. Moreover, Mill assumes that the value of different instances of happiness can be thought of as summed up to generate a larger good. These assumptions are explicit in a letter Mill wrote regarding the move from (3A) to (3B):

> As to the sentence you quote from my *Utilitarianism*, when I said the general happiness is a good to the aggregate of all persons I did not mean that every human being's happiness is a good to every other human being, though I think in a good state of society and education it would be so. I merely meant in this particular sentence to argue that since A's happiness is a good, B's a good, C's a good, etc., the sum of all these goods must be a good.[22]

His assumptions are even more explicit in a footnote to Chapter V of *Utilitarianism*. There, answering the objection that the principle of utility presupposes the anterior principle that everybody has an equal right to happiness, Mill says:

> It may be more correctly described as supposing that equal amounts of happiness are equally desirable, whether felt by the same or by different

persons. This, however, is not a presupposition, not a premise needful to support the principle of utility, but the very principle itself; . . . If there is an anterior principle implied, it can be no other than this—that the truths of arithmetic are applicable to the valuation of happiness, as of all other measurable quantities.[23]

It seems clear, then, that the "to each person" in (3A) and (5A) does not represent a "point of view," but simply the location or embodiment of welfare that cannot exist without location or embodiment, and the "to the aggregate of all persons" in (3B) and (5B) refers to the location or embodiment of welfare in a group of individuals, not a point of view. A good to the aggregate of A, B, C, etc., is interpreted by Mill to be a sum of goods to A, plus goods to B, plus goods to C, etc. He assumes both that happiness is arithmetical, capable of being summed up to find a total, "general" happiness, and that goods to different people are arithmetical, capable of being summed up to find a total good "to the aggregate of all persons."

With these assumptions, (3B) does follow from (3A), for to say that the general happiness is a good to the aggregate of all persons is merely to say that A's happiness, plus B's happiness, plus C's happiness, etc., constitutes a good to A, plus a good to B, plus a good to C, etc. And (5B) follows from (5A). If nothing is a good to each person but insofar as it is a part of his happiness (or a means to it), then nothing will be part of the sum of goods to A, plus goods to B, plus goods to C, etc., but insofar as it is a part of the happiness of A or part of the happiness of B, etc., or a means to these. This interpretation explains why Mill did not bother to state (5A) and (5B) explicitly and why he passed from (3A) to (3B) in one sentence. The evidence of desire shows that happiness is the *kind* of thing desirable as an end. It is not a different kind of thing when it is located in A's experience from what it is when it is located in B's experience. Thus, whether or not any single individual desires the general happiness, if each of its parts is shown to be desirable by the evidence of desire, because of the kind of thing each part is, then the sum of these parts will be desirable because it is simply a summation of instances of the same kind of thing.[24] Given this interpretation the "utilitarian doctrine" represented by (6), is perhaps better stated by making clear that Mill believes happiness, wherever it occurs, is what is desirable as an end. This could be restated with the following reinterpretation:

(6) Happiness is [the kind of thing which is] desirable, and the only [kind of] thing desirable, as an end, all other things being desirable only as means to that end.

From this, the connection with morality is said to follow:

(7) The promotion of [happiness] is the test by which to judge of all conduct from whence it necessarily follows that it must be the criterion of morality, since a part is included in the whole.[25]

If my earlier elucidation of Mill's argument for happiness as the kind of thing that makes the objects of desires desirable was convincing, then the argument has some plausibility. Desire does not confer desirability; it is evidence for what kind of thing constitutes welfare. Thus, that one desires only his own happiness does not restrict the desirability of happiness to one's own happiness. If the desirability of happiness *as such* is identified (and not created) by one's own desire for it in one's own experience, its desirability—wherever it is located—can be admitted by the intellect.

That the value of different instances of happiness is arithmetical is certainly controversial, but not, I think, indefensible. Without an operational definition for measurement, it is difficult to know how happy two different individuals are, but it seems plausible that if two people do happen to be equally happy, then twice as much happiness exists. Mill recognizes the difficulty in determining how happy a person is. He thinks Bentham's measures of intensity and duration are inadequate to capture the complex hedonic dimensions of experience, asserting that the only test of the comparative pleasure of two experiences is the unbiased preference of those who have experienced both. This is not a direct measurement of felt experience, since the experiences are seldom if ever simultaneous. It is a judgment based on memory. In making interpersonal comparisons, it is even less reliable, since one can assume only a rough equality of sensibility between persons or make a rough estimate of difference in case evidence based on behavior or physiology shows a basis for difference. Thus summations of instances of happiness will be imprecise, but we do make judgments that one course of action will make oneself or another person more or less happy. These are not meaningless judgments; even if only rough estimates, they assume (and, I think, justifiably) that different instances of happiness are commensurable.

That the general happiness is simply the sum of the happiness of all individuals and that the good to the aggregate of all is simply the sum of the goods to each is, like Mill's methodological principle, primarily negative in its import. He is denying that there is any happiness or any value that cannot be analyzed without remainder as the happiness or the good of some individual or individuals. To prove this would require refutation of every claim to such an irreducible social good. So, again, I simply assert that I find his skepticism plausible.

If Mill's proof is plausible, as I have suggested, it does not follow that anyone will act on it. The intellect may be convinced that it is plausible or even that it is correct, without one thereby being moved to conduct his life in such a way as to maximize his own happiness or thereby being moved to identify the general happiness with his own and become a practicing utilitarian. That, according to Mill, requires a good state of society and education. But convincing the intellect may be a first step.

NOTES

1. John Stuart Mill, *Utilitarianism*, Chapter II, Paragraph 2. *Utilitarianism*, published in 1861, is reprinted in *Collected Works of John Stuart Mill*, Volume X: *Essays on Ethics, Religion and Society*, ed. J. W. Robson (Toronto: University of Toronto Press, 1969), pp. 203–259, and in various other editions. References will be to chapter and paragraph. Unless otherwise noted, references will be to paragraphs of Chapter IV.

2. Chapter I, Paragraph 5.

3. "Introduction" to *Mill's Ethical Writings*, edited with an introduction by J. B. Schneewind (London: Collier-Macmillan Ltd., New York: Collier Books, 1965), p. 31. In the years following 1965 when Schneewind wrote this, the frequency of essays on the topic even increased.

4. Chapter I, Paragraph 5.

5. Paragraph 11. (Emphasis added).

6. Book VI, Chapter XII. For an analysis of these complex views, see D. P. Dryer, "Mill's Utilitarianism," in *Collected Works of John Stuart Mill*, Volume X: *Essays on Ethics, Religion and Society*, pp. lxiii–cxiii, especially xcv–cxiii, and David Lyons, "Mill's Theory of Morality," *Nous* 10 (1976): 101–120.

7. In her essay, "Mill's Theory of Value," *Theoria* 36 (1970): 100–115, Dorothy Mitchell makes a distinction between "desirable" and "good" based on an analysis of the use of "desirable" in contexts of ordinary language. I think she is correct that they are not synonyms in English, but I think, nevertheless, that Mill is using them as such in this essay.

8. For a discussion of this point, see H. R. West, "Reconstructing Mill's 'Proof' of the Principle of Utility," *Mind* 81 (1972): 256–257.

9. This part of Mill's psychological doctrine is stated explicitly in his essay on "Whewell's Moral Philosophy." He quotes Whewell as saying that "we cannot desire anything else unless by identifying it with our happiness." To this Mill says he should have nothing to object, "if by identification was meant that what we desire unselfishly must first, by a mental process, become an actual part of what we seek as our own happiness; that the good of others becomes our pleasure because

we have learnt to find pleasure in it; this is, we think, the true philosophical account of the matter." ("Whewell's Moral Philosophy," *Collected Works,* Volume X: *Essays on Ethics, Religion and Society,* p. 184 note; Schneewind, ed., *Mill's Ethical Writings,* p. 192 note.)

10. George Edward Moore, *Principia Ethics* (Cambridge: Cambridge University Press, 1948 [first edition 1903]), p. 66.

11. Moore's interpretation of Mill as committing the "naturalistic fallacy" is analyzed and refuted by E. W. Hall in "The 'Proof' of Utility in Bentham and Mill," *Ethics* 61 (1950–51): 66–68. R. F. Atkinson in "J. S. Mill's 'Proof' of the Principle of Utility," *Philosophy* 32 (1957): 158–167, calls attention to the continuing difficulty presented by a footnote in Chapter V where Mill says ". . . for what is the principle of utility, if it be not that 'happiness' and 'desirable' are synonymous terms." This is a puzzling use of "synonymous" but I do not think that it has to be interpreted (absurdly) as claiming that "Happiness is desirable" is a tautology. He may simply mean that the two terms are applicable to the same phenomena, one descriptively, the other normatively.

12. This is found in Book VI, Chapter XII, Section VI of the *Logic* where he says that a first principle of an Art (including the Art of Life, which embodies the first principles of all conduct) enunciates the object aimed at and affirms it to be a desirable object. It does not assert that anything is, but enjoins that something should be. "A proposition of which the predicate is expressed by the words *ought* or *should be,* is generically different from one which is expressed by *is,* or *will be.*"

13. Another of Moore's charges, in *Principia,* p. 67.

14. Paragraph 3.

15. Paragraph 11.

16. Paragraph 4, J. S. Mill's father, James Mill, apparently did hold such a view: ". . . we have a desire for water to drink, for fire to warm us, and so on." But, ". . . it is not the water we desire, but the pleasure of drinking; not the fire we desire, but the pleasure of warmth." (James Mill, *Analysis of the Phenomena of the Human Mind,* 2nd edition, ed. John Stuart Mill, Chapter XIX.)

17. Paragraph 10.

18. For example, he says that "the peculiar character of what we term *moral* feelings is not a question of ethics but of metaphysics." ("Whewell's Moral Philosophy," p. 185.) This interpretation of the term "metaphysical" is argued forcefully in M. Mandelbaum, "On Interpreting Mill's *Utilitarianism,*" *Journal of the History of Philosophy* 6 (1968): 39.

19. James Mill, *Analysis of the Phenomena of the Human Mind,* 2nd edition, Chapter XIX. The passage continues: "The idea of a pleasure, is the idea of something good to have. But what is desire, other than the idea of something good to have; good to have, being really nothing but desirable to have? The term, therefore, 'idea of pleasure,' and 'desire,' are but two names; the thing named, the state of consciousness, is one and the same."

20. James Mill, *Analysis of the Phenomena of the Human Mind,* 2nd edition, Volume II, Note 36.

21. Paragraph 5 and Paragraph 6.

22. *The Letters of John Stuart Mill,* 2 volumes, ed. H. S. R. Elliot (London: Longmans, Green, and Co., 1910), Vol. 2, p. 116; *Collected Works of John Stuart Mill,* Vol. XVI: *The Later Letters of John Stuart Mill 1819–1873,* edited by Francis E. Mineka and Dwight N. Lindley (Toronto: University of Toronto Press, 1972), p. 1414. Quoted in Schneewind (ed.), *Mill's Ethical Writings,* p. 339.

23. Chapter V, the second from the last paragraph of the chapter.

24. John Marshall, in "The Proof of Utility and Equity in Mill's Utilitarianism," *Canadian Journal of Philosophy* 3 (1973–74): 13–26, especially p. 16, points out the ambiguity in the question, "What is desirable as an end?" It can be taken to ask "What kind of thing?" or "What specific thing?" He interprets Mill as thinking more in terms of the first question in arguing that each person's happiness is desirable. I am claiming that Mill's proof is concerned only with the first question and believe that Marshall is reading in too much in finding a proof of equity as well. For a further statement of Marshall's position, see "Egalitarianism and the General Happiness" in *The Limits of Utilitarianism,* ed. by Harlan B. Miller and William H. Williams (Minneapolis: University of Minnesota Press, 1982).

25. Paragraph 9.

· 8 ·

How Thinking about Character and Utilitarianism Might Lead to Rethinking the Character of Utilitarianism

Peter Railton

I

" One cannot properly judge actions by their outcomes alone. The motive from which an act is performed is independently important, and makes a distinctive contribution to moral assessment not only of the actor, but of the action. Moreover, if morality is to achieve a secure place in individual lives and social practices, it is necessary that agents develop firm characters to guide their choices and to provide others with a stable basis of expectation and trust. Any sensible moral theory therefore must give a central role to the encouragement and possession of virtuous character."

When such thoughts are heard, can it be more than a moment before a condemnation of act utilitarianism follows? Still, many critics of *act* utilitarianism remain drawn to what I will call the guiding utilitarian idea, namely, that the final ground of moral assessment—including assessment of character—must lie in effects on people's well-being.[1] For such critics, a favored strategy has been to turn to indirect forms of utilitarianism, such as rule utilitarianism. And indeed, moral philosophers in general appear increasingly to be convinced that *if* utilitarianism is to be defensible, it will be in an indirect form.

Perhaps, then, with the above remarks about the importance of character fresh in our minds and with some sympathy for the guiding utilitarian idea alive in our hearts, we should consider the possibility of formulating an indirect utilitarianism worthy of the name *character utilitarianism*. And that is indeed what I propose to do, by considering two forms character utilitarianism might take. In the end, however, it will seem doubtful whether either form can satisfactorily accommodate our concerns about character, and this will in a roundabout way tell us something about how utilitarianism has been conceived and about how a reconception of it might better serve the guiding utilitarian idea. Sometimes in philosophy, getting there is half the fun. In the case of character utilitarianism, not getting there will have to be all of it.

II

One form character utilitarianism might take would follow the model of rule utilitarianism and hold that an act is right just in case it would be done by someone having a character,[2] the general possession of which would bring about at least as much utility as any alternative.

To assess this possibility, let us look directly to the model. Rule utilitarianism sometimes is defended along lines that echo the remarks about character voiced at the outset: "We need rules in moral life because it is a poor idea to send moral agents into the world without the guidance they afford. Moral decisions often involve complex problems that call for large amounts of information and stable, coordinated responses. Further, individuals inevitably slant deliberation in their own favor. If moral agents were left to their own devices it would be worse overall than if they were to follow shared rules of the kind that would be chosen on broadly utilitarian grounds."

For present purposes, let us define rule utilitarianism as the moral theory that deems an act right just in case the act conforms to a set of rules the general acceptance of which would bring about at least as much utility as any alternative.[3] Do the above reflections about the need for rules lend support to rule utilitarianism?

Nothing in rule utilitarianism as here defined inherently mitigates against case-by-case deliberation by individual moral agents. Since it is highly unlikely that the rules prevalent in any given agent's society are optimal, it is as much the task of a rule-utilitarian deliberator to figure out which sets of rules would be optimal as it is the task of an act-utilitarian deliberator to figure out which acts would be.[4] In answering such questions the rule-utilitarian deliberator would face essentially similar problems arising from changing or incomplete information, tendencies toward personal bias, and the like. And a society of rule-utilitarian deliberators would have problems of coordination akin to those afflicting act-utilitarian deliberators. Indeed, since multiple sets of rules may be optimal, even well-informed, unbiased, continent rule-utilitarian deliberators could fail to coordinate.[5] Finally, although rule utilitarianism places the question whether an act *would conform to* certain rules at the center of moral evaluation, it characteristically attaches no direct significance to the question whether an act *is in fact done from respect for* a rule.

Rule utilitarianism is a theory of the moral rightness of individual acts, not a moral endorsement of rules or rule-following deliberation or rule-governed action. To be sure, it is an indirect theory, for it applies the test of utility to rules rather than individual acts. But its appeal to rules in giving a criterion of the rightness of acts must not be confused with its according actual, shared rules—and their many benefits—a prominent place in moral life. It might of course turn out that acts promoting the widespread adoption and following of useful rules would be approved by rule utilitarianism; but then equally it might turn out that such acts would be approved by act utilitarianism. The case of rule utilitarianism should make us wary of the idea that if one is concerned about *X*'s, one should be an *X*-utilitarian.

Similarly, character utilitarianism, if defined as above, is a theory of the rightness of individual acts, and although it appeals to character in giving a criterion of rightness, it no more than act utilitarianism assigns a special place to the cultivation or exercise of character in practice, and it no more than act utilitarianism makes the moral evaluation of an act depend upon the motive from which the act was actually performed.

III

Perhaps, then, character utilitarianism should be built on a different model. We might take its lines from motive utilitarianism, as recently discussed by Robert M. Adams,[6] and adopt as its ultimate concern the moral value of actual possession of character. Suppose we were to define character utilitarianism as the moral theory according to which a character is morally better the higher the utility of general possession of that character. Would this give us what we want?

Not obviously. Once again, let us examine the model before the copy. The characterization of motive utilitarianism that Adams seems to prefer is the following: A motive, among those humanly possible, is morally better the higher the average utility of anyone's having it on any occasion.[7]

Motive utilitarianism begins with the moral evaluation of actual possession of motives—but it also ends there. It does not, for example, tell us whether right action depends upon motive. Indeed, it has no implications, even indirect, for the assessment of actions. The having of a motive is not an action; and though the cultivation of morally good motives normally would involve various sorts of actions, motive utilitarianism is silent on whether we should act in such a way as to encourage good motives in ourselves or others (as Adams notes, p. 481). Moreover, in the assessment of motives it ignores a range of questions that would be central to any discussion of the appropriate role of motives in our moral life, e.g., questions about the cost or likelihood of bringing people to have certain motives, and so on.

Motive utilitarianism is what William K. Frankena has called an *aretaic* theory—a normative theory of moral *value*—and thus stands in contrast with *deontic* theories—normative theories of moral *obligation*.[8] Deontic theories take as fundamental the question what it would be morally right or wrong to do, whereas aretaic theories take as fundamental the question what would be morally good or bad. Among deontic theories are divine command ethics, natural law ethics, Kantian ethics, and act and rule utilitarianism; among aretaic theories, ethics of virtue and motive utilitarianism. Adams draws this distinction in his own way by distinguishing the (deontic) question 'What should I do?' from the (aretaic) question 'Have I lived well?' and he remarks that motive utilitarianism is concerned with questions of the latter sort (p. 474). He in effect observes that an aretaic theory need not be bound by a constraint comparable to the "*ought* implies *can*" restriction on deontic theories, for he notes that one may be liable to the judgment that one has not lived well even though one's life has been among the best of those "causally possible" for one to lead (p. 475). It is, for example, legitimate within an aretaic theory to ask, "Is Jack morally perfect?" where this question is only minimally bounded by the bare constraints of what it takes to be a person.[9] It is legitimate to ask this, and not to worry about whether Jack is actually capable of moral perfection, because an aretaic judgment of perfection does not imply that he *ought* to be perfect, or is *obligated* to be perfect, or is *wrong* for being imperfect.[10]

It comes as something of a surprise, then, when Adams speaks of motives as "right" (p. 471), says that "from a motive-utilitarian point of view Jack ought . . . to have been as weakly interested in maximizing utility as he was" (pp. 471–72), and worries therefore about "incompatibility" between "right action, by act-utilitarian standards" and "right motivation, by motive-utilitarian standards" (p. 475). However, since rightness in action concerns choice among causally possible options, whereas having the best motives (at least, according to motive utilitarianism) does not, it is not obvious that there is a common dimension of assessment along which this incompatibility could arise.

To adapt an example of Adams's: Wretch that I am, I cannot have the best motives humanly possible, and so I could not bring myself to "love righteousness and my neighbors"; instead, "I did my duty out of fear of hellfire for the most part" (p. 475). Act utilitarianism says that if indeed I did do my duty, then I acted rightly, for doing my duty amounted to acting in ways, of those available to me, most conducive to net utility. Motive utilitarianism does not contradict this by telling me I did anything wrong. Rather, it simply says that, whatever I did, I failed to possess the best sort of motives humanly possible. Is there any incompatibility here? (Is there any incompatibility in saying, "Lefty pitches the baseball as fast as he can, as fast as any coach could ask him to, but he still is not the best fastball pitcher humanly possible"?)

Perhaps incompatibility is more likely to arise when we shift from general to specific standards of excellence, and confine ourselves to that which is causally possible for given individuals. We might for example ask not whether Jack has perfect motives, but whether he has the best motives among those possible for him. Here 'best possible' presumably means "bringing about—directly by their possession or indirectly by their effects—at least as much net utility as any others he might actually have had." However, this last phrase is ambiguous. One way Jack might have had better motives is that he might have been brought up differently, had better luck in his youth, and so on. (Lefty pitches as fast as he can, but still is not the best fastball pitcher he could have been, since he might have had better coaching in Little League.) Such possibilities raise no issues about the rightness of Jack's actions, for they are not acts on his part.

Alternatively, Jack might have had better motives as a result of having made different choices or tried harder. Would this show that he did not act rightly? Whenever a choice is made that affects what motives one will have, the utility or disutility of the consequences of this choice will in part be the direct or indirect result of one's possession of these motives. Suppose Jack has made motive-affecting choices in ways that did not bring him to have the best possible motives of those available to him. Still, he may have acted rightly, since the costs that would have been involved in acquiring motives that would subsequently have made the greatest possible contribution to utility—as opposed to more easily acquired motives whose subsequent contribution was less—might have been sufficiently high to offset the gains. Thus an act–utilitarian standard of right action need not recommend choosing in such a way as to have the best possible motives among those causally accessible to the agent.[11] This might be thought to be a kind of incompatibility between act and motive utilitarianism.

Consider now the other direction of comparison. Could it be the case that if Jack had the best possible motives (of those causally accessible to him) he would in some circumstances act wrongly by act-utilitarian standards? It

may bring about the greatest utility on the whole if Jack is strongly motivated to be honest, so strongly that he does not even try to deceive—
though he would succeed were he to try—in some cases in which this
would be optimal. This could come about if the psychological changes
necessary for Jack to become more likely to deceive in such cases would
inevitably increase Jack's tendency to deceive in many non-optimal cases
as well. Thus there is no necessary coincidence between having the best
motives by motive-utilitarian standards and acting rightly by act-utilitarian
standards. This, too, might seem an incompatibility.

It can be replied that there is no strict incompatibility in either case,
since judgments of the rightness of acts and judgments of the goodness of
(possession of) motives lack a common subject matter. (Lefty has the best
strikeout record in the league, but a mediocre earned-run average.) Motive
utilitarianism, even in its individualistic form (p. 480), does not imply that
one ought to have the best motives among those available. And act utilitarianism, because it does not until supplemented—e.g., by motive utilitarianism—contain a theory of moral value, does not imply that the moral value
of motives is determined exclusively by their contribution to right action.

IV

Yet one who aspires to be a character utilitarian may find this rather beside
the point. For, to him, the issue is not one of incompatibility in a logical
sense. Rather, he has the concerns about the place of character in morality
expressed in the opening paragraph of this paper, and he thinks, "If I accept
both character utilitarianism and act utilitarianism, then an evaluative dualism may arise in which what I deem right in action lacks an appropriate
connection with what I deem good in character. In a number of cases, the
two aspects of evaluation will simply go their separate ways, whereas my
hope was to integrate them."[12]

Suppose, for example, that part of the best character available to Mel
is a powerful sense of parental responsibility. This is so, we may suppose,
because with this sense he will receive great satisfaction for helping his
child—a highly useful thing that he is more likely to do, and do well, if he
finds enjoyment in it—and because without it he would become more self-
absorbed and less motivated to take into account the interests of others in
general. Consider now a choice he faces between conferring a smallish
benefit upon his young son and conferring a considerably larger benefit
upon people unknown to him. Mel could spend an afternoon taking his
son and a friend on an outing he knows they would especially like, or he

could find a sitter to mind his son at home while he goes out to spend the afternoon canvassing for grassroots economic development in Central America.

We need not imagine that the sort of parental concern that would be part of the best character available to Mel is one which would dispose him in such cases *always* to elect to spend time with his child—surely there would be room for activities of both sorts. But suppose that on this particular Saturday Mel has just returned home from an extended, utility-maximizing trip. An act-utilitarian computation reveals that it nonetheless would bring about more intrinsic good were he to go door-to-door for agricultural self-help projects. All things considered—including, for example, long-term effects on his character and his relation with his son—it would be wrong according to act utilitarianism for Mel to take his son on the outing, and he accordingly is morally obliged not to do so. Yet it may also be the case that if Mel had the best sort of character available to him he would on this Saturday deliberately sidestep his all-things-considered obligation and go on the outing. And here there is a rub. The normative force of claims about "the best sort of character" available to one is unclear and perhaps unimpressive or unpointed in comparison to claims about one's "all-things-considered moral obligation." It is not unusual in ethics to come across conflicts among duties each of which is weighty, but this case is of a different nature. An all-things-considered duty stands on one side, while on the other there is no duty at all, for motive utilitarianism does not enjoin us to act as someone with good character would. So if, contrary to duty, Mel does go on the outing—either because he has a good character or because he is trying to act as someone with good character would—how is Mel to regard the moral status of what he is doing? And how can Mel really embrace his character in a moral sense? Yet it may be crucial to achieving the good effects of this character that he so embrace it.

An act utilitarian can respond that the impression that judgments of character are inconsequential in guiding action is something like an illusion of perspective. When we broaden our gaze to take in decisions that will affect the sort of character we have—and many of our decisions have such effects—we will find within act utilitarianism all the injunctive force we need to give weight to character. Act utilitarianism does not tell us to maximize episodes of right action; its concern is only and always with maximizing utility.[13] Thus when Mel contemplates his past, and considers choices that would have altered his commitment to his child in such a way as to have made it likely that he would have decided to go door-to-door that Saturday, he will see that, on our hypothesis,[14] he was at the time under an all-things-considered act-utilitarian injunction to act to promote instead a parental commitment that would lead him to favor going on the outing. Here, the act utilitarian argues, is the sought-after normative affirmation of character: the best way to achieve good results almost always involves taking seriously the development of firm character, where "taking seriously" includes embracing a character even though it will sometimes lead to wrong action.

If our would-be character utilitarian complains that what he wanted was an affirmation of the intrinsic rather than strategic value of character, the act utilitarian has two lines of reply. First, to the extent that the character utilitarian has in mind whatever intrinsic *non*moral value character may have, the act utilitarian of course affirms this and allows it to enter directly into his calculations of utility. Second, to the extent that the character utilitarian has in mind whatever intrinsic *moral* value character may have, then he is in effect supposing the falsity of his own view, since the point of character utilitarianism is to give an account of moral value without appealing to any notion of *intrinsic* moral goodness.

Of course, the sorts of character that act utilitarianism would recommend that we develop will not in general be exactly the ones that an aretaic character utilitarian would identify as "best (among those available) to have." For, as we have already noted in connection with motives, act utilitarianism takes into account not only how much utility arises from the having of a character, but also how much is lost or gained in the acquiring, teaching, or encouraging of a character, and how much utility arises from act-affected sources other than character and the consequences of character. However, the value of having a character will certainly figure prominently in act-utilitarian assessment, and so character-utilitarian evaluations will certainly have a place in the scheme. Moreover, one can accept an act-utilitarian account of rightness in action without being (what might be called) a *hegemonic* act utilitarian, that is, without believing that all moral evaluation is based at bottom upon evaluations of the rightness of acts. One could, for example, hold that whenever there is direct concern with moral evaluation of character, character utilitarianism can stand entirely on its own alongside act utilitarianism, fielding whatever questions come its way.

V

Still, the aspiring character utilitarianism may have the uncomfortable sense that his concerns have somehow been shoved to the periphery. Perhaps act utilitarianism can issue an endorsement of cultivating firm traits of character, but some of the issues raised by the remarks about character and action with which this paper began remain unresolved.

First, what of the idea that motives make a distinctive contribution to the moral assessment of an act, a contribution in some ways independent of the consequences of the act?

Suppose that Frank has a character that is among the best available to him, and that indeed is among the best humanly possible. But he is human, and in order that he be sufficiently sensitive to, and critical of, unjustified inequality he must also harbor a trace of resentment of just about any inequality. As a result, he finds a certain satisfaction in seeing those of high status taken down a peg or two. An opportunity presents itself for him to facilitate this in the large firm for which he works. He is asked his candid opinion of Richard, a superior in the firm who is being considered for an employee reward. Now Frank is honest and cooperative. And his honest opinion is that Richard is worthy, though overrated. Ordinarily, Frank's reluctance to damage a candidate's chances for something as peripheral as an employee award would outweigh his cooperative desire to supply an honest answer to a legitimate question, and he would find some polite way—undamaging to the candidate—to beg off. In this case, however, he reflects for a moment, and then quite deliberately says, "I think he's overrated, though, of course, there is no question of such a choice actually embarrassing you." Frank is giving a candid opinion, and one that he has reason to believe will have good effects, since it seems likely to advance the candidacy of some less senior employees whom Frank believes to be at least as deserving of the award as Richard and also to be more likely to benefit significantly from it. But deep down Frank is also hoping that his carefully chosen remark will tilt the decision against Richard, and what lies behind his hope is largely the idea that this would be something good *not* happening to Richard, to whom so many good things have already happened. However, without realizing it, Frank has said exactly what his questioner wanted to hear—the only thing holding up giving the award to Richard was precisely this person's idiosyncratic fear that the choice would somehow prove embarrassing.

Suppose now that for the award to go to Richard would for complicated reasons do considerably more good than Frank had imagined—so much more that Frank's response turns out to have been utility maximizing. Yet don't we feel a bit queasy about the moral status of Frank's action? Are we content to call it right, as an act-utilitarian standard would indicate?[15] And if the function of a character-utilitarian standard is simply to answer questions about the moral value of character within the realm of what is causally possible for humans, then it too will find nothing to criticize about Frank—he is as good as a human can be. What would seem to be needed is a way of reaching a motivation-related evaluation that applies to individual actions and that is not a function solely of consequences.

Second, we have not fully quieted the earlier worry about chafing between acting from good character and the act–utilitarian insistence that it is always all-things-considered obligatory to maximize the good. The possibility of chafing does not exist because, as it is sometimes said, act utiltarianism requires that agents actually consult the test of utility in deliberating about their choices.[16] Insofar as deliberation is an action, or can be influenced by action, act utilitarianism requires optimality, whether or not this involves distinctively utilitarian deliberation or a resolve to act in an optimal way, and it may on occasion (or even always) involve neither, but rather a tendency to act, say, from character.[17]

Instead, chafing threatens largely because it seems to us so plausible that acting optimally will not infrequently require action that in one way or another goes against good character. The conflict suggested in the case of Mel, between optimal action and the natural action-tendencies of parental concern, arises not only on the odd Saturday afternoon, but daily, whenever he faces a decision about how to make use of his time or money or energy. And it arises not only for parental concern, but for any special relation he might have with other individuals or groups, or with his work or avocations. The ubiquity of such potential for conflict in Mel's life—and in our lives—is the joint product of human psychology and the world in which we and Mel now find ourselves. On the one side, there are many in severe need who could benefit dramatically from reallocation even of small resources. On the other, there are few among those with ample resources who could be unstintingly responsive to this need except at great personal cost. Not all of this cost would be due to selfishness in any narrow or pejorative sense. For some will arise from possible impairment of an individual's ability to have in any deep way the more particular attachments and engagements of family, friendship, and work that anchor the self and supply much of the structure and interest of life.

To be sure, act utilitarianism does not tell us to set out to destroy these attachments in order to clear the way for doing impersonal good. It can recognize that people will be able to act reliably to promote the general good only if they can sustain the integrity and interest of their own lives. Act utilitarianism, therefore, may school us in the importance of acting so as to develop and maintain practices and characters that merge a tendency to promote general well-being with other psychological characteristics that lend integrity and interest to lives. So far so good. But it tells us one thing further: Someone with as good a character as possible in this sense nonetheless does what is morally *impermissible* whenever, owing to such character, he fails to the slightest degree to optimize when given the chance.

There will be cases in which it is uncontroversial that the best character available to an agent can lead to wrong action. Consider the example involving Frank, but remove the supposition that Frank could have had reasonable confidence that his remark would have positive effects overall. Assume, perhaps, that he knows Richard to be aware of being in the running for the award and to be prone to respond in an exaggerated way to anything that hints of failure. Assume that Frank can (correctly) see that these considerations would be just enough to make it optimal in the circumstances to keep his opinion of Richard to himself. And assume that, when voiced, Frank's opinion will—as he hopes—steer the award away from Richard. Thus re-described, Frank's action would count as wrong by an act-utilitarian standard. And it would probably strike most of us as morally wrong, even though it would stem from the best character available to him.

But there are many cases on the other side. It is rather unintuitive, for example, to judge it morally wrong for Mel to go on the Saturday afternoon outing. In a more general example, the most generous people I know give something like 15 percent of their income to charities and other worthwhile causes. Assume that this approaches the "maximum sustainable yield" for most people. Perhaps anyone who committed himself on a regular basis to giving substantially more, say, 30 percent, would after several years feel so cramped that he would lose interest in the whole thing. Or perhaps he would have so hardened his heart against providing for his own or his family's "less needy" desires as to become a crank whose example leads his children to swear off all but minimal charitable contributions for the remainder of the natural lives. Yet, on any given occasion of making a gift, any of my generous friends could give more than 15 percent without noticeable harm and to considerable good effect. Thus, on each occasion when they give 15 percent they act wrongly, contrary to their moral duty. That is, with regard to charitable giving, they act wrongly almost all the time. In that respect, they act like me, even though I give only a few percent. Wrong is wrong, after all.

But most of us would be inclined to say that they do not really act like me—they act much better. Indeed, it would accord with ordinary usage to say that when they give 15 percent they not only act better, they act rightly, even beyond the call of duty. This would sit comfortably alongside the idea that they have something close to the best character available to them. But it contradicts act utilitarianism.

Now act utilitarians will rush to tell us that they have the wherewithal to explain the moral distinction between my acts and those of my more generous friends. For example, act utilitarians can distinguish the question whether an act is wrong from the question whether it would be right to blame the agent for it. Yet I may be morally countersuggestive while my generous friends, bless them, respond constructively to moral criticism. If criticized, they would nudge their annual charitable contributions still closer to the sustainable limit and add some further, exceptional gifts from time to time. Thus it could be right in act–utilitarian terms to blame them for giving "only" 15 percent, but not to blame me for giving a paltry few percent. Similarly, to heap praise upon the charitable acts of such people might simply embarrass them and fill the rest of us with envy and self-loathing, making us less charitable out of a mixture of spite and increased consumption as we apply to our wounded self-esteem the balm of luxury.

If indirect act–utilitarian approaches seem not to yield the judgments wanted, an act utilitarian might attempt to generate the judgments directly by introducing a vocabulary of degrees of wrongness in which to say that, for example, while both my giving 2 percent and their giving 15 percent are wrong, mine is wronger. Yet wrongness may not be the concept for the job.

For a start, 'right' and 'wrong' mark a binary distinction—hence the oddness of 'wronger'—and it may be useful in moral theorizing to keep them that way, especially since we already have a serviceable vocabulary of degree in moral assessment: 'better' and 'worse', 'more valuable' and 'less valuable', and so on.

More importantly, the binary character of 'right' and 'wrong' reflects deeper facts about their use. Right and wrong are quasi-juridical notions, linked to requirement and impermissibility, and it is clear why this is usually seen as a dualism—perhaps with a vague boundary—rather than as a matter of degree.

Now it seems inconsistent with anything like our ordinary understanding of 'morally right' to say that the boundary separating the right from the wrong is to be sharply drawn infinitesimally below the very best action possible. 'Wrong' does mark a kind of discontinuity in moral evaluation, but one associated with real unacceptability. For this reason 'right', though not itself a matter of degree, covers actions that are entirely acceptable given reasonable expectations as well as those that are optimal. 'Wrong' comes into clear application only when we reach actions far enough below normal expectations to warrant real criticism or censure.

As quasi-juridical notions, rightness and wrongness are to be found ready-made in some conceptions of the basis of morality, such as those of divine command and natural law. Not so in the case of the underlying conception of utilitarianism, which consists not in laws or commands directed at individuals, but in overall states of affairs that realize varying amounts of value. Individual acts are parts of these states of affairs, and are both bearers and causes of value. But they are not the only parts, the only bearers, or the only causes. Intrinsic good is realizable in human lives through being and doing alike—through experience, acts, characters, institutions, and practices. All of these phenomena interact, and the utilitarian perspective upon them—and the value they realize—is global rather than local, symmetrical rather than agent-centered. (Perhaps for these reasons, a direct utilitarian standard has always had greater plausibility as a criterion of choice in public policy than in personal ethics.[18]) Obviously a complex treatment will be needed to accommodate within a scheme of global, symmetrical evaluations of continuously valued states of affairs an account of one multiply entangled, discontinuous, asymmetrical, local component of moral evaluation, such as rightness in action.

The utilitarian can—and typically does—pull out one contributor to value and one component of moral evaluation and link them in a fairly simple, direct or indirect way. The act utilitarian does this in giving his account of moral rightness. 'Right' becomes as a result a term of art, and incongruities arise partly because most of us will continue to understand the term as carrying many of its traditional connections—for example, with reasonable expectations, praising and blaming, etc.—and partly, too, because the utilitarian himself continues to draw upon some traditional connections—for example, with all-things-considered obligation. A dilemma may present itself. Either the act utilitarian is also making, say, 'all-things-considered obligation' a term of art—with a change in its role that removes obligation so far from reasonable expectation that we no longer expect most people in our society to come close to carrying out their obligations—or the act utilitarian is retaining our familiar sense of, and role for, 'all-things-considered obligation', in which case most people will be amazed at what is expected of them and at what they are liable to criticism for failing to do.[19]

The source of this dilemma is familiar in contemporary philosophy. Once one accepts a reasonable degree of holism about discourse and practice, one accepts that any attempt to introduce new meanings or roles into this network will involve two complementary processes. First, it will bring about alterations in the meanings and roles of other elements of discourse and practice, and thus run the risk of changing the subject. Second, it will itself be vulnerable to alteration beyond original specification as a result of "backward linkages" from the rest of the network, and thus run the risk of saying something unintended. The utilitarian who is attempting a quite systematic account of ethics must be very careful which part of the network of moral discourse and practice he seizes upon when he begins his reconstruction. It may be inadvisable to proceed as the act utilitarian does, by initially taking up the threads that converge on the notion of moral right-ness. Although reconstruction must eventually come to this notion, if a utilitarian ties a tight knot between the goodness of states of affairs and the rightness of individual actions he may find that he is unable to get back the slack he needs for successful reconstruction except by unraveling the strands connecting right action to obligation, reasonable expectation, blamewor-thiness, and so on—increasingly changing the subject. The importance of where the utilitarian takes—or makes—his slack becomes especially evident when, out of a concern with character, we look up from the traditional focus upon right action and glimpse the multiple dimensions and questions of moral assessment that need to be tied together without creating excessive strain.

VI

What is the alternative to commencing utilitarian reconstruction deonti-cally, with a theory of right action? Some distinctly nonutilitarian philoso-phers appear to favor outright abandonment of the categories of right and wrong in ethics, but it seems to me that in morality as in law, there is a highly useful function to be served by the particular sort of guidance such notions provide to agents. We thus do have a reason for attempting to give some account of deontic judgments within moral theory, but it is a further question whether moral theory should start with such judgments.

Aretaic theories afford an example of how one might start elsewhere, namely, with assessments of moral value. But as the name suggests, such theories have largely been concerned with virtue, and what is needed is a broader category than *arete*. For want of anything better, I will forego the felicity of Greek roots and introduce the harsh latinate term *valoric* to cover direct assessments of what is better or worse from a moral point of view, whether these assessments be made of acts, agents, characters, institutions, or whatever. When the moral point of view in question bases its assessments ultimately upon an impartial reckoning of the nonmoral good realized, we have what may be called *valoric utilitarianism*.

Valoric utilitarianism starts out from the guiding utilitarian idea that no sort of act or motive or institution has intrinsic moral value and that what-ever value it has from a moral point of view depends in the final reckoning upon how it affects human well-being. There are, of course, multiple val-oric utilitarian positions, depending upon how well-being is understood and upon whether effects on well-being are evaluated in terms of total amount of utility realized, average amount, distributed amount,[20] or whatever. In what follows I will be concerned only with a maximizing valoric utilitarianism. Although I will not defend this choice here, it must be admitted to be a choice—nothing in the theory of nonmoral value tells us that for purposes of moral evaluation greater total nonmoral value is always superior to lesser, a claim that belongs to the realm of moral theory proper.

Is it therefore a claim about moral value? In a sense, yes, for it is a matter of what is "better rather than worse from a moral point of view." It would however be confusing to appropriate the familiar term 'moral value' for such claims. A maximizing[21] valoric utilitarian assessment of an action or a character would consist in asking directly how much net nonmoral value would be realized by, and as a result of, its occurrence or existence. But notoriously, an act or character can strike us as morally bad even though it happens to bring about very good results. Like 'right' and 'wrong', 'morally good' and 'morally bad' owe their content in part to judgments about *kinds* of actions or characters and about what *characteristically* goes along with them, and in part as well to judgments about the *normal range* of human variation. Moreover, 'morally good' tends in ordinary use to be applied only to the limited range of human thought and action that involves *moral conscientiousness,* and so would not be applied to actions of, say, spontaneous affection that, although highly beneficial, lack distinctively moral motivation.

Valoric utilitarians thus should not assume that their notion of "better or worse from a moral point of view" coincides with our notion of moral value. They will almost certainly have to use complex and indirect means to give an account of judgments of moral value (in the ordinary sense) and thus should insist that they are using 'better or worse from a moral point of view' as a technical term. To emphasize this while at the same time avoiding a cumbersome phrase, let us remint an expression coined by Bertrand Russell, and speak of acts or character traits that are better rather than worse from a moral point of view as more or less *morally fortunate.*[22] Thus one could speak of Frank's unenthusiastic remark (under the original assumptions) as morally most fortunate relative to available alternatives, even if not morally right or morally good as we ordinarily understand these terms. Frank's overall character, too, would be morally most fortunate relative to available alternatives, and here ordinary usage might deem this character morally good. Moreover, valoric utilitarianism would say that it is unfortunate, relative to a perhaps unattainable ideal of character, that Frank's moral outrage at unjustified inequalities must be allied to his rather spiteful resentment of all inequalities, just as ordinary usage would say that owing to this spiteful streak Frank, though good, is not perfect. Put another way, among the motives underlying Frank's act are some which, even though they are part of a character both fortunate and good, are not themselves either fortunate or good.

As this example suggests, valoric utilitarianism has direct application not only to acts, but to any object of moral assessment. In this way it differs not only from familiar indirect utilitarianisms, but also from direct act utilitarianism. One can ask how morally fortunate an individual act is, or how morally fortunate actions of that kind usually are, or how morally fortunate it would be if everyone regularly took such actions, and so on. And one may ask how morally fortunate it is that on a given occasion an individual possesses or acts from a given character, or how morally fortunate a character of that kind usually is, or how morally fortunate it would be if most people had such characters, and so on. And thus far, we have spoken only of valoric utilitarian judgments based upon the *absolute* amount of nonmoral value that is or would be brought about.

In moral practice we have a special interest in judgments based upon the *relative* amount of nonmoral value that acts, characters, etc. would bring about, especially those within the range of alternatives causally accessible to us. For example, we often want to know which acts, among those the agent would succeed in performing if he tried, would bring about at least as much nonmoral value as any others.[23] I suppose one could call the view that such acts are morally most fortunate "act-token valoric utilitarianism," but this view would not as such be a theory of moral rightness, nor would it be in competition with "act-type valoric utilitarianism" or "rule valoric utilitarianism" or "character valoric utilitarianism." "Rule valoric utilitarianism" and "character valoric utilitarianism," for example, are direct views about the fortunateness of rules or characters, not indirect views about the fortunateness of acts.

Consider again my generous friends. According to valoric utilitarianism, (1) it is very fortunate relative to available alternatives that they give 15 percent of their income to worthy causes—since this does a large amount of good compared to most other uses of these funds—but (2) it would be still more fortunate if on occasion or regularly they were to give 30 percent. Yet (3) it is most fortunate relative to available alternatives that they have the characters they do, even though these characters lead them not to give more than 15 percent. For although it would be more fortunate for them to have characters that would lead them always to give 30 percent, such characters are not causally accessible to them, and we have supposed that it would in fact be less fortunate were they to have characters that would lead them to be strongly inclined to try to give 30 percent. Moreover, (4) their acts of donation are substantially more fortunate than mine, despite the fact that (5) chastising them for not giving more would, owing to their more measured and appropriate response, be more fortunate than chastising me.

Consider, too, Mel's Saturday afternoon. The valoric utilitarian would say that (1) it would be more fortunate were Mel to go off canvassing, but (2) less fortunate were he to have the sort of character that would make it highly likely for him to do so. Valoric utilitarianism would also say that, (3) given the resources available to Mel and the world as it is, it would be more fortunate were his psychology such that he would reliably do more for Central American peasants and others in great need, even if this meant doing less for his kith and kin. Yet valoric utilitarianism would also say that (4) it would be more fortunate were the world and Mel's psychology such that he could live a life in which contribution to his own good and the good of kith and kin were more consonant with maximizing the general good, at least, so long as this were achieved by raising the resources available to others rather than simply lowering the resources available to Mel.

So far the valoric utilitarian's judgments do not strike me as either morally complacent or grossly at odds with our moral concepts. For example, although the value of doing more nonmoral good has been recognized, no claim has been made to the effect that it is always wrong to fail to optimize.

However, the rejoinder will be made: perhaps nothing jarring has been said about right or wrong, but that may only be because nothing has been said about them. And it must be admitted that, as described thus far, valoric utilitarianism is indeed an incomplete, and to that extent unspecific, moral theory. Note, however, that it is also in its own way quite a bit more comprehensive theory than familiar deontic utilitarianisms, for it furnishes assessments of what is better or worse from a moral point of view not only with regard to acts, but also motives, characters, distributions of resources, and so on. Moreover, in its hegemonic form—the form with which we are concerned here[24]—valoric utilitarianism is quite specific in at least one respect about how it is to be completed. For it tells us that all moral evaluations—evaluations of moral rightness, moral goodness, and the like—are to be traced back to assessments of the total amount of nonmoral good realized in the world, i.e., to what is more rather than less fortunate. Upon this base would be built accounts of these other species of moral evaluation, and once the valoric utilitarian moves beyond judgments of what is more or less morally fortunate, about which he is relentlessly direct, he is free to beome indirect. Indirect and intricate. For in view of what has been said about the holism of moral discourse, any plausible account of, say, moral rightness can be expected to be quite elaborate, involving not only questions about rules or principles, but also about motivations, dispositions to feel guilt or attribute blame, and so on. Thus a valoric utilitarian account of rightness might deem an action right if it would conform to normative practices—comprising rules, motivations, dispositions, etc.—that would be fortunate.[25] But if it is to overcome some of the difficulties facing existing indirect utilitarianisms, the valoric account may have to avoid certain idealizations and abstractions. For example, it may have to attach primary significance not to the question "Which practices would be most fortunate if generally observed?" but rather "Which practices are most fortunate given circumstances as they are and will be?" And it may also have to attach importance not simply to whether an action *would* be performed if the agent had fortunate motives, dispositions, etc., but also to whether it actually was the result of such causes.

Given the characteristic structure of valoric utilitarianism, it may be able to escape the charge of "rule worship" that has been laid against various forms of deontic indirect utilitarianism. For in an instance in which an act in conformity with fortunate normative practices would lead to bad outcomes, the valoric utilitarian is able to say that it would be morally more fortunate—i.e., better from a moral point of view—if the practice were violated and a more beneficial act performed. This application of direct utilitarian assessment is not, it must be noted, a judgment of rightness. The act in violation of fortunate normative practices remains wrong, and this accommodates the commonsense thought that certain sorts of action—torture, deception, the sacrifice of innocents—are wrong even when, owing to unusual circumstances, they are beneficial.

This may seem puzzling. "What am I to do," an agent seeking moral advice in such circumstances may ask, "that which is most fortunate or that which is right?" Shouldn't there be a definite answer as to which evaluation to follow? There are definite answers, but there is no one question. If the agent wants to know which acts, of those available to him, are most highly valued from a moral point of view, he receives one answer. If he wants to know which acts would be right or wrong, he receives another. It is a familiar feature of ordinary moral life that in doing something right, one is not always doing the best—there is, after all, supererogation. Moreover, in doing something right, for example, in rejecting certain sorts of deception, one may be doing a good bit of harm. Insofar as the moral point of view is concerned, it is preferable if the most fortunate act is performed. But the most fortunate act may be blameworthy by the sorts of standards that ground judgments of right and wrong. This is a bit like the fact that the morally fortunate thing to do may be illegal and appropriately punished. It is a bit more like the fact that the best thing to do from the standpoint of promoting the law itself may be illegal.

Perhaps, however, the agent is asking a different question still. He may want to know whether he has more reason to do what is morally fortunate or what is morally right. This, however, is not a question to refer to moral standards or even to the moral point of view. For it is the office of practical reason to answer questions about the place of morally fortunate—or morally right—action in a rational life.

It would be a very large task to develop a valoric utilitarian reconstruction of the discourse and practice of assessments of moral rightness, or, for that matter, of moral goodness or social justice. Such a reconstruction would have to withstand stresses from several directions at once—from the need to retain continuity with existing language and practice as well as the need to avoid complacency and make appropriate improvements. Whether such a reconstruction could give character and rules a significance in morality closer to roles suggested by the imagined defenses of character and rules quoted in the initial sections of this paper cannot be judged until we have before us a more definite idea of what such a reconstruction might look like.

Still, those drawn to the guiding idea of utilitarianism may wish to consider the possibility that valoric utilitarianism gives the most direct expression of what they find attractive in that idea. And it is possible to say something about what valoric accounts of rightness or goodness might look like. For act and rule utilitarianism could be seen as more or less simple prototypes of how one might develop an account of moral rightness in action within a valoric framework; and motive and character utilitarianism (in the second form discussed) could be seen as prototypes of how one might develop an account of moral goodness of motive or character within such a framework. The difficulties these prototypes have faced in meeting the simultaneous stresses of necessary continuity with existing practices and appropriate reform are instructive, for they show where the valorist needs to work outward from the guiding utilitarian idea with greater sophistication. Of course, if, even after considerable time, more successful prototypes were not forthcoming, then this failure might provide a different sort of instruction, to the effect that the fault lies with the guiding idea itself. Those who are already impatient with utilitarianism may feel they have seen more than enough to reach such a judgment—Is utilitarianism asking for our patience for another century or two? To them I can only say that, by this standard, the grace period of deontology would also have expired.

VII

We have taken a curious route from our starting point. Consideration of how judgments of character might figure in a utilitarian moral theory have led us not to new advancements in utilitarianism, but rather to a new starting point, one further back than where we began. That could be fortunate for utilitarianism. Progress sometimes comes from taking a fresh start. But at the same time, the view from the valoric starting point is not entirely cheering to the utilitarian, since from this vantage utilitarianism as it stands seems to lack a satisfactory account not only of goodness of character, but even of the category of moral assessment with which it has most preoccupied itself, right action. And it will be cold comfort to the valoric utilitarian to learn that, in the eyes of many moral philosophers, that much of valoric utilitarianism is obviously true.[26]

NOTES

1. One might expand this guiding idea to include all sentient beings. In this paper it will be restricted to people, though not on principled grounds.

2. Throughout I will speak of having a character rather than having specific traits of character. The view could be formulated in either way, but there may be something to be said for the more holistic notion, just as in contemporary rule utilitarianism reference is usually made not to individual rules, but to sets of rules or "moral codes."

3. Many formulations of the notion of 'general acceptance' exist. Some, for example, ignore questions of teaching or socialization and simply assume widespread—or even ideal—compliance. Others more plausibly incorporate costs of teaching, difficulty of internalization, and so on, in assessing optimality and do not assume anything like ideal compliance. Similarly, rule utilitarians may differ over whether they are recommending *action in accord with optimal rules* or *active consultation of optimal rules in deliberation*. Since there can be no guarantee that the former always requires—or even always permits—the latter, and since in cases of conflict it seems at odds with a broadly consequentialist spirit to treat a form of deliberation as intrinsically required, I have taken for our definition a version of rule utilitarianism that adopts the former line.

4. I mean by 'rule-utilitarian deliberator' to designate, not someone who—in deliberation or action—actually lives up to the requirements of rule utilitarianism, but someone who *tries* to do so in the following sense: he accepts the rule–utilitarian account of rightness and he conscientiously endeavors to determine which acts, of those available to him, would satisfy it. Similarly for 'act-utilitarian deliberator'. It is important to see that neither theory need set forward such conscious, conscientious striving as a moral ideal. We will return to this point below, in connection with act utilitarianism.

5. It is perhaps a defect of rule utilitarianism that it could turn out that agents would escape rule-utilitarian criticism despite their failure to coordinate if each could correctly claim to be conforming to one of the optimal sets of rules. (I sup-

pose any optimal set of rules would somewhere contain an injunction to coordinate, but our example supposes that the injunctions of the equi-optimal sets of rules have already been taken into account.) Actual-outcome act utilitarianism, by contrast, would condemn an agent's failure to coordinate optimally whenever it was in his power to do so. This, of course, would leave untouched the interesting problems of how agents might actually go about achieving coordination.

6. See R. M. Adams, "Motive Utilitarianism," *The Journal of Philosophy* 73 (1976): 467–81, esp. p. 480. Otherwise unattributed page citations in the text refer to this work.

7. For the sake of consistency with the rest of this paper, I have put his definition (p. 480) in terms of actual rather than expected utility.

8. See William K. Frankena, *Ethics,* 2nd ed. (Englewood Cliffs, N.J., 1973), 121, 122.

9. Adams restricts the question of what motives "the morally perfect person" would have to "patterns of motivation that are causally possible for human beings" (p. 470), but we may also wish to consider persons more broadly. A Kantian might, for example, want to say that a morally perfect *person* would have a holy will, while a morally perfect *human* would have at best a good will.

10. But doesn't calling something good entail a claim that it "ought to exist"? Philosophers have indeed often spoken as if this were so, but to whom or what would this 'ought' be addressed in those cases where we speak of the goodness of impossible perfection?

11. Because the difference in question arises from the fact that the act utilitarian casts his evaluative net wider, this situation could arise even if the acquisition of motives were assumed to be effortless. For example, it may be that, of the sets of motives available to me, M would bring about more utility than any other, and *a fortiori* more than N. However, perhaps in order to have motives M, I must also as a matter of psychological necessity have beliefs B, which themselves directly bring me a certain amount of utility; on the other hand, in order to have motives N I must have beliefs C, which, we will suppose, directly bring me more utility than B. The beliefs are not caused or otherwise brought about by having the motives, and so their direct utility does not figure in the evaluation of the motives or the effects of these motives. It therefore could turn out that although motives M would bring about more utility than motives N, the motive-belief package $M + B$ would bring about less utility than $N + C$. If we consider a choice among acts that would determine which of these packages I would (effortlessly, we suppose) come to have, an act-utilitarian standard would favor promoting $N + C$.

12. Adams may be expressing a similar concern when he speaks of "the way that the motives, and especially the kind of conscience, regarded as right must be related to the acts regarded as right in anything that is to count as a morality" (p. 479), and it may be this concern that lies behind his talk of incompatibility.

13. Contrast here the claim of Bernard Williams that act utilitarianism "contains something which a utilitarian would see as a certain weakness, a traditional idea which it unreflectively harbors. This is, that the best world must be one in which

right action is maximized." B. Williams, "A Critique of Utilitarianism," in *Utilitarianism: For and Against,* edited by J. J. C. Smart and B. Williams (Cambridge, 1975), 129.

14. That is, on the assumption that, were Mel's parental attachment to weaken, the result would be that he would bring about less utility in the long run. Note that this assumption is in a relevant sense more inclusive than the assumption that strong parental attachment is among the motives it would be best for him to have. See below.

15. I have tried to formulate the example so that the act would be right on either a prospective or an actualist account of act-utilitarian duty.

16. Williams disagrees, arguing that "There is no distinctive place for *direct* utilitarianism unless it is, within fairly narrow limits, a doctrine about how one should decide what to do" ("A Critique of Utilitarianism," 128).

17. For discussion, see P. Railton, "Alienation, Consequentialism, and the Demands of Morality," *Philosophy and Public Affairs* 13 (Spring 1984): 134–71, esp. 148–56.

18. Presumably the global, symmetrical character of the underlying conception of utilitarianism—which yields "no comprehensible difference which consists just in my bringing about a certain outcome rather than someone else's producing it"— helps account for Williams' criticism that utilitarianism cannot give a plausible account of agency and moreover leaves individuals forever at the mercy of a "universal satisfaction system" ("A Critique of Utilitarianism," 96, 118). Although I would emphasize that these are features of the *underlying* utilitarian conception, and not necessarily of all accounts of right action justified by appeal to that conception, it must be said that Williams' criticism has made vivid an important part of what would be involved in giving a satisfactory utilitarian account of right action.

19. I was guilty of failure to take the full measure of this dilemma when, in a footnote to "Alienation, Consequentialism, and the Demands of Morality," I attempted without saying as much to pick and choose among the connections the expression 'right'—as used by an act utilitarian—would retain with existing usage (p. 160n).

20. The role of distribution here would be distinct both from the role distribution would play if it had intrinsic *non*moral value—which could then be figured directly into a maximizing or averaging scheme without loss—and from the role distribution would play if it had intrinsic *moral* value in the narrow sense. I suppose that a defense of allowing distribution the role in question would have to take the form of showing distributive constraints to be partly *constitutive* of the moral point of view.

21. Hereinafter, this qualification will be dropped.

22. See B. Russell, "The Elements of Ethics," reprinted in *Readings in Ethical Theory,* 2nd ed., edited by Wilfred Sellars and John Hospers (Englewood Cliffs, N.J., 1970), 12. Russell uses the term for a somewhat different purpose, to pick out those acts that actually (as opposed to prospectively) have good consequences.

23. This is what we would like to know, although of course we seldom do, and

so settle instead for some prospective estimation of the value that would be realized. It seems to me that valoric utilitarianism is most plausibly formulated in terms of *actual* nonmoral value realized, although the valorist's account of such notions as moral rightness, goodness, and so on, may well appeal to *prospective* value. It is, I think, because of utilitarians' undue focus upon the question of right action that it has seemed so natural to formulate their view, at base, in terms of prospective value. For how can one say that agents are *obliged* to act as full information would indicate, given that they never will have full information? Once, however, we see the problem of constructing an account of moral obligation from the standpoint of what I have called the guiding idea of utilitarianism, it becomes more plausible that it is actual well-being that matters at bottom, and that prospective value matters because it is predictive of actual value.

24. Just as act utilitarianism could be held in a nonhegemonic way (e.g., in tandem with motive utilitarianism), so can valoric utilitarianism (e.g., in tandem with act utilitarianism). However, since our aim here is to get some idea of what a nondeontic utilitarianism might look like, and in particular to see how an integrated valoric utilitarian approach to the various species of moral evaluation might be made, it will best suit our purposes to focus upon hegemonic valoric utilitarianism, which denies deontic judgments any independent foundation.

25. Compare here Richard B. Brandt's notion of a "moral code," as presented in *A Theory of the Good and the Right* (Oxford, 1979), chap. 9.

26. I would like to thank William K. Frankena for very helpful comments on an earlier draft of this paper.

· 9 ·

JOHN STUART MILL AND EXPERIMENTS IN LIVING

Elizabeth S. Anderson

John Stuart Mill thought that we learn about the good through "experiments in living."[1] As an empiricist, he rejected the traditional view that we know about the good through a priori intuitions. Conceptions of the good must be tested by the experiences we have in living them out, not merely by comparing them with ethical intuitions. This article offers a reconstruction of Mill's theory of experiments in living. I argue that Mill regarded his own early life as an experiment in living which revealed the superiority of his conception of the good over Bentham's.

Mill's dispute with Bentham illuminates two debates of contemporary significance in moral philosophy. One concerns the limitations of ethical theories that are "self-effacing."[2] When a theory of the good is self-effacing, a person cannot realize the good if he believes the theory; such theories instruct individuals to believe some other theory of the good. Derek Parfit has argued that the fact that a theory is self-effacing has no bearing on its truth.[3] I will show that Mill's arguments imply that Bentham's theory of the good is self-effacing, and that this feature of his theory ultimately undermines it.

The second debate concerns empirical naturalism—the claim that evaluative concepts can and must be constructed out of empirical nonevaluative concepts, so as to arrive at objective criteria of the good and the right which do not refer to or rely on people's disputable value judgments.[4] Bentham insisted that if judgments were to have any objective meaning, they must ultimately be understood in terms of empirical concepts. Mill rejected empirical naturalism, for he thought that concepts of the higher pleasures must be explicated in terms which ultimately refer to the value judgments of experienced people. Nevertheless, he still insisted that ethical theory be empirically testable. Mill's ethical empiricism, which admits evaluative concepts not constructed out of nonevaluative concepts, is akin to postpositivist scientific empiricism, which admits theoretical terms not constructed out of observational terms, so long as the former figure in empirically testable theories.

Mill's dispute with Bentham over the empirical basis of ethics is closely tied to the conflict between proponents and critics of a hierarchy of goods. Empirical naturalistic theories tend to be hostile or indifferent to conceptions of higher goods, or ideals of higher ways of life.[5] They typically explicate the good in terms of empirical concepts such as preference, desire satisfaction, or pleasure. Such accounts typically leave a person no room to appeal to ideals which claim that some goods are intrinsically higher than others to criticize her preferences, desires, or pleasures. In recent times, Charles Taylor has relentlessly criticized empirical naturalism for its refusal to acknowledge a hierarchy of goods as essential to understanding human agency.[6] Mill similarly criticized Bentham's empirical naturalism for its failure to grasp the ways in which conceptions of higher goods are inherent in the structure of human desire. His theory is especially significant for those who wish to reconcile empiricism with a hierarchy of goods.

In the following sections, I shall reconstruct Mill's theory of experiments in living. Mill's attempt to affirm a hierarchy of goods consistent with empiricism arose from a deep dissatisfaction with Bentham's conception of the good. In order to understand Mill's views, then, we must first examine Bentham's.

BENTHAM'S CONCEPTION OF THE GOOD

Bentham's conception of the good follows straightforwardly from his psychology. As a psychological hedonist, Bentam held that pleasure is the sole end which human beings intrinsically desire. Assuming that nothing can be intrinsically good which people do not intrinsically desire, and that something is intrinsically good, it follows that pleasure is the only intrinsic good. The rest of Bentham's doctrine largely follows from his conception of the psychological state of pleasure. Pleasures differ only in quantity (intensity and duration), not in quality or rank. The good for a human being consists in a life of the maximum net balance of pleasure over pain.[7]

Bentham insisted that all value judgments which purported to refer to other intrinsic values besides pleasure were fraudulent. Nonhedonic evaluative terms were fictional terms which falsely purported to refer to really existing entities. To understand what people are really doing when they make value judgments containing such terms, Bentham offered a "paraphresis" or explication of them: for any sentence containing such terms, he substituted a sentence referring only to real (empirical) entities that performed all of the functions of the original sentence. His subversive explication of "the principle of sympathy and antipathy" illustrates the technique. Whenever someone claimed that something was tasteful, beautiful, just, fitting, or nonhedonically intrinsically valuable in any other way, the speaker was doing nothing more than holding up his own capricious feelings of pleasure (likings and approvals) and insisting that other people act as he pleases. Non-hedonic intrinsic value judgments were not only fraudulent but tyrannical, arbitrary, and dangerous.[8]

If we accept Bentham's denial of distinctions of intrinsic value not based upon pleasure, then we cannot critically evaluate the intrinsic worth of pleasures and pains. We cannot judge that sadistic pleasures are intrinsically nonmorally bad. Qualities of character may be valuable as they promote utility but not as they embody standards of excellence defined in nonhedonic terms. Personal integrity, dignity, sensitivity, individuality, honor—all of those excellences so central to Mill's conception of the good—cannot be real intrinsic values differing in kind from ordinary pleasures, since these concepts correctly refer to nothing beyond our own states of ordinary pleasure.

Bentham drew the alarming conclusion from his theory that intense feelings and fervent moral sentiments are dangerous states of mind which should be repressed. When people are caught up in intense feelings, they tend to express their feelings in the form of nonhedonic value judgments. They point to their own sentiments of approval or repugnance as overriding reasons for other people to do their bidding. Since these feelings are merely reflections of the individual's arbitrary sensations of pleasure, they threaten the utilitarian goal of maximizing total happiness. Insofar as people are guided by their sentiments when they make moral judgments, they consider only their own states of pleasure and despotically disregard the pleasures of others.

A moral decision procedure which takes all people's pleasures and displeasures equally into account must therefore reject intuitionist claims that the sentiments justify or refer to authentic evaluative standards. It must base itself upon rational calculations which refer only to real entities whose existence is confirmable by empirical observation, independent of disputable, subjective opinions. By defining the right in terms of maximizing the good, and the good in terms of pleasure, which could presumably be empirically measured, Bentham thought he had constructed such an objective procedure for determining the right act. To ensure that its conclusions could be implemented, it would be necessary to repress the sentiments which oppose these conclusions. A rational social order would not stimulate intense feelings in children and would discourage activities which arouse such feelings.[9]

MILL'S CONCEPTION OF THE GOOD: HIGHER AND LOWER PLEASURES

Mill's conception of the good officially shared with Bentham the same basic premises: ethical and psychological hedonism and implacable opposition to intuitionism.[10] Intuitionism was a refuge for political reaction: against utilitarian arguments for social change, such as those in favor of religious tolerance or liberalizing divorce laws, reactionaries invoked their sentiments of moral repugnance, claiming that their sentiments reflected an a priori perception of moral truths. Neither Bentham nor Mill tolerated this parade of prejudice masquerading as moral argument. They agreed that moral claims were only justified by empirically accessible standards and not by appeal to the supposedly a priori standards of internal conviction.[11]

The points of disagreement between Bentham and Mill seem even sharper, however. Mill thought that the cultivation of the nonutilitarian sentiments was one of the chief constituents of the good life. He also viewed the achievement of ethical ideals to be intrinsically, not merely instrumentally, valuable.[12] How could he fit ethical ideals and sentiments into the confines of an empiricist and apparently hedonist doctrine? Mill's claim that pleasures differ in quality and rank provides the key to this puzzle. If pleasures differ in rank, then there may be room for higher modes of life or ideals to find a place in the good life. Mill's famous decided preference criterion in *Utilitarianism* performs the function of providing an empirical test for higher pleasures.[13]

Mill's decided preference criterion appears to be a straightforward empirical test. Of two pleasures, A and B, A is a higher pleasure than B if all or most people equally experienced with both decidedly prefer A to B. A person decidedly prefers A over B if and only if (1) she would not "resign" her portion of A for any amount of B, (2) she would prefer A even if it were attended by more discontent than B, (3) her preference is not based upon any feeling of obligation to choose A over B, and (4) her preference is not based upon the greater circumstantial advantages of A. (That is, it should not be based upon the fact that the pleasures of A are more pure, more lasting, or more productive of future pleasures.)

Consider these conditions in more detail. Condition 4 is needed to distinguish pleasures superior in quantity from those superior in quality. Quantitative hedonists could grant that philosophy affords more pleasure than skiing, since it can be pursued for longer periods of time and after bodily infirmity renders one incapable of more energetic pleasures, and since it does not carry risk of physical injury. But these considerations show only that philosophy provides more net pleasure than skiing, not that it provides higher pleasures. Condition 3 is needed to make the decided preference test useful to a utilitarian. Since utilitarianism defines the right in terms of the good, it cannot allow the measure of the good to depend upon conceptions of moral obligation or right. Condition 2 is a plausible test for a higher pleasure: one would not prefer it, given the cost in discontentment (quantity of pleasure), if it did not have some other dimension of superiority besides quantity.

Condition 1 seems to be a sufficient condition for marking a difference in quality. If two pleasures differ only in quantity, then one would not mind giving up one entirely for unlimited amounts of the other. But it is not a criterion for a difference in the rank of pleasures, since the relation it refers to is often symmetrical. I would not give up reading books for any amount of the pleasures of eating dessert, but neither would I give up desserts for unlimited opportunities to read books. Perhaps condition 1 marks a difference in rank only if the relation is not symmetrical for the pleasures compared. This cannot be a necessary condition for a difference in rank among goods, however. It is not unreasonable to prefer a life which balances the pursuit of higher and lower pleasures to one singlemindedly devoted to the higher ones alone.[14]

Suppose that a workable interpretation of the first condition can be found.[15] Then Mill has apparently provided an empirical test for distinguishing higher from lower pleasures which does not depend upon any unexplicated value judgments. This appearance unravels as soon as we probe more deeply into Mill's reasoning for the decided preference criterion. Mill ultimately bases the distinction among pleasures on nonhedonic value judgments.[16]

Consider Mill's reply to the following objection: Don't people experienced with and capable of enjoying both pleasures sometimes postpone the higher pleasures for the sake of the lower? Mill argued that this is compatible with appreciating the higher pleasures as intrinsically superior to the lower ones. It shows only that some people suffer from weakness of will: they sometimes choose actions contrary to their judgment of what is best.[17] This reply suggests that we must reform the first condition of the decided preference criterion. The test for the higher pleasure is not whether experienced people would be willing to give up A for B but whether they would judge it worthwhile to do so. Mill says that the experienced make such judgments of relative worth by considering how the pleasures being compared fit into their conception of happiness. Their conception of happiness is in turn informed by the "higher faculties." "The comparison of the Epicurean life to that of beasts is felt as degrading, precisely because a beast's pleasures do not satisfy a human being's *conceptions of happiness*. Human beings have faculties more elevated than the animal appetites and, when once made conscious of them, do not regard anything as happiness which does not incude their gratification."[18] Mill identified the elevated faculties as "the intellect, the feelings and imagination, and . . . the moral sentiments" and attributed the decided preference of experienced people for a life which "employs their higher faculties" over one which does not to "a sense of dignity."[19]

Thus, people experienced with both rank the pleasures of certain faculties higher than the pleasures of others because they judge the former to be more dignified. Our capacity to make such a nonhedonic value judgment explains our capacity to rank pleasures. And our sense of dignity enables us to make such judgments.

Mill's account of higher and lower pleasures raises three difficult questions. If happiness just consists in "pleasure and the absence of pain," how can Mill use a person's conception of happiness as an independent standard by which to rank pleasures?[20] Can Mill square his acknowledgment of nonhedonic values such as dignity with his official ethical hedonism? What is the nature of the sentiments which are so central to Mill's account of happiness?

Consider first the relation of happiness to pleasure. Bentham regarded happiness as a large quantity of pleasure. Mill granted that happiness is comprehensively made up of pleasure while denying that the sole standard for happiness is the amount of pleasure it contains. He conceived of happiness as a second-order good—as an arrangement of pleasures of different kinds into an ordered whole.[21] Happiness is not just a large amount of pleasure, it is "not a life of rapture, but moments of such, in an existence made up of few and transitory pains, many and various pleasures, with a decided predominance of the active over the passive."[22] An individual's conception of happiness governs her estimate of the relative worth and priority she is to give to different kinds of pleasure. It includes a conception of other values realized in a life—dignity, independence, nobility, beauty—as different kinds of pleasures. While an increase in the sheer quantity of pleasure in a life will contribute to its happiness, a person will prefer a life containing fewer but higher pleasures if it conforms more closely to her ideal of happiness.

On this interpretation of Mill's view, a person's conception of happiness constitutes the primary standard of evaluation.[23] This conception consists of a complex ordering of different kinds of pleasures in a life, emphasizing the pleasures which satisfy the higher faculties of imagination and feeling. Chief among the higher faculties Mill cited in various works are the senses of dignity, beauty, sympathy or fellow-feeling, self-respect, honor, conscience, and imagination.[24] Mill's emphasis on the intrinsic desirability of gratifying these sentiments strongly suggests that he believed that dignity, beauty, honor, and so forth are values distinct from pleasure.

Mill confirmed this view in his essay "Bentham." There he distinguished three evaluative perspectives—the moral, aesthetic, and sympathetic—each of which is characterized by a specific higher faculty to which it appeals, the peculiar feelings aroused by its stimulation, and the objects which it evaluates.[25] The moral perspective appeals to our conscience, arouses feelings of approval and disapproval, and is directed solely at the pleasurable or painful consequences of actions and their causes. The aesthetic perspective appeals to our imagination, arouses feelings of admiration and contempt, and is directed at the beautiful or noble qualities of mind evidenced in people and their actions.[26] The sympathetic perspective appeals to our fellow-feeling, arouses feelings of love, pity, and dislike, and is directed at the lovable qualities of mind evidenced in people and their actions. Any conception of happiness acceptable to a cultivated person will include ideals of excellent character to be pursued, admired, and loved for their own sakes, apart from those approved of from a moral point of view—that is, just for their instrumental value in promoting pleasure and preventing pain.

How does the subordination of pleasure as a standard of evaluation to conceptions of happiness containing ideals of excellence square with Mill's apparent ethical hedonism? Mill stated his position in a way which concealed his differences with Bentham: "Nothing is a good to human beings but in so far as it is either itself pleasurable or a means of attaining pleasure."[27] This claim is consistent with denying the basic premise of ethical hedonism, that pleasure is the sole respect in which things can be intrinsically valuable. It requires only that the realization of any other kind of intrinsic value, such as dignity or beauty, is pleasurable. I suggest that Mill's higher pleasures are best understood as pleasures taken in the realization of excellence. This conveys both the idea that excellence is a distinct intrinsic value from pleasure and that the recognition of excellence by a conscious being is pleasant.[28] Thus, Mill's conception of the good is not hedonistic but pluralistic and hierarchical.[29]

Mill's conception of the good presupposes a complex theory of sentiments. The nobler sentiments are dispositions to experience feelings which are directed at the objects of nonhedonic value judgments (at what is judged to be beautiful, noble, lovable) and which motivate us to seek them in preference to the lower pleasures. The higher feelings are motives or causes of action which embody nonhedonic value judgments: they have a cognitive, not merely a phenomenal, dimension.[30] Mill claimed that pleasure is the original motive of any action. So higher feelings are pleasures taken in thoughts of nonhedonic excellence, which cause us to seek the objects of these thoughts. Action from a higher feeling, although caused by a pleasurable thought, does not aim at pleasure but at excellence.[31] When we consciously realize these excellences in action, the result is the gratification of our sentiments—that is, a higher pleasure.[32]

Mill departed from Bentham chiefly in his acceptance of authentic nonhedonic value judgments and in his conviction that people need the sentiments to recognize and appreciate nonhedonic values. In nonhedonic value judgments, Mill found a basis for distinguishing pleasures in rank, for promoting ideals of excellence as intrinsically worthy ends, and for advocating the cultivation of the sentiments rather than their repression. He claimed that evidence for the superiority of one conception of the good over another can be found in experiments in living. If we wish to discover how Mill thought experiments in living could provide such evidence, we are well advised to consider Mill's own experiment in living Bentham's conception of the good, as reported in his *Autobiography*.

MILL'S EXPERIMENT IN LIVING

John Stuart Mill led his early life strictly according to Benthamite principles. Mill's father, James Mill, gave Mill an intensive, highly disciplined education, following Bentham's belief that the happiest life was a life of rational calculation. James Mill agreed with Bentham that the sentiments were potentially dangerous dispositions which should not be stimulated, so he did not express strong feelings toward his son or encourage the development of his son's imagination.[33] He conceived of the education of the sentiments as a matter of training, not of cultivation. The association of ideas explained how sentiments could be trained to cling to the right objects through a program of conditioned reinforcement. If an object were frequently paired with a pleasurable (or painful) consequence, eventually the mind would raise the idea of pleasure (or pain) upon the presentation of the object, even if the actual consequence no longer followed—that is, the object would become pleasurable or painful in itself. It was thought that by conditioning, a child could be raised to desire and take pleasure in nearly anything.[34] John Mill was raised to desire the maximization of social utility as his primary end and became an enthusiastic propagandist for it.

Mill's life came as close as any experiment in living could to fulfilling the conditions for a valid test of a conception of the good. It was nearly free from all contrary influences to Bentham's view, such as religion.[35] Mill possessed all of the faculties needed for successfully living out Bentham's conception of the good, and lived in secure circumstances highly favorable to calculation and the pursuit of pleasure. He was zealously committed to Bentham's view, so no doubts of the validity of the experiment could be brought on grounds of lack of dedication to it.

Mill's experiment encountered a crisis when he fell into a depression in 1826. Mill saw his subjection to and recovery from depression as the crucial experiences which gave him evidence for the superiority of his mature conception of the good over Bentham's.[36] Most conceptions of the good depend on psychological claims of the following sort: if one follows the view under reasonably favorable conditions, then, barring identifiable problems, one will experience one's life as flourishing. And if one encounters a particular problem, one may overcome it by following a remedy prescribed by the view. If these psychological claims can be undermined in experience, then their associated theories of the good will also be undermined. To improve one's conception of the good, one must engage in a joint quest for a new way of life which overcomes the problems inexplicable and insoluble on the old theory and for a new psychological theory which explains the success of the new way of life in overcoming these problems as the result of its superior grasp of the good.[37]

Mill's experiences disconfirmed Bentham's psychology in two ways. First, Bentham's theory could neither explain the onset of Mill's depression nor offer a successful remedy. Bentham's psychology predicted that a person could lift his spirits by engaging in the pursuits which habitually please him. Mill tried every such pursuit, to no avail.[38] Second, Bentham's psychology failed to explain Mill's recovery from depression through reading poetry. Mill's experiences in reading poetry could be explained only by a more sophisticated theory of the sentiments than Bentham's.

While seeking a recovery from his depression, Mill also sought a superior psychological theory which could explain his predicament. Mill's first attempt to explain his ailment by modifying Bentham's psychology generated the grim prediction that he would be incapable of recovering from depression. He saw his depression as the product of a conflict between the habits of analysis and the sentiments. His well-developed habits of analysis were "a perpetual worm at the root both of the passions and of the virtues." They "fearfully undermine all desires, and all pleasures, which are the effects of association," by "enabl[ing] us mentally to separate ideas which have only casually clung together."[39]

Mill says just enough to permit us to speculate on the mechanism by which he thought analysis tended to undermine his desires. Analysis makes us separate the idea of an end from the idea of its pleasantness, and hence makes us think of it without being motivated to pursue it. Analysis suggests that the object sought may not really have worth in itself: we desire it only because its attainment was artificially associated with pleasures during our earlier upbringing, not because it is intrinsically valuable. So analysis eats away at our final ends by making us view them in an entirely indifferent light and destroying any thoughts of their intrinsic worth.

Mill's modified psychological theory thus accepted Bentham's account of the origins and training of the desires but added to it the un-Benthamite hypothesis that attachment to some of our final ends depends on viewing them as intrinsically valuable. This new theory predicted that his deeply entrenched habits of analysis would unnerve all of his nonphysical desires, and hence that he would never recover from depression. Mill discovered that his new theory was mistaken when, reading a maudlin memoir of Marmontel, he was brought to tears and came to recognize that he still possessed capacities for human feeling. He was "not a stock or a stone," not a mere "reasoning machine," but a human being who retained the capacity to feel as others felt.[40] His recognition of this fact started him on the path to recovery.

Mill's self-discovery also led him to formulate a new theory of psychology and happiness. Once he realized that he still had human sentiments, Mill had to determine which of the claims of his modified Benthamite psychology were mistaken. Three hypotheses were candidates for rejection: (1) that analysis tends to undermine sentiments born of artificial association; (2) that a lasting attachment to objects of pleasure (besides physical ones) depends on viewing them as intrinsically valuable; and (3) that the only sentiments we have are either instinctive (physical) or brought about through association. Mill would not reject the first hypothesis. It accounted too well for the onset of his depression.

Mill's experiences in reading Wordsworth's poetry convinced him to reject the third hypothesis and retain the second: for poetry alerted him to the higher sentiments, which enabled him to take lasting pleasure in things seen to be intrinsically valuable, apart from the merely "casual" associations they had with external pleasures. Mill had read poetry earlier in his life, but did so in a utilitarian spirit, for amusement and instruction.[41] Only when he came to see poetry as cultivating his sensibilities to dimensions of nonhedonic value did he find real inspiration in it. A Benthamite would claim that Mill's pleasure in reading Wordsworth's poetry came from its presentation of images of rural landscapes, images which had given Mill pleasure since childhood. Mill observed, however, that even though second-rate landscapes presented more vivid images, Wordsworth's poetry gave him a special pleasure which real landscapes did not. This pleasure did not result just from an image but from arousing "states of feeling, and of thought coloured by feeling, under the excitement of beauty."[42]

According to Mill, poetry depicts and addresses itself to feelings. If it depicts outward objects, it is as they are felt by the poet's mind.[43] Poetry alerts us to and arouses in us the poet's feelings for what he depicts. The image of a landscape does not immediately cause a pleasure of beauty in us. When a poet depicts it, this image is mediated by a sentiment of beauty, an aesthetic sensibility, which arouses our own feeling for the landscape through our feeling for the qualities of mind the poet depicts. Aesthetic sentiments attune us to nonhedonic values of beauty and nobility and make us take pleasure in and desire them. In reflecting on his reaction to poetry, Mill had thus discovered that some pleasures are mediated by recognitions of nonhedonic worth and that some nonphysical pleasures could be founded on sentiments, not just by artificial association.

Mill thus rejected the third hypothesis of his modified Benthamite psychology: the claim that all sentiments are either instinctive or acquired by association. There is a third kind of sentiment, resulting from "cultivation" through poetry and the other imaginative arts.[44] They do not dissolve under the habits of analysis because they continue to present their characteristic objects under aspects of intrinsic worth which cannot be unnerved by any representation of empirical facts.[45] Their arousal explained Mill's ability to recover from his depression without abandoning his analytical habits.

Mill's psychology thus departed in significant ways from Bentham's. To explain his depression and his manner of recovery, Mill postulated psychological states and causal processes not found in Bentham's theory. First, there was a new kind of sentiment whose characteristics and causal properties differed from the sentiments born of association. The new sentiments aroused a recognition of values distinct from pleasure; they were cultivated through the imaginative arts, and they were resistant to the force of analysis. Cultivation aroused the sentiments, not by associating their objects with external pleasures but by attuning the agent to dimensions of value internal to the sentiments—values which could not be experienced apart from the sentiments. These sentiments lifted him out of depression by enabling him to recognize himself as a person who had fellow-feeling. Second, there was a new kind of pleasure, consisting in the pleasures we take in the conscious realization of other values. These were the pleasures which gratified the new sentiments—the higher pleasures.

Mill's psychology proved superior to Bentham's in its ability to explain his experiences in living out Bentham's conception of the good. But what implications did this scientific superiority have for their rival ethical theories? First, it caused Mill to change his views of how to attain happiness. Mill's psychology predicted that the sentiments had to be cultivated if one were to lead a happy life while exercising analytical skills. The impersonal, artificially induced zeal for the improvement of humanity could not survive analysis unless it was reinforced by a genuine, cultivated feeling of unity with other people. Mill's psychology also explained why happiness could not be attained by attempting to directly pursue pleasure—that is, by interested behavior, which sees actions as merely instrumental to pleasure. Interested behavior misses out entirely on the higher pleasures, which are pleasing only because they are seen to be valuable in some other respect. Since the higher pleasures consist in pleasurable recognitions of the achievement of distinct excellences, one cannot experience these pleasures without aiming at and recognizing the intrinsic worth of excellence. To aim at excellent action for its own sake, apart from any idea of its pleasurable consequences, is to be motivated by feeling, not interest. On this more Aristotelian view, (higher) pleasure is an unintended by-product of the passionate pursuit of other ends, considered worthy in themselves.[46]

Every theory of the good is vulnerable to criticism insofar as it misconceives the things it identifies as good. Mill charged Bentham's ethical theory with such a misconception. Against Bentham, he contended that pleasure is not homogeneous in quality and does not motivate solely in respect of its quantity. Pleasures differ in quality because they embody recognitions of distinct dimensions of intrinsic value. People experiencing these pleasures understand themselves to be enjoying other values. Mill's psychology thus forces Bentham to concede that to have certain kinds of pleasure, people must understand themselves to be experiencing nonhedonic values, for these pleasures are inextricably bound up with experiences understood in this way.

Psychology and the Authenticity of Nonhedonic Values

Do these criticisms undermine the core normative commitments of Bentham's view? One could argue that Mill's observations about how to achieve happiness show only that Bentham's theory is indirectly self-defeating: in order to achieve the good as Bentham defines it, we cannot aim directly at it. One could also argue that Mill's claims about how to conceive of happiness show only that Bentham's theory is self-effacing: in order to realize Bentham's good, people have to believe some rival theory of the good, such as Mill's. The fact that aiming at some other ends, or believing some rival theory of the good, is a causal condition for realizing the good as defined by another theory shows neither that the rival theory is true nor that the first theory is false.[47] A quantitative hedonist can still argue that his perspective is the only valid one from which to justify evaluative claims.

Here we reach the deeper disagreement between Bentham and Mill: are there genuine nonhedonic values, or not? Are beauty and dignity values distinct from pleasure? If so, then the perspective from which we justify claims about the good is informed by sentiments which embody such nonhedonic value judgments. Mill's psychology can resolve his deeper disagreement with Bentham if there are empirical conditions a theory of the good must meet for it to constitute a normatively valid perspective.

The solution I propose on Mill's behalf can only be speculative, for Mill himself never squarely confronted this problem. We know at least that if Mill's psychology is correct, then Bentham's theory of the good can be defended only if it self-effacing. Given two reasonable empirical constraints on a self-effacing theory of the good, Mill's psychology can show that Bentham's theory of the good is not acceptable even as a self-effacing doctrine. First, any theory of the good must have normative force: we must be capable of being moved to action for the reasons it offers us. Second, if a theory is self-effacing, then its perspective of evaluation must be one from which we are convinced that the theory it tells us to believe is mistaken. A self-effacing theory must meet this second constraint, for if the self-effacing theory is true, then at least two theories of the good satisfy the first constraint: the self-effacing theory and the theory it tells us to believe.[48]

Mill's psychology implies that a self-effacing quantitative hedonism does not satisfy the first condition. It predicts that there are agents whose preferences satisfy the conditions laid out by the decided preference criterion of higher pleasures. These agents do not find the perspective of quantitative hedonism to have normative force: upon reflection, they are unwilling to sacrifice the higher pleasures for any amount of the lower. No self-respecting or dignified agent, on Mill's view, can be moved by quantitative hedonism.[49]

Mill's psychology also claims that a self-effacing quantitative hedonism fails the second condition. The perspective it offers people moved by the "nobler sentiments" does not convince them that Mill's conception of the good is mistaken. Mill's psychology addresses the even broader dispute between empirical naturalists and those who claim that valid normative perspectives must be informed by unreduced evaluative distinctions. Quantitative hedonism is one way to construct a normative perspective from empirical facts that do not refer to unexplicated value judgments. One motivation for attempting such a construction is the view that some error is being made when we employ evaluative categories such as the dignified and the beautiful to justify or guide our actions. For Bentham, the error was the thought that these evaluative categories correctly referred to something more than the speaker's arbitrary states of pleasure, states which could be comprehensively explicated without employing an unreduced evaluative vocabulary.[50] According to Mill's psychology, the pleasures we feel cannot all be explicated independently of an evaluative vocabulary: the higher pleasures are pleasures taken in the realization of distinct excellences. And Mill denied any incompatibility between a full scientific understanding of something and justifiably employing an evaluative vocabulary with respect to it. A purely empirical, factual perspective does not tell us that any error is being made when we call something beautiful, for instance.[51]

Thus, Mill's empirical investigations undermine the core claims of Bentham's conception of the good. Nonhedonic values are essential parts of a viable conception of the good, not just because we must believe in them in order to be happy but because they are an inescapable component of any evaluative perspective which has normative force for us. Granting that Mill can escape Bentham's reductionism, does he not risk falling into the intuitionist camp? The intuitionists whom Mill attacked also believed that our ability to make valid judgments about the good was governed by sentiments, and that such judgments involved nonhedonic normative distinctions. How could Mill consistently reject appeals to the sentiments undertaken for reactionary purposes, while defending his own appeals to the sentiments? Mill needed to find an empirical basis for distinguishing ethical sentiments which attune us to authentic distinctions of worth from sentiments which do not.[52]

Mill provided a model for dealing with this problem in his analysis of the sentiment of justice.[53] By examining the origins and composition of a sentiment, one can test whether it is a response to a distinctive, reflectively endorsable dimension of worth or whether it is merely an amalgam of responses to other things, some of which have no normative force. The sentiment of justice appears to respond to a standard of worth distinct from and potentially in conflict with the standard of utility. But Mill argued that this sentiment is really reducible to a mixture of other sentiments, including an instinct for self-protection and revenge and a concern for the general utility. The only part of this mixture which has normative force for us—the only part which we can reflectively endorse—is the concern for general utility. Since the only normatively valid part of the sentiment of justice is derived from the principle of utility, the sentiment of justice does not attune us to values distinct from utility itself. Empirical psychology thus provides a test for valid appeals to the sentiments, regarded as responses to distinct dimensions of worth: the appeal is not valid if, after analyzing the sentiment, we cannot reflectively endorse its parts, or we can reflectively endorse only those parts of it which are reducible to other standards.[54]

EXPERIMENTS IN LIVING, EMPIRICISM, AND INTUITIONISM

Mill's analysis of his transition from Bentham's to his own conception of the good offers a general model of how experiments in living bear upon conceptions of the good. This model views conceptions of the good as dependent upon empirical theories in several ways. These theories explain the nature of the things the ethical theory identifies as good, the means by which people achieve the good, how they come to appreciate and seek the good, and so forth. A person may enter a period of crisis if, having faithfully followed the recommendations of the conception of the good under reasonably favorable conditions, she experiences her life as one of suffering rather than one of flourishing. This crisis has two dimensions: it is a crisis of life, since she is not realizing what she can recognize as good; and it is a theoretical crisis, since the theories linked with her conception of the good cannot account for her felt suffering. The experience of crisis prompts a twofold quest, for a way of life which relieves the suffering and sets new goals she recognizes as worthwhile, and for a new theory which can explain the failures of the old way of life and the successes of the new.

This quest is largely a quest for self-understanding. To discover her good, a person must come to terms with her experiences and motivations—with what she finds to be good according to understandings which she finds compelling.[55] The crucial test for a conception of the good is that it provide a perspective of self-understanding which is both personally compelling (has normative force for the agent) and capable of explaining and resolving her predicament—the reasons for crisis and for recovery from it. Mill's conception of the good, with its associated psychology, met these conditions for superiority over Bentham's conception of the good. Mill adopted an expansive understanding of what was intrinsically valuable and sought out these new goods. By adopting this new conception of the good, he was able to overcome his depression and lead a life he found to be fulfilling.

If Mill had succeeded only on a practical and not on a theoretical plane, one could have charged that he had only shown that believing his theory has instrumental value, not that it was better. The theoretical success of Mill's conception of the good consisted in its ability to account for the defects of Bentham's view and the successes of his own. It showed that

Bentham's view was insensitive to the fundamental human needs to cultivate and gratify the higher sentiments. Mill's failure to tend to these needs accounted for his lapse into depression, and his fulfillment of the need, for his recovery from it. Bentham's psychology could not even describe this need, much less explain it. Hence, Mill could explain the practical success of his new conception of the good as coming about in virtue of its superior account of and sensitivity to fundamental human needs which could be described and recognized only within the perspective of his conception of the good.

My elaboration of Mill's theory of experiments in living has both exploratory and critical parts.[56] The critical part determines if and how a conception of the good is defective, by testing its underlying empirical claims. It makes comparative assessments of two given conceptions of the good. But it does not by itself lead us to a superior theory. To discover a superior conception of the good, we must be free to explore different ways of life under conditions of toleration, as Mill outlined in *On Liberty*. I have emphasized the critical part of Mill's views because the exploratory part is more familiar. Yet the exploratory part is apt to be more crucial for many people. As a pluralist, Mill thought that even after defective conceptions of the good such as Bentham's were eliminated, there would remain numerous rival views compatible with empirical psychology. Not every choice among conceptions of the good can be resolved on the basis of underlying empirical disagreements. At this level, an individual trying to decide between rivals can only explore both and consult her decided preference. But if she comes to question whether her decided preferences are based upon authentic evaluative distinctions, then she must use the critical theory.

One might object to the critical theory that it is incompatible with a credible philosophy of science. How could Mill draw definite conclusions about the good from just one experiment (his own life), and for human beings generally? And isn't a life too messy to count as a good test of any conception of the good? To be sure, Mill cannot lay claim to a definitive refutation of Bentham's conception of the good, but only to reasonable grounds for rejecting it. However, few empirically based theories are ever decisively refuted. They usually contain resources for evading refutation, and the more resources, the more complex the conditions of experiment are. Mill's life was no more complex than the phenomena upon which social scientific theories are routinely built. Nor did it contain just a single test of Bentham's views; it contained numerous tests which repeatedly failed to solve his overriding problem of depression. As with any other theory, at some point, certainly reached by Mill, it becomes reasonable to try a new conception of the good rather than to continue tinkering with an old one which has repeatedly failed to deliver on its promises.

Nevertheless, the demands of Mill's critical theory are daunting. Critical theory requires an extraordinary degree of self-understanding. Mill supposed that people can make themselves relatively self-transparent through determined and thoughtful introspection. A credible critical theory today must provide a more complex account of how people can gain access to their unconscious motivations, and will likely be less sanguine about the prospects for success. Mill's critical theory also demands that the principles underlying people's conceptions of the good be precise and articulate enough to be undermined through scientific inquiry. Most people's conceptions of the good are vague and unsystematic, and hence difficult to bring into contact with empirical theory.

Even if Mill should not be faulted for drawing unreasonable conclusions about his own good, what about his generalizations to other people? Mill would agree that his conception of the good is not valid for people incapable of cultivating the higher sentiments. Mill could reasonably apply his theory only to those who share his psychology, and it is an open question how many people do. Mill based part of his confidence in the generality of human sentiments on the communicability of poetry, which he held to be a prime vehicle for generating shared feelings with others.

Mill's empiricism departed in fundamental ways from empirical naturalism. Empirical naturalism begins with a conception of the facts which is borrowed not from people's self-understandings but from natural science. This conception of moral theory almost inevitably compels one to abstract from the evaluative distinctions which people actually find to have normative force. These distinctions are never recovered in their full variety, since they cannot be built up out of the spare construal of the facts from which this brand of empiricism begins. Most scope for genuine distinctions between higher and lower values drops out of this kind of empiricist theory of the good.

Mill's conception of empiricism in moral theory does not make any substantive presuppositions about what distinctions may count as authentic. What makes a conception of the good an empirically grounded one is that it leaves itself vulnerable to criticism by the felt experiences of those who attempt to live up to it. Unreduced value judgments are susceptible to refutation by experience because our ethical experiences are not mere creatures of our beliefs: as Mill's own life shows, it is possible to judge one way about what is good, but to feel quite differently about it. The conflict between one's beliefs about what is valuable and what one finds in one's experiences to be moving or valuable provides the first evidence that a theory of the good is mistaken. The explanation for this conflict provides the first evidence for a rival theory of the good. This way of conceiving of the relation of theories of the good to experience provides a way to reconcile Mill's commitment to empiricism with his recognition of fundamentally diverse and hierarchical distinctions of value.*

NOTES

*I thank Stephen Darwall, Virginia Held, Don Herzog, Joel Kupperman, Andrew Levine, Peter Railton, Marion Smiley, David Velleman, and anonymous referees for *Ethics* for helpful comments and criticisms. I also thank my research assistant, Lynette Simmons, for her tireless investigations of the literature on John Stuart Mill.

1. See J. S. Mill, *On Liberty,* vol. 18 of *Collected Works of J. S. Mill,* ed. J. M. Robson (Toronto: University of Toronto Press, 1977), pp. 260–67, esp. p. 261 (herafter cited as *Collected Works*).

2. The term is Derek Parfit's. See Parfit, *Reasons and Persons* (Oxford: Clarendon, 1984), p. 23.

3. Ibid., p. 24.

4. "Naturalism" is intended to echo Moore's usage of the term to refer to the view that "good" can be defined; the naturalism I am interested in is "empirical" because the terms of the definition are part of empirical science. However, my usage departs from Moore's in including, besides definition in Moore's sense, any kind of reduction, construction, or explication of evaluative terms which is supposed to convey to us what we ought to mean in using them, or how they function. Empirical explication includes but is not confined to defining "good" as an empirical property. Bentham did not believe "good" could be defined—only that it could be explicated by "paraphresis" in terms of empirical concepts. Richard Brandt and Peter Railton, who are both empirical naturalists in my sense, do not propose to define the present meaning of "good" but to offer reforming definitions of it. R. M. Hare is also an empirical naturalist, since he analyzes evaluative concepts in terms of prescriptions and preferences, although he is a noncognitivist and hence denies that "good" names a natural property. See Amnon Goldworth, "Bentham's Concept of Pleasure: Its Relation to Fictitious Terms," *Ethics* 82 (1972): 332–43; Peter Railton, "Moral Realism," *Philosophical Review* 95 (1986): 163–207; Richard Brandt, *A Theory of the Good and the Right* (Oxford: Clarendon, 1979); R. M. Hare, *Moral Thinking* (Oxford: Clarendon, 1981).

5. For example, Bentham ridiculed such ideas; R. M. Hare has consistently tried to portray the proponents of ideals as vicious "fanatics"; ideals are absent from Brandt's discussions of the good.

6. See Charles Taylor, "The Diversity of Goods," in *Philosophy and the Human Sciences* (Cambridge: Cambridge University Press, 1985), pp. 230–47, "What Is Human Agency?" in *Human Agency and Language* (Cambridge: Cambridge Univer-

sity Press, 1985), pp. 15–44, and *Sources of the Self* (Cambridge, Mass.: Harvard University Press, 1989).

7. Jeremy Bentham, *The Principles of Morals and Legislation* (New York: Hafner, 1948), pp. 1–2, 29. I leave aside the question of whether the distribution of pleasures across time makes a difference for the goodness of a life.

8. Ibid., pp. 13–20. Ross Harrison offers an excellent account of Bentham's method of paraphresis and its impact on his moral theory in his *Bentham* (London: Routledge & Kegan Paul, 1983). Bentham's theory of fictions combines elements of subjectivist, emotivist, and error theories of meaning. All nonhedonic value judgments involve error because they purport to refer to real external standards, such as the "eternal and immutable Rule of Right" or "the Fitness of Things," which are merely fictional, imaginary standards. Bentham's further explication of such judgments is ambiguous between a subjectivist and emotivist interpretation. If, in making such judgments, one is "holding up that approbation or disapprobation as a sufficient reason for itself" (p. 16), one is referring to these feelings, as a subjectivist account would hold. But Bentham also suggests an emotivist account in claiming that all that the judgment that something is unnatural "can serve to express is, the disposition of the person who is talking of it . . . to be angry at thoughts of it" (p. 18, n. 1). Harrison points out this ambiguity and argues that emotivism cannot be Bentham's considered position (pp. 101, 192–93). At any rate, a person cannot correctly use a nonhedonic evaluative term to refer to anything beyond his own feelings of pleasure or displeasure, nor can he sincerely use it if he does not have such feelings.

9. For this reason, Bentham was hostile to poetry. With a rationalism rivaling Plato's, Bentham condemned all poetry as "misrepresentation." Quoted by J. S. Mill in "Bentham," in *Essays on Ethics, Religion, and Society*, vol. 10 of *Collected Works*, p. 114. (Compare Plato's claim that poetry is "thrice removed from reality" [*Republic* 10.599a1].) By exaggerating the facts and offering as universal value judgments the caprice of the author, poetry arouses the sentiments of its readers and threatens the possibility of rational calculation.

10. In fact, Mill embraced much weaker hedonistic claims than those endorsed by Bentham. See below, pp. 13–15.

11. J. S. Mill, *Autobiography* (Boston: Houghton Mifflin, 1969), pp. 133–35, 162–63 (on reactionary tendencies of intuitionism), and "Whewell on Moral Philosophy," in *Essays on Ethics, Religion, and Society*, vol. 10 of *Collected Works*, pp. 197–200 (on Whewell's use of intuitionism to attack religious tolerance and liberalized divorce law).

12. On sentiments: Mill, *Autobiography*, pp. 86, 91, J. S. Mill, "Inaugural Address at the University of St. Andrews," in *John Stuart Mill on Education* (New York: Teachers College Press, 1971), pp. 223–27; on ideals of character: J. S. Mill, "Utilitarianism," in *Essays on Ethics, Religion, and Society*, vol. 10 of *Collected Works*, 4:5 (all references to "Utilitarianism" are cited by chap. and par.), and Mill, "Bentham," pp. 95–96, 98.

13. Mill, "Utilitarianism," 2:5–6.

14. Alternatively, condition 1 could be read as saying that A is a higher pleasure than B only if one would not give up *any* amount of A for any amount of B. But I cannot think of any worthwhile pleasures which satisfy this condition. Even if I regard philosophy as a higher pleasure than skiing, I may still go skiing when I could be doing philosophy. The only exceptions are for pleasures regarded as base or contemptible. Since Mill does not deny that some lower pleasures are worth pursuing, this cannot be the model for all distinctions of higher and lower pleasures. Mill's examples of lower pleasures include both worthwhile and contemptible ones. Compare, e.g., Mill, "Utilitarianism," 2:14 (a person will not give up the pleasures of participating in the project to overcome human suffering for any amount of "selfish indulgence") with J. S. Mill, "Subjection of Women," in *Three Essays* (Oxford: Oxford University Press, 1975), p. 543 (a citizen of a free country will not give up his freedom no matter how well his affairs will be managed by others).

15. In fact, for the reasons stated above, I do not think that any lexical ordering of choices or preferences will adequately distinguish higher from lower pleasures. I explain below that Mill's distinction among pleasures need not turn upon crude criteria of lexical preference, for it is ultimately grounded in value judgments.

16. My interpretation thus follows G. E. Moore in arguing that Mill distinguished pleasures qualitatively by appealing to nonhedonic value judgments. See Moore's *Principia Ethica* (Cambridge: Cambridge University Press, 1903), pp. 77–81. Moore judged Mill inconsistent on this point, since he interpreted Mill as affirming the hedonist thesis that pleasure alone is intrinsically valuable. I read Mill as denying this strong hedonist thesis. Some commentators have proposed ways in which Mill could avoid Moore's argument and remain a hedonist while continuing to distinguish qualities of pleasure. See Daniel Holbrook, *Qualitative Utilitarianism* (Lanham, Md.: University Press of America, 1988); Rex Martin, "A Defense of Mill's Qualitative Hedonism," *Philosophy* 47 (1972): 140–51; and Henry West, "Mill's Qualitative Hedonism," *Philosophy* 51 (1976): 97–101.

17. Mill, "Utilitarianism," 2:7.

18. Ibid., 2:4, emphasis mine.

19. Ibid., 2:6.

20. Ibid., 2:2.

21. This discussion is indebted to Robert Hoag, "Mill's Conception of Happiness as an Inclusive End," *Journal of the History of Philosophy* 25 (1987): 417–31, esp. p. 421.

22. Mill, "Utilitarianism," 2:12. See also 4:5: "The ingredients of happiness are very various, and each of them is desirable in itself, and not merely when considered as swelling an aggregate." Compare J. S. Mill, *The Logic of the Moral Sciences,* bk. 6 of *A System of Logic* (La Salle, Ill.: Open Court, 1988), p. 143, where Mill contrasts the "humble sense" of happiness as "pleasure and freedom from pain" with its "higher meaning, of rendering life . . . such as human beings with highly developed faculties can care to have."

23. Thanks to the work of Fred Berger and John Gray, this interpretation of Mill's conception of happiness deserves to become the received view. See Fred

Berger, *Happiness, Justice, and Freedom* (Berkeley: University of California Press, 1985); and John Gray, *Mill on Liberty: A Defense* (London: Routledge & Kegan Paul, 1983). Their interpretation leaves open how far one may emphasize the centrality of nonhedonic conceptions of excellence in Mill's view. In emphasizing this idealistic side of Mill, my interpretation is close to Robert Hoag's (see n. 21).

24. Mill, "Utilitarianism," 2:4, 6, "Bentham," pp. 95–97.

25. Mill, "Bentham," pp. 112–13. Compare Mill, *The Logic of Moral Sciences*, pp. 140–41, which divides the "Art of Life" into three departments: morality, prudence, and aesthetics; and Mill, "Inaugural Address at the University of St. Andrews," p. 219, which outlines three kinds of education: moral, intellectual, and aesthetic.

26. Mill linked ideals of noble character to the imagination, because imagination enables us to frame ideas of as-yet-unexperienced perfection. Without the imagination, we could desire only what we have already experienced. Hence Mill attributed Bentham's failure to recognize the importance of ideals of character to his lack of imagination (Mill, "Bentham," pp. 91–92). "The Imagination which he had not, was . . . that which enables us . . . to conceive the absent as if it were present . . . and to clothe it in the feelings which, if it were indeed real, it would bring along with it" (p. 92). Bentham's empirical naturalism—his insistence that authentic moral standards refer only to really existing entities (actual pleasures and the things we already take pleasure in) and not to imaginary ones (ideals in which we could cultivate our pleasures)—foreclosed any acknowledgment of higher intrinsic goods. Mill regarded the imagination as a higher faculty, and its gratification as a higher pleasure, because through it we conceive and are moved by feeling to aspire to ideals. He called the higher pleasures aesthetic, in contrast with physical, pleasures, because they are caused not by sensation alone but by ideas and feelings associated with sensation. See esp. Susan Feagin, "Mill and Edwards on the Higher Pleasures," *Philosophy* 58 (1983): 244–52, explaining the connections among imagination, ideals of excellence, and aesthetic pleasure; and Brian Anderson, "Mill on Bentham: From Ideology to Humanized Utilitarianism," *History of Political Thought* 4 (1983): 341–56.

27. Mill, "Utilitarianism," 4:11. One passage often cited as evidence of Mill's hedonism is 4:2–3, where Mill claims that happiness is the sole thing intrinsically desirable as an end. But if happiness is distinguished from pleasure, then this passage supports the rejection of ethical hedonism, as Berger argues. See Fred Berger, "Mill's Concept of Happiness," *Interpretation* 7 (1978): 95–117, 104.

28. To speak of honor, dignity, and so forth as pleasures is consistent with some of Mills's usage—he also speaks of music and the consciousness of virtue as pleasures (Mill, "Utilitarianism," 4:5, 8) and recognizes the notion of taking pleasure in virtue (4:8). But he also speaks of such things as giving us pleasure, or as sources of pleasure, thus suggesting that pleasure is a sensation existing independently of ethical ideals, which serve as mere means to pleasure (2:4; 4:8).

29. See Robert Hoag, "Happiness and Freedom: Recent Work on John Stuart Mill," *Philosophy and Public Affairs* 15 (1986): 188–99, esp. p. 189.

30. Mill treats feeling and judgment as closely associated. See his "Utilitarianism," 2:8: "What is there to decide whether a particular pleasure is worth purchasing at the cost of a particular pain, except the feelings and judgment of the experienced?" And it is the "feelings and judgment" which "declare the pleasures derived from the higher faculties to be preferable *in kind*" to the pleasures we share with animals.

31. The key texts on Mill's theory of motivation are "Remarks on Bentham's Philosophy," in *Essays on Ethics, Religion, and Society,* vol. 10 of *Collected Works,* pp. 12–15, and Mill, *The Logic of the Moral Sciences,* pp. 28–29. Pleasure and pain are the original causes of all action, but they have different causal roles, depending on whether action is from interest, habit, or feeling. When people act from interest, their aim is (as Bentham thought it always was) to obtain pleasure and avoid pain, and their action is instrumental to this aim. Action from interest is caused by thoughts of pleasures and pains in prospect. When people act from feeling, their aim is the action itself, considered apart from its pleasurable or painful consequences. Action from feeling is caused by the pleasurable and painful thoughts of the action itself. If the thought of the act is pleasant or painful, it prompts us to perform or avoid it, respectively. Action from habit also aims at the action apart from its consequences, but it was originally motivated by interest. Actions from habit persist even after the pleasurable consequences which originally motivated them have ceased, thereby explaining how things originally pursued as mere means, such as money, can come to be pursued for their own sakes. See "Utilitarianism," 4:6–7, 10–11.

32. Mill's psychology poses a difficulty in that higher feelings, i.e., pleasures taken in thoughts of excellence, both motivate us to action and constitute the higher pleasures. If the higher pleasures already exist prior to action, why need we act to realize them? Mill did not carefully distinguish feelings as motivators (expressions of the sentiments) from feelings as higher pleasures (gratifications of the sentiments), but presumably the distinction is this: the motivating feeling consists in a pleasure taken in the thought that an action would be excellent; the higher pleasure consists in the pleasure taken in the conscious performance of the excellent action.

33. Mill, *Autobiography,* pp. 31, 67–68.

34. Ibid., p. 82. Compare "Utilitarianism," 4:5–7, where Mill gives a similar account of the origin of the desire for virtue.

35. An exception to this claim may be found in Mill's recollection that his father rated intellectual enjoyments above all others as pleasures, even discounting their circumstantial advantages (Mill, *Autobiography,* p. 31). This suggests that James Mill implicitly taught his son that there was a distinction between higher and lower pleasures, a clear deviation from Bentham's teachings. I thank Richard Dees for pointing out this exception to me.

36. This account is found in ibid., pp. 80–90.

37. A successful psychological adjustment is evidence of acquisition of a better set of values only if we have a theory which explains its success in these terms. An alternative explanation of successful adjustment could explain a depression as the result of trying to live out a worthwhile conception of the good in unfavorable

circumstances, and recovery as the result of cultivating a certain callousness toward higher ends.

38. A more relaxed Benthamite than James Mill could object that John Mill's life was not a proper test of Benthamite hedonism because his father worked him too hard. An excessively harsh and disciplined upbringing could bring on a depression in later life. Nevertheless, Bentham's view failed to guide Mill out of his depression, or to explain how Mill's own techniques succeeded.

39. Mill, *Autobiography,* p. 83.

40. Ibid., pp. 85, 66.

41. Ibid., p. 11.

42. Ibid., p. 89.

43. J. S. Mill, "What Is Poetry?" in *Essays on Poetry by John Stuart Mill,* ed. F. P. Sharpless (Columbia: University of South Carolina Press, 1976), pp. 6, 11.

44. Aesthetic education differs from scientific education by the sentiments it arouses and the way these sentiments are linked with ideas. In persons of scientific or business education, "objects group themselves according to the artificial classifications which the understanding has voluntarily made for the convenience of thought or practice." But in persons of aesthetic education, "emotions are the links of association by which their ideas, both sensuous and spiritual, are connected together" (J. S. Mill, "The Two Kinds of Poetry," in *Essays on Poetry by John Stuart Mill,* pp. 31–32, 33). Mill thought it essential that a person's moral training appeal to sentiments cultivated by aesthetic and not just scientific training. For "moral associations, which are wholly of artificial creation . . . yield by degrees to the dissolving force of analysis." To be firm and lasting, they must be connected by the natural social sentiment of "unity with our fellow creatures" ("Utilitarianism," 3:9). Aesthetic education provides this connection, linking the moral sentiments with the sympathetic sentiments through the aesthetic ones. Aesthetic education cultivates our desire for ideal aims, giving us a "higher conception of what constitutes success [happiness] in life." Since the nobler pleasures are shared, not competitive, poetic cultivation "brings home to us all those aspects of life which take hold of our nature on its unselfish side and lead us to identify our joy and grief with the good or ill of the system of which we form a part" (Mill, "Inaugural Address at the University of St. Andrews," p. 224). Thus, aesthetic education inspires the feeling of unity with mankind which Mill thought necessary to support a utilitarian morality. It ties together the higher sentiments underlying the three evaluative perspectives he distinguished in "Bentham."

45. See Mill, *Autobiography,* pp. 91–92, where Mill argues that there is no inconsistency between "the intensest feeling of the beauty of a cloud" and a full understanding of the laws of nature which account for its physical characteristics.

46. Ibid., pp. 85–86. Compare Aristotle, *Nicomachean Ethics* 1174b20–1175a21.

47. See Parfit, pp. 5, 11–12, 19–24. One can agree that to have valuable experiences one must have certain beliefs yet deny that the value of these experiences can only be understood in terms of these beliefs. A child's pleasurable experience of the Christmas holiday might be heightened and colored by her belief in Santa Claus.

But our ability to evaluate her experience does not depend upon belief in Santa Claus. Similarly, one might have to believe in the validity of nonhedonic value judgments to have certain pleasurable experiences, but be able to evaluate these experiences from an empirical naturalist perspective which explicates all values in terms of empirical criteria that make no reference to people's value judgments.

48. Two (or more) theories of the good might have normative force for us, although they do not stand in the relation of a self-effacing theory to a theory it tells us to believe. I believe that this possibility is realized on a widespread scale. This need not be disturbing—it may simply be strong evidence for pluralism about the good. Pluralists do not have to be relativists: even if there are many valid conceptions of the good, others might be mistaken, and some might be superior to others. I believe that this is Mill's view of the matter as well.

49. An exception must be made for weakness of will. But this condition reflects a perspective which the agent himself views as normatively invalid. I argued above that it is difficult to believe that people actually do or ought to satisfy the lexical component of the decided preference criterion. It is enough to refute Bentham's quantitative view, however, that people satisfy condition 2 of the criterion: they are willing to sacrifice significant quantities for qualities of total pleasure.

50. Bentham's objection cannot rest solely on his error theory of the meaning of value judgments. The issue at hand is not ontological—Does beauty really exist independently of how we regard it?—but, rather, normative—Is beauty an authentic and distinctive evaluative category, properly used in justifying normative judgments? As Harrison notes, Bentham's theory implied that all value judgments, including utilitarian ones, involve fictions, so ontology alone does not settle this question. Bentham thought that the normative issue could be settled by the requirement that an authentic evaluative standard be objective and empirically determinable. He thought that only those value judgments which could be paraphrased by sentences referring only to real nonimaginary entities could satisfy this requirement, and that only hedonist and utilitarian judgments did so. Other standards referred to imaginary entities about which people could disagree (Harrison, pp. 80–81, 102–3, 173–74). Mill accepted the normative requirement but rejected Bentham's empirical naturalist interpretation of it. Since the sentiments were widely shared and susceptible of nearly universal cultivation, standards that referred to imaginary entities (unrealized ideals) that inform the sentiments could be objects of intersubjective agreement among experienced people. This is all the objectivity they need to properly figure in evaluative reasoning.

51. Mill, *Autobiography,* pp. 91–92. See n. 45 above.

52. Mill consistently denied all claims to evaluative distinctiveness made on behalf of the moral sentiments—i.e., those sentiments which embody standards of right and wrong. He only defended the evaluative distinctiveness of some nonmoral sentiments. But this distinction among sentiments does not provide us with a justification for accepting the deliverances of sentiments of one kind and rejecting those of the other.

53. "Utilitarianism," 5.

54. See also the *Autobiography*, pp. 162–63, where Mill showed how moral claims based upon sentiments can be undermined by showing that they arose under special circumstances from utilitarian concerns, and hence lack any validity apart from these circumstances. Another strategy Mill used to undermine purportedly authentic nonutilitarian standards was to show that they are incoherent. See esp. his critique of nature as a moral standard, in "Nature," in *Essays on Ethics, Religion, and Society*, in vol. 10 of *Collected Works*, pp. 373–402.

55. This is a central theme of Mill's *On Liberty*. See esp. pp. 260–67.

56. I am indebted to Andrew Levine for raising some of the issues in these paragraphs.

· 10 ·

MILL'S DELIBERATIVE UTILITARIANISM

David O. Brink

Whatever the appeal of particular strands in Mill's moral theory, it is commonly thought that he is not a very systematic moral philosopher. In particular, Mill's moral theory is usually thought to be seriously inconsistent in at least two ways. First, his version of utilitarianism is thought to be internally inconsistent. Though Mill appears to want to defend hedonistic utilitarianism, his doctrine of "higher pleasures" seems antihedonistic.[1] Second, Mill's strong defense of individual liberty in *On Liberty* seems inconsistent with his defense of utilitarianism in *Utilitarianism* for the perfectly general reason that utilitarianism cannot accommodate moral and political rights.[2] Nor is this second inconsistency simply a matter of reconciling two individually consistent but jointly incompatible works, though this, of course, would be bad enough. In *On Liberty* Mill insists that his defense of liberty rests on utilitarian foundations (*OL*, I 11), and in *Utilitarianism* he attempts to account for rights on utilitarian grounds (*U*, V, esp. 25).[3]

I think that these two familiar charges of inconsistency are mistaken and that both mistakes rest on a misunderstanding of Mill's theory of value. Mill can be shown to reject hedonism consistently; instead, he defends (consistently) a conception of human happiness whose dominant component consists in the exercise of one's rational capacities. This deliberative conception of happiness not only provides a better account of his claims in *Utilitarianism* but also explains how he can provide a strong defense of an individual right to certain liberties on utilitarian grounds.[4] If so, these interpretive claims are important not just for our understanding of Mill, but because they outline a distinctive and resourceful form of utilitarianism.

1. INTERPRETIVE PROBLEMS

It is unproblematic that Mill accepts some form of utilitarianism. What is problematic is the exact form of his utilitarianism.

One problem, about which I will say little, concerns his theory of right action. Mill is not a straightforward act–utilitarian or rule–utilitarian, for in chapter V of *Utilitarianism* he construes an action's rightness or permissibility as consisting neither in the value of its consequences nor in its conformity to rules with positive or optimific acceptance value. Rather, he claims that an act is permissible just in case it is not wrong and that an action is wrong just in case some kind of external or internal sanction attached to it (punishment, blame, or self-reproach) would have good—perhaps optimific—consequences (V 14). Nonetheless, other passages point toward act-utilitarianism (II 2), and much of his discussion is neutral on these issues of right action. It will be simpler for our purposes and produce no relevant distortion if we assume that he accepts a familiar maximizing version of act-utilitarianism according to which an act is right or obligatory just in case its consequences for human welfare are at least as good as any alternative act available to the agent.[5]

Another problem, which will be my primary focus, concerns Mill's evaluative views and their effect on his utilitarianism. Mill is usually thought to accept a *subjective* conception of happiness or welfare in which a person's happiness or welfare consists in or depends importantly on certain of her contingent psychological states.[6] When he introduces utilitarianism, he seems clearly to endorse *hedonism* and its claim that happiness consists in pleasurable mental states or sensations (*U*, II 1–2). However, he also makes claims that seem to imply a *desire-satisfaction* or *preference-satisfaction* theory that makes a person's happiness depend on what she wants and consist in the satisfaction of her desires or preferences. For he links higher value with the preferences of competent judges (*U*, II), and he takes desire to be proof of desirability or value (*U*, IV).

By contrast, Mill holds an *objective* theory of happiness or welfare if he claims that happiness or welfare consists in the possession of certain character traits, the exercise of certain capacities, and the development of certain relations to others and the world and that the value of these traits, activities, and relationships is independent of the amount of pleasure that they produce or their being the object of desire. And one reading of some of Mill's texts suggests an objective interpretation of his conception of happiness. For his version of utilitarianism rests on a conception of happiness appropriate to progressive beings (*OL*, I 11) in which the exercise of one's higher faculties seems to be a dominant component (*U*, II 4–8).

An objective conception of happiness may seem strange; it is easy for us to think of happiness in completely subjective terms. We usually count a person as happy insofar as she is contented, pleased, or meeting her own goals and aims. This may seem to be simply part of what we mean by calling someone "happy." But we also think of a happy life as a full life, a life that goes well, or a life well lived, and we can understand judging of someone that she did not lead a full life—indeed, that she was not really happy—even though she was contented or pleased and satisfying desires and preferences that she held at the time. This would be natural if the person's pleasure or desires were based on false beliefs, or if we thought that the activities that were the objects of her desires and the source of her pleasure were unimportant or inappropriate. If so, it is a substantive question whether the correct conception of happiness or welfare is subjective or objective, and we should not decide which conception Mill holds in advance of the evidence.[7]

2. Mill as a Hedonistic Utilitarian

Mill's apparent sympathy with hedonistic utilitarianism is clear; early in *Utilitarianism* (chap. II) he appears to endorse it and its claims that pleasure is the one and only good and that things are good and right insofar as they are pleasurable:

> The creed which accepts as the foundations of morals "utility" or the "greatest happiness principle" holds that actions are right in proportion as they tend to promote happiness; wrong as they tend to produce the reverse of happiness. By happiness is intended pleasure and the absence of pain; by unhappiness, pain and the privation of pleasure. (II 2; cf. II 1)

It is worth making explicit what Mill commits himself to in any endorsement of hedonistic utilitarianism.

Hedonism claims that pleasure is the good (that pleasantness is the one and only good-making property) and that pain is the bad (that painfulness is the one and only bad-making property). Different versions of hedonism correspond to different theories of pleasure and pain. According to *simple hedonism*, pleasure is a simple qualitative mental state or sensation that varies only in duration and intensity, and the same is true of pain. According to *preference hedonism*, pleasure and pain are functional states: pleasure is a mental state or sensation such that the person having it wants it to continue and will, *ceteris paribus*, undertake actions so as to prolong it, while pain is a mental state or sensation such that the person having it wants it to cease and will, *ceteris paribus*, take action to make it stop. There is no apparent reason why mental states having one of these functional profiles need be qualitatively similar or have the same feel. These two versions of hedonism are different.[8] Where the differences are important, I shall mark the distinction.

Hedonism implies that the mental state of pleasure is the only thing having *intrinsic* value—that is, the only thing good in itself, good whatever its consequences, or necessarily good (and the mental state of pain is the only intrinsic evil). All other things have only *extrinsic* value; they have value just insofar as they bring about, mediately or directly, intrinsic value (or disvalue). It follows that actions, activities, and so on can have only extrinsic value and that their value depends entirely on the *quantity* of pleasure that they produce. The quantity of pleasure that anything produces is a positive function of both the pleasure's *intensity* and its *duration*. This should be true of both simple hedonism and preference hedonism.[9] One activity is more valuable than another if and only if it produces a greater quantity of pleasure than the other. So, as Bentham noticed, intellectual pursuits (e.g., poetry) are intrinsically no more valuable than voluptuous pursuits (e.g., push-pin); if the former are more valuable than the latter, it can only be because, as it happens, the intellectual pursuits tend in the long run to produce a greater quantity of pleasure than voluptuous pursuits do.

3. Higher "Pleasures"

But in defending the value of higher pleasures against that of lower pleasures (II 4–8), Mill rejects these hedonistic claims. In discussing the greater value of intellectual pleasures, in comparison with voluptuous ones, he agrees with the strict hedonist that the former produce a larger quantity of pleasure and so are extrinsically more valuable, but he also insists that the greater value of intellectual pleasures can and should be put on a more secure footing (II 4). Mill explains these higher or more valuable pleasures, and links them with the preferences of a competent judge, in the following manner.

> If I am asked what I mean by difference of quality in pleasures, or what makes one pleasure more valuable than another, merely as a pleasure, except its being greater in amount, there is but one possible answer. If one of the two is, by those who are competently acquainted with both, placed so far above the other that they prefer it, even though knowing it to be attended with a greater amount of discontent, and would not resign it for any quantity of the other pleasure which their nature is capable of, we are justified in ascribing to the preferred enjoyment a superiority in quality so far outweighing quantity as to render it, in comparison, of small account. (II 5)

Indeed, Mill appears here to claim not just that these higher pleasures are more valuable than lower pleasures, but that their value is infinitely or perhaps lexically greater than that of lower pleasures, because he claims that no quantity of lower pleasures could ever outweigh the value of higher pleasures (cf. *U*, II 6).

Now when Mill discusses higher and lower "pleasures," we might expect him to be discussing certain kinds of mental states or sensations, for instance, simple pleasures or preference pleasures. When hedonists say that pleasure is the one and only good, they use the word "pleasure" to refer to a mental state or sensation of some kind. But a more objective reading of Mill's claims about higher pleasures is appropriate here. On the more objective reading, "pleasure" refers to nonmental items, such as actions, activities, and pursuits that do or can cause pleasurable mental states. Higher pleasures are those activities or pursuits that exercise our higher (e.g., intellectual) capacities.

This objective reading of "pleasures" may sound less natural than the mental state reading. But there is good reason to suppose that Mill intends the objective reading of the higher pleasures doctrine. First, he often does use "pleasure" to refer to activities and pursuits, especially those that typically cause pleasurable mental states—we might call these "objective pleasures." (Compare the way in which someone might refer to sexual activity as a bodily pleasure.) As we shall see in Section 4, in the second part of the "proof" of the principle of utility Mill counts music, virtue, and health as pleasures (*U*, IV 5). These are objective pleasures. And elsewhere in his discussion of higher pleasures in chapter II, Mill equates a person's pleasures with his "indulgences" (II 7) and with his "mode of existence" (II 8). Here too he must be discussing objective pleasures. Second, when Mill introduces higher pleasures (II 4) he is clearly discussing, among other things, intellectual pursuits and activities. He claims to be arguing that what the quantitative hedonist finds extrinsically more valuable is also intrinsically more valuable (II 4, 7). But what the quantitative hedonist defends as extrinsically more valuable is (intellectual) activities and pursuits, not mental states.[10] Because Mill claims that these very same things are intrinsically, and not just extrinsically, more valuable, his higher pleasures would appear to be intellectual activities and pursuits, rather than mental states. Finally, in paragraphs 4 through 8 Mill links the preferences of competent judges and the greater value of the objects of their preferences. But among the things Mill thinks competent judges would prefer are activities and pursuits. And, in particular, in commenting on the passage quoted above (II 5), Mill writes:

> Now it is an unquestionable fact that those who are equally acquainted
> with and equally capable of appreciating and enjoying both do give a
> most marked preference to the *manner of existence* which employs their
> higher faculties. (*U,* II 6; italics mine)

Here Mill is identifying the higher pleasures with activities and pursuits that
exercise our higher capacities.

For these reasons, Mill's discussion of higher pleasures appears to be a
discussion of the value of intellectual activities, rather than a discussion of
the value of certain sorts of mental states. If so, his explanation of the greater
value of these activities appears to be antihedonistic for two reasons. First,
he claims that the intellectual pursuits have value out of proportion to the
amount of contentment or pleasure (the mental state) that they produce.
This contradicts the hedonist claim that the extrinsic value of an activity is
proportional to the quantity of pleasure associated with it. Second, Mill
claims that these activities are intrinsically more valuable than the lower
pursuits (II 7). But the hedonist must claim that the mental state of pleasure
is the one and only intrinsic good; activities can have only extrinsic value,
and no activity can be intrinsically more valuable than another.

But perhaps we can salvage a hedonistic reading of the higher pleasures
doctrine. This interpretation concedes that Mill's doctrine of higher and
lower pleasures draws a distinction between kinds of activities. But this
distinction may help him distinguish different kinds of pleasure (the mental
state) if he picks out qualitatively different mental states in terms of different
sorts of activities associated with them. On this interpretation, Mill might
claim that higher pleasures, pleasures caused by higher activities, are intrinsically more valuable than lower pleasures, pleasures caused by lower activities.

If this proposal is to provide a hedonistic explanation of the fact that
higher pleasures pick out activities, then it must presumably claim not just
that we can describe pleasures in terms of their causes but that the causes of
pleasure are constituents of pleasures. But there is an apparent problem
with this interpretation if it holds that mental states have as constituents
their own causes. For this appears to violate the independence we require
between cause and effect.[11]

However, the hedonist can respect the independence of cause and
effect by treating different kinds of pleasures as mental states that are com-
pounds of pleasure *simpliciter* (simple pleasure or preference pleasure) and
different kinds of activities. On this view, different kinds of activities cause
pleasure, and different kinds of pleasure (e.g., higher pleasure) are com-
pounds of the pleasure caused by different kinds of activities (e.g., intellec-

tual activities) and those activities. So intellectual activities (can) cause pleasure (simple pleasure or preference pleasure), but not higher pleasure; they are constituents of higher pleasure. The interdependent relata are the whole (higher pleasure) and its parts (intellectual activities and pleasures that these activities cause). But the parts are independent of each other. The causal relata are these independent parts of the higher pleasure. Hence, the hedonist can treat activities as constituents of kinds of pleasure without violating the independence required between cause and effect.

We may wonder whether the compound of an activity and the mental state that it causes is itself a mental state. If not, higher pleasures will not be mental states, and this interpretation will presumably not yield a hedonistic reading of the higher pleasures doctrine. However, we need not resolve this issue; there are other problems for this hedonistic reading of the higher pleasures doctrine.

First, even if there are qualitatively different kinds of pleasures, because of their different kinds of constituent activities, the hedonist should claim that the value of the activities or the compound ought to be proportional to the amount of simple pleasure or preference pleasure associated with them. But Mill denies this; as we have seen, the higher pleasures doctrine asserts that higher "pleasures" are valuable out of proportion to the amount of contentment or pleasure associated with them.

Second, even if Mill can claim that intellectual pleasures (the mental states) are qualitatively *different* from voluptuous pleasures (the mental states), because of their constituent activities, he would have no hedonistic ground for asserting, as he does, that the former are *intrinsically superior* to the latter. For one kind of pleasure to be a superior pleasure to another is presumably for it to contain more simple pleasure or preference pleasure. But whether this is true of intellectual pleasures vis-à-vis voluptuous pleasures must be a contingent psychological matter and so could not establish the intrinsic superiority of intellectual pleasures.

Third, any version of hedonism must claim that the only intrinsic goods are pleasures (the mental states). But Mill denies this. As I have argued, his use of "pleasure" in his statement of the higher pleasures doctrine refers to certain activities and pursuits, rather than the mental state in which they are constituents or the mental states that they cause. If, as he claims, these "pleasures" are intrinsically more valuable than others, it is the activities and pursuits themselves that are intrinsically valuable. And this makes a difference. Higher activities can fail to produce simple pleasure or preference pleasure, even if when they do, there exists a higher pleasure that has the associated activity as a constituent.[12] If activities are valuable only as parts of higher pleasures, they will not be valuable when they do not produce pleasure. However, if, as Mill seems to claim, the activities themselves are valuable, then they have value when they do not produce pleasure and their value is independent of the pleasure they cause when they do produce pleasure (the pleasure, of course, representing additional value).

I conclude that we should read the higher pleasures doctrine as the claim that activities and pursuits that exercise our higher capacities are intrinsically more valuable than voluptuous activities and pursuits, rather than as a claim about the greater value of certain mental states. This reading explains Mill's claim that the doctrine of higher pleasures transcends the quantitative hedonist claim about the greater extrinsic value of intellectual pursuits (II 4), but it also makes his position antihedonist. Higher activities have intrinsic, not simply extrinsic, value that is not dependent on their causing pleasure, though, of course, taking pleasure in such activities is also valuable.

4. The Components of Happiness in Mill's "Proof"

Nor is the higher pleasures doctrine the only place in which Mill contradicts a commitment to hedonism. His claims about the nature of happiness in the second part of his "proof" of the principle of utility in chapter IV of *Utilitarianism* imply an apparently objective conception of happiness. Mill there claims that happiness consists of a number of distinct, nonmental components, such as virtue, health, and music. As *components* or *parts* of happiness, these things are intrinsic goods.

> This opinion [that virtue is desired for its own sake] is not, in the smallest degree, a departure from the happiness principle. The ingredients of happiness are very various, and each of them is desirable in itself, and not merely when considered as swelling an aggregate. The principle of utility does not mean that any given pleasure, as music, for instance, or any given exemption from pain, as for example health, is to be looked upon as a means to a collective something termed happiness. They are desired and desirable in and for themselves; besides being means, they are a part of the end. (*U*, IV 5)

The proof itself raises difficult questions about how claims about what is desired support conclusions about what is desirable. But I am here concerned only with Mill's conclusions about what is desirable for its own sake or intrinsically good.[13] His conclusion in the second part of the proof implies two antihedonistic claims.

Mill claims that there is a plurality of intrinsic goods. This is incompatible with the simple hedonist claim that the only intrinsic good is a homogeneous mental state or sensation. On a natural interpretation, it is also incompatible with preference hedonism, because the preference hedonist claims that there is only one intrinsic good, namely, pleasure. And in a certain sense, the preference hedonist thinks that all pleasures are homogeneous: those mental states are pleasures by virtue of a single common characteristic, namely, their functional role. So it is at least misleading for the preference hedonist to claim that there is a plurality of intrinsic goods. But the preference hedonist can perhaps think that there are qualitatively different preference pleasures, having different qualia or feels. If so, he could allow that the good—pleasure—is a complex notion that has distinct constituents.

But there is a second antihedonist claim here that undercuts preference hedonism as well. This is the claim that the components of happiness are not the sort of mental items that the hedonist requires. Rather, the term "pleasures" refers to objective pleasures, that is, activities, states, and abilities (e.g., music and virtue). And, as parts of happiness, Mill claims, they are intrinsic goods. But, as we have seen, neither form of hedonism can allow that such activities, states, and abilities are intrinsic goods.

5. MILL'S DELIBERATIVE CONCEPTION OF HAPPINESS

Someone might agree that the doctrine of higher pleasures and the claims of chapter IV about happiness are inconsistent with hedonism but resist any commitment to objectivism, because it is (in chap. II) the *preferences* of competent judges and (in chap. IV) facts about what people *desire* that determine which activities are valuable. Mill may not distinguish hedonism and a desire-satisfaction theory, as he should, but perhaps these passages reflect his sympathies with desire-satisfaction theories of value and so allow us to represent him as a consistent subjectivist, even if not as a consistent hedonist.

In order to decide between objective and desire-satisfaction readings of Mill's antihedonist aspects, it may help to look at his substantive evaluative views. In *On Liberty* Mill claims that his defense of liberty relies on claims about the happiness of people *as progressive beings* (*OL*, I 11; cf. chap. III) and about the abilities of progressive beings to form, revise, and implement plans, projects, and commitments. It is these abilities that distinguish fully human beings from nonhuman animals and whose exercise constitutes a major component of human happiness.

> He who lets the world, or his own portion of it, choose his plan of life for him has no need of any other faculty than the ape-like one of imitation. He who chooses his plan for himself employs all his faculties. He must use observation to see, reasoning and judgment to foresee, activity to gather materials for decision, discrimination to decide, and when he has decided, firmness and self-control to hold his deliberate decision. And these qualities he requires and exercises exactly in proportion as the part of his conduct which he determines according to his own judgment and feelings is a large one. It is possible that he might be guided in some good path, and kept out of harm's way, without any of these things. But what will be his comparative worth as a human being? (*OL*, III 4)

Moreover, his contrast between higher pleasures and the pleasures of swine in chapter II of *Utilitarianism* suggests similar claims about human happiness. Happiness consists in large part in the exercise of those higher capacities that distinguish us from other animals. Our higher capacities include our rational capacities, especially our capacities for practical deliberation. Call this a *deliberative* conception of happiness or welfare.

A deliberative conception is also reflected in claims Mill makes elsewhere. In *Considerations on Representative Government* Mill claims that a principal aim of government is the improvement of its citizens and that this improvement consists in the development of their intellectual, deliberative, and moral capacities (*CRG*, esp. chaps. II–III). In *The Subjection of Women* he explains the unhappiness for women in their subjection in terms of the way sexist institutions and attitudes prevent them from developing their rational and deliberative powers (*SW*, IV/542–48). And in various places Mill also expresses reservations about charities that encourage dependence of the beneficiary on her benefactor and so undermine the beneficiary's self-development and self-respect (*SW*, IV/532; *PPE*, V.xi.13/960–62).

The most important exercise of deliberative capacities, Mill thinks, is in the reflective choice and implementation of structured plans. It is important *that* one form, revise, assess, choose, and implement one's own set of plans and projects and not simply that these plans and projects have certain kinds of *content*. This is why in *On Liberty* Mill defends the importance of diversity and experimentation in life-styles and the freedom to make substantively poor decisions.

Presumably, content is important too; one's projects should exercise one's higher capacities. But these capacities can be exercised in a wide variety of projects and life-styles (cf. *OL*, III 2; *A*, V/101). For example, the skilled craftsperson who controls important aspects of her own craft (e.g., production and distribution decisions) will exercise important creative and deliberative capacities in the regular pursuit of her craft every bit as much as the intellectual. Because Mill specifies the constituents of happiness abstractly in terms of capacities for practical deliberation, which can be exercised in multiple ways, his theory allows for a kind of pluralism about the good life.

6. AN OBJECTIVE INTERPRETATION OF THE DELIBERATIVE CONCEPTION

It is this deliberative conception of happiness that is the most important part of my interpretation of Mill's utilitarianism and the consistency of his moral and political views. But we may also wonder whether these deliberative activities are valuable because they are the object of desire, as a desire-satisfaction interpretation would claim, or because of their intrinsic nature and independently of their being the object of desire, as an objective interpretation would claim.

Because it is the preferences of competent judges that are in some sense determinative of higher pleasures, the value of an agent's activities is more or less independent not only of the pleasure *he* derives from those activities but also of *his* desires to perform those activities. The swine is failing to realize higher pleasures even if he is meeting self-imposed goals and satisfying his own desires. This shows that Mill believes that the value of an agent's activity is independent of its being the object of his *actual* desires.

However, these claims are compatible with the subjectivist claim that the value of an activity depends on its being the object of *informed* or *counterfactual* desire, that is, of desire the agent would have in a preferred epistemic state in which he was a competent judge.

But it is possible and reasonable to hold that the competent judges' preferences are *evidential*, rather than *constitutive*, of higher value. Mill can deny that these higher activities have comparatively greater value because competent judges prefer them and claim that competent judges prefer them because they have greater value. On this view, competent judges provide us with our most reliable access to those things that are objectively valuable.

The objective or evidential reading of the relation between the preferences of competent judges and the comparatively greater value of the objects of their preferences helps explain a feature of Mill's higher pleasures doctrine that the subjective or constitutive reading does not. Higher pleasures, we saw, are those things (e.g., activities) that a competent judge would prefer, even if they produced less pleasure *in her* than the lower "pleasures" would (*U,* II 5). But *why* should competent judges prefer activities that *they* often find less pleasurable unless they believe that these activities are more valuable? Mill does want to explain the fact that competent judges prefer activities that exercise their rational capacities, and he does so by appeal to their sense of *dignity:*

> We may give what explanation we please of this unwillingness [on the part of a competent judge ever to sink into what he feels to be a lower grade of existence] . . . but its most appropriate appellation is a sense of dignity, which all human beings possess in one form or other, and in some, though by no means in exact, proportion to their higher faculties. . . . (*U,* II 6)

In claiming that it is the dignity of a life in which the higher capacities are exercised and the competent judge's sense of her own dignity that explains her preference for those activities that exercise these higher capacities, Mill defends the objective reading of the relation between the preferences of competent judges and the greater value of the objects of their preferences. Their preferences reflect judgments about the value that these activities have for beings such as themselves prior to and independenly of their being the object of desire. If so, it is the (perceived) value of the activities that explains the preferences of the competent judge, rather than her preferences explaining the value of the activities.[14]

There is another argument for an objective interpretation of Mill's deliberative conception of happiness. As we have seen, both the higher pleasures doctrine and Mill's proof represent various nonmental items, including higher activities that exercise our deliberative capacities, as intrinsic goods. If higher activities are intrinsic goods, they must be good in themselves. If so, they must be necessarily good or good whatever else is true (even when they are outweighed by competing goods). While these conditions are met for higher activities on the objective interpretation, they are not on the subjective interpretation. For on the subjective interpretation, it must be a contingent psychological fact, assuming it is a fact, that suitably informed people would prefer activities that exercise their deliberative capacities. Perhaps this is a deep psychological fact about human beings, but it is a contingent fact. This implies that on the subjective interpretation higher activities cannot be necessarily valuable, and this implies that they cannot be intrinsic goods, contrary to what Mill claims.[15]

Though it is the deliberative conception of happiness that is most basic to our understanding of Mill's utilitarianism, these are reasons to interpret the deliberative conception in objective as well as antihedonist terms.

7. MILL'S CONSISTENCY

Do the antihedonistic elements reveal an inconsistency in Mill's utilitarianism? The apparently hedonistic formulation at the beginning of *Utilitarianism* (II 2), Mill insists, is only a first approximation that needs articulation. The passage continues as follows:

> To give a clear view of the moral standard set up by the theory, much more requires to be said; in particular, what things it includes in the ideas of pain and pleasure, and to what extent this is left an open question. (II 2).

This should be a puzzling claim if we assume that "pleasure" refers to a simple, qualitative mental state or sensation, as the simple hedonist would so understand it. On this reading, no further analysis of happiness should be necessary or even possible (though we could identify these mental states ostensively).[16] This may be less of a puzzle for the preference hedonist, because she can recognize, at least in one sense, the existence of qualitatively different kinds of pleasure.

There is no puzzle if Mill is speaking of objective pleasures. Because he often uses the word "pleasure" to refer, not to any mental state, but to the activities that typically produce pleasurable mental states (II 1, 5, 7, 8; IV 5; cf. Section 3), he can consistently say that happiness consists in pleasure—objective pleasure—and offer an objective conception of happiness whose dominant component is the exercise of deliberative capacities. And this is just what he does. His defense of higher pleasures in the paragraphs immediately following this initial statement of utilitarianism should be read as an important articulation of this initial statement that yields a nonhedonistic conception of happiness. Indeed, given Mill's other claims about happiness, the objective reading of "pleasure" in these passages is both a necessary and a sufficient condition of a consistent reading of his views. This objective conception of happiness may run counter to some common usage of the term "happiness," but this fact by itself should not and does not trouble Mill (*U,* IV 4; Section 1).[17]

Of course, Mill's break with hedonism would have been clearer if he had avoided defining utilitarianism in terms of pleasure and pain and eschewed talk of "higher pleasures" and simply argued for a conception of happiness that recognizes the intrinsic superiority of the higher activities. But, I have claimed, this is how we should understand the doctrine of higher pleasures. The fact that he uses the word "pleasure" to refer to activities as well as mental states allows us to recover a consistent and coherent doctrine from his somewhat misleading claims.

8. Utilitarianism, Rights, and Liberty

As we have seen, it is also claimed that Mill's defense of utilitarianism is incompatible with his defense of a right to liberty. This alleged difficulty is just a special case of the more general complaint that utilitarianism is unable to account for moral and political *rights*.

Notoriously, writers disagree over what rights we have. Some asssert only *negative* rights to liberty and protection from harm from others, while others assert *positive* rights to particular goods and services. But there is rough agreement about what a right *is*. Rights are normative considerations that have a distinctive dialectical force in moral and political debate. They protect important or fundamental interests that individuals have by placing a limit on what may be done to individuals even in pursuit of otherwise valuable social goals. Nozick, for example, understands rights as "side-constraints" on the pursuit of the good, and Dworkin understands rights as "trumps" over considerations of policy or the promotion of valuable goals.[18] The basic idea is that if an agent has a right to something, then she cannot be deprived of it—it would be *wrong* to deprive her of it—merely on the ground that we could promote the general welfare by doing so. This conception of a right would explain why Mill thinks that a right is a claim that an individual has that society ought to protect and enforce (*U*, V 24–25); it also explains the apparent tension between utilitarianism and rights.

The apparent hostility between utilitarianism and rights presents a problem for Mill not only because *Utilitarianism* defends a version of utilitarianism and *On Liberty* seems to defend a strong right to liberty, but because in *On Liberty* Mill actually claims to base his defense of liberty on utilitarian foundations:

> It is proper to state that I forego any advantage which could be derived to my argument from the idea of abstract right as a thing independent of utility. I regard utility as the ultimate appeal on all ethical questions; but it must be utility in the largest sense, grounded on the permanent interests of man as a progressive being (*OL*, I 11)

If we bear in mind this apparent conflict, there are three views about the compatibility of Mill's utilitarianism and his defense of liberty. First, the apparent conflict between utilitarianism and rights is genuine; Mill does defend rights to liberties, but, contrary to what he claims, this is incompatible with his utilitarianism. Second, the apparent conflict between utilitarianism and rights is genuine; Mill's claims about utilitarianism and liberty are compatible, because he does not defend *rights* to liberties. Third, the apparent conflict between utilitarianism and rights is only apparent; Mill's commitments to utilitarianism and rights to liberties are compatible. We can decide which view is appropriate only if we look at his claims about liberty and his defense of these claims.

9. Mill's Defense of Liberty

Mill distinguishes paternalistic restrictions of liberty from restrictions of liberty based on the harm principle. At one point he suggests that a restriction on someone's liberty is legitimate if and only if it satisfies the harm principle (*OL,* I 9, IV 1–4, V 2). The harm principle allows A to restrict B's liberty in order to prevent harm to someone other than B. Exactly what, in Mill's view, will count as a harm for purposes of the harm principle is complicated. He clearly denies that any inconvenience or annoyance is a harm. Rather, in order to satisfy the harm principle, an action must actually violate or threaten imminent violation of those important interests of others in which they have a right (*OL,* I 12, III 1, IV 3, 10, 12, V 5). Major provisions of the criminal law (e.g., laws against murder, rape, assault), for example, satisfy the harm principle. Mill thinks that restrictions of liberty based on the harm principle are unproblematic (but see *OL,* V 3). By contrast, he sometimes claims, paternalistic restrictions of liberty are never justified.[19] A's restriction of B's liberty is paternalistic if it is done in order to prevent B from harming himself or in order to provide B with benefits that B would not secure on his own.

10. Against Paternalism

Mill's position on paternalism already raises the question of the consistency of his overall position. He (sometimes) accepts a *blanket* prohibition on paternalism, but one would expect a utilitarian to take a more cautious attitude. A utilitarian might be able to explain why paternalistic restrictions on liberty often fail to promote the interests of the person whose liberty is restricted and so why there should be a presumption against paternalistic interference, but she ought to be prepared to override this presumption if the harms that paternalism would prevent or the benefits that it would secure would be great enough.

Mill offers two general arguments against paternalism. First, state power is liable to abuse. Politicians are corruptible and will use a paternalistic license to limit the freedom of citizens in ways that promote their own interests and not those of the citizens whose liberty they restrict (*OL*, V 20–23). Second, even well-intentioned rulers will misidentify the good of citizens. Because an agent is a more reliable judge of his own good, even well-intentioned rulers will promote the good of the citizens less well than would the citizens themselves (*OL*, IV 4, 12).

These are the sort of strategic arguments against leaving paternalistic interference to the state's discretion that we might expect utilitarians to offer. They provide no *principled* objection to paternalism—no objection to successful paternalistic restrictions on B's liberty that *do* benefit B.

Though these are Mill's explicit arguments against paternalism, he has the resources for another, stronger argument. These resources are clearest in his defense of free speech. Indeed, Mill thinks that there is general agreement on the importance of free speech and that, once the grounds for free speech are understood, this agreement can be exploited to support a more general defense of individual liberties (*OL*, I 16, III 1).

11. Against Censorship

The usual justification of censorship, Mill believes, is the suppression of probable falsehood (and the social value that this represents) or the suppression of unpopular and offensive or annoying views.[20] Mill offers four reasons for maintaining free speech and opposing censorship.

(1) A censored opinion might be true (*OL*, II 1–20, 41).
(2) Even if literally false, a censored opinion might contain part of the truth (*OL*, II 34–39, 42).
(3) Even if wholly false, a censored opinion would prevent true opinions from becoming dogma (*OL*, II 1–2, 7, 20–33, 43).
(4) As a dogma, an unchallenged opinion will lose its meaning (*OL*, II 26, 43).

Like the two general arguments against paternalism, (1) and (2) represent liberty as extrinsically valuable: freedom of speech is valuable, because it tends to produce true belief or increase the ratio of true belief to false belief, which, Mill assumes, is (at least extrinsically) valuable. If, even if only contrary to fact, we had extremely knowledgeable and reliable censors who censored all and only false beliefs, (1) and (2) would provide no argument against censorship. Indeed, if the question is what policies are likely to increase the ratio of true belief to false belief, it would seem that we should employ conservative criteria of censorship and censor those opinions for whose falsity there is especially clear evidence. We would be on good ground in censoring flat-earthers.[21]

Reasons (3) and (4) really represent just one ground of freedom of speech. They offer a more secure defense of freedom of speech and expression; they are supposed to rebut the case for censorship even on the assumption that all and only false beliefs would be censored (II 2). Mill's claim is that these freedoms are necessary conditions for the exercise of people's deliberative capacities and for fulfilling our natures as progressive beings (II 20). Here he can appeal to the conditions of exercising both (i) *intellectual* reason and (ii) *practical* reason.[22]

(i) The justification of true beliefs is valuable, because it realizes our capacities for theoretical reason. Consideration of various possible opinions is necessary if one is to be justified in one's beliefs, and freedom of speech is a precondition of consideration of competing opinions (II 7, 23). Free discussion is essential for rational beings who are not cognitively self-sufficient if they are to justify their beliefs. Because we are individually limited cognitively, free discussion with others is essential to the *identification* of alternative positions, whose consideration is part of the justification of beliefs and values. But confrontation among and *discussion of* alternative positions, already identified, is also essential to the proper articulation of true beliefs and their grounds, and freedoms of speech are required for this discussion to take place. If so, censorship, even of false belief, robs both those whose speech is suppressed and their audience of resources that they need to justify their beliefs and values (II 1).

(ii) In a similar way, the exercise of practical reason in the assessment, selection, revision, and implementation of projects and plans requires that agents deliberate about alternative plans and projects and their appeal. Proper deliberation requires both identification and discussion of alternatives, and this requires various freedoms of thought and speech.

12. The General Argument for Basic Liberties

The defense of free speech is just an instance of a more general defense Mill offers for various liberties in chapter III of *On Liberty*. Those activities are more valuable that exercise a person's higher capacities (*OL*, I 11, II 20, III

1–10). A person's higher capacities include her deliberative capacities, in particular, capacities to form, revise, assess, select, and implement her own plan of life. This kind of autonomous self-expression requires, among other things, various liberties of *thought* and *action*. If the choice and pursuit of projects and plans is to be reflective, it must be informed as to the alternatives and their grounds, and this requires intellectual freedoms of speech, association, and press. If there is to be choice and implementation of choices, there must be liberties of action such as freedom of association, freedom of worship, and freedom to choose one's occupation.

If this interpretation is right, Mill cannot be claiming that liberty is intrinsically valuable. He insists that his defense of liberty applies only to those who have rational capacities and are in a position to exercise them effectively:

> It is, perhaps, hardly necessary to say that this doctrine is meant to apply only to human beings in the maturity of their faculties. . . . Liberty, as a principle, has no application to any state of things anterior to the time when mankind have become capable of being improved by free and equal discussion.[23] (*OL,* I 10)

This restriction makes no sense if liberty itself is a dominant intrinsic good, for then it should always be valuable to accord people liberty—a claim that Mill here denies. This restriction makes perfect sense if the liberties in question, though not intrinsically valuable, are necessary conditions of realizing dominant goods, for then there will be, or need be, no value to liberty where, as in these circumstances, other necessary conditions for the realization of these higher values (namely, sufficient rational development) are absent.[24]

As long as people have some rational capacities, Mill can claim that it is valuable that they be exercised, and this requires various freedoms of thought and action. This does not imply that everyone should have unrestricted freedom. Freedom can still be restricted when its exercise would harm important interests of others (harm principle) and perhaps when its exercise would cause substantial or irreversible self-injury or would otherwise substantially compromise the agent's ability to exercise her practical reason effectively in the future (weak paternalism).

Mill is forced to qualify his blanket prohibition on paternalism in these ways in order to maintain his claim that no one should be free to sell herself into slavery:

> The ground for thus limiting his power of voluntarily disposing of his own lot is apparent, and is very clearly seen in this extreme case. . . . [B]y

selling himself for a slave, he abdicates his liberty; he foregoes any future use of it beyond that single act. He, therefore, defeats in his own case, the very purpose which is the justification of allowing him to dispose of himself. (*OL*, V 11)

Because it is the importance of exercising one's deliberative capacities that explains the importance of certain liberties, the usual reason for recognizing liberties provides an argument against extending liberties to do things that will permanently undermine one's future exercise of those same capacities.

It would also seem that we can and should distinguish liberties that are *central* to the exercise of higher capacities from those that are not. For instance, restrictions on speech, writing, worship, association, and choice of profession violate liberties that are much more important than those restricted, say, by seat belt laws or traffic regulations, because the former restrict our practical deliberation about the sort of persons we will be, and so the exercise of our rational capacities, in much more significant ways than the latter restrictions do. If so, some liberties are more important than others, and it is these *basic liberties*, rather than *liberty* per se, that Mill's arguments defend.[25]

This restriction on the scope of the argument is important if he is to be able to defend the permissibility of familiar kinds of social welfare legislation that generate revenue to be redistributed within the community and to be spent on community projects. And Mill does accept many forms of social welfare legislation. He thinks that local and central government are empowered to enact various kinds of legislation pursuant to the community's interest (*PPE*, V.i.2/803–4; *CRG*, XV/368, 369). He explicitly includes the following items on the governmental agenda: the redistribution of wealth (through taxes on earned and unearned income and inheritance) so as to ensure a decent minimum standard of living,[26] Poor Laws that provide work for the able-bodied indigent (*PPE*, II.xii.2/359–60, V.xi.13/960–62), labor regulation (e.g., regulation of the hours of factory laborers) (*PPE*, V.xi.12/956–58), provision for a common defense (*OL*, I 11; *PPE*, V.viii.1/880), development of a system of public education (*OL*, V 12–13; *PPE*, II.xiii.3/374–75, V.xi.8/948–50; *CRG*, VIII/278; *A*, V/128), maintenance of community infrastructure (e.g., roads, sanitation, police, and correctional facilities) (*PPE*, V.viii.1/880; *CRG*, XV/368, 371, 373), and state support for the arts (*PPE*, V.xi.15/968–70).

Now social welfare legislation is a challenge to those who prize liberty per se, because, as Bentham noted, almost all legislation restricts liberty in some way; certainly, the tax measures to support such social welfare legislation do.[27] The challenge is to explain why these restrictions on liberty are permissible, while paternalistic, moralistic, and other restrictions on liberty are not.[28]

Some of the goods provided by such social welfare legislation—in particular, personal security, a decent minimum standard of living, and education—are important preconditions of exercising one's capacities for practical deliberation well. In this way, Mill can defend the importance of access to certain positive conditions for realizing dominant components of happiness in much the same way that I have claimed he can and does defend claims to certain negative conditions—certain freedoms of thought and action (cf. *OL,* V 12–13; *U,* V 25; *A,* V/128). If Mill can defend negative rights to these liberties of thought and action (see Section 13), he can also defend positive rights to these basic goods. But the objects of other forms of social welfare legislation do not have this status. If Mill is to defend the latter form of social welfare legislation at all, and if he is to avoid a confict between positive and negative rights in the case of social welfare legislation of the former type (granting access to basic goods), then he must also claim that the liberties restricted by these sorts of social welfare legislation are less important liberties than those restricted by paternalistic and moralistic legislation. He can begin to do this if he can distinguish, as I have suggested he can, the importance of different liberties in terms of their role in practical deliberation and if he can show that permissible social welfare legislation restricts less important liberties in small and predictable ways and does not constrain practical deliberation significantly. Social welfare legislation may restrict some people's freedom to dispose of their gross income and assets as they please, but it does not significantly constrain anyone's ability to choose or implement projects and plans that express her own deliberations, as paternalistic and moralistic legislation does.

Thus, a proper understanding of Mill's defense of liberty requires us to modify or better articulate some of his conclusions. Paternalism is not always impermissible; weak paternalism is defensible. The harm principle is not the sole legitimate ground for restricting liberty; various forms of social welfare legislation are acceptable.[29] And there are rights to basic liberties, but no right to liberty per se. These claims should seem well motivated once the nature of Mill's argument and its appeal to deliberative capacities is understood.

13. A DELIBERATIVE UTILITARIAN ACCOUNT OF RIGHTS

Once we recognize the way in which Mill's defense of basic liberties relies on his deliberative conception of happiness, it is less clear that there is an inconsistency between his utilitarianism and his defense of a right to certain liberties. Mill holds a pluralistic theory of welfare in which higher activities are dominant components. Exercise of higher capacities has greater value than other intrinsic goods such as pleasure or the satisfaction of desire, and magnitudes of it cannot be exchanged one-for-one with magnitudes of these other goods without significant loss of value. Indeed, as we have seen (Section 3), Mill thinks that the higher activities have value that is infinitely or lexically greater than that of mere pleasures, because he claims that their value cannot be outweighed by any quantity of lower pleasures (*U,* II 5, 6).[30] Even though liberty is not intrinsically valuable, some liberties are necessary conditions to the realization of the dominant component in human welfare, namely, the exercise of rational capacities. For this reason the liberties that are essential to the exercise of rational capacities are themselves dominant (though not intrinsic) goods and have the status of rights; they trump or defeat claims that we could promote lesser goods (e.g., pleasure or preference satisfaction) by interfering with these liberties. Recognizing a right to these liberties, therefore, is the way to maximize value.

This interpretation of Mill's theory of rights should be contrasted with a "strategic" interpretation, according to which a right to liberties is a reliable strategy for promoting values that have no necessary or intrinsic connection with liberty.[31] This strategy conception of rights is just a special case of the strategy conception of moral rules.

Appeal to a moral rule, rather than application of the utilitarian principle itself, is justified on utilitarian grounds, according to the strategy conception, if (a) acceptance of the rule generally, but not always, produces optimific acts, and (b) the suboptimific acts that adherence to the rule produces cannot reliably and efficiently be identified in advance. Rules that satisfy condition (a) often satisfy condition (b); there are a number of advantages to operating with fairly coarse-grained rules, even though adherence to them will produce some suboptimific acts. We may mistakenly identify cases in which adherence to the rule produces suboptimific results and so our deviations from the rule may be suboptimific; even when we get the calculations right, case-by-case calculation is itself costly; and a simpler, more coarse-grained rule will be easier to internalize and less subject to various forms of bias and self-deception in its application than extremely complex rules or case-by-case evaluation.

This strategy conception of moral rules explains Mill's regular insistence on the need for "secondary principles" that function in our practical reasoning in lieu of direct appeals to the utilitarian first principle (*SL,* VI.xii.7/951–52; cf. *U,* II 19, 24–25; B, 110–11; *A,* V/100).[32] When conditions (a) and (b) are met, the associated moral rule should be appealed to and applied automatically in most cases and should be set aside in favor of direct appeal to the utilitarian principle only in very unusual circumstances (e.g., where it is obvious that adherence to the rule would have disastrous consequences) and in cases of conflicts among moral rules each of which has a utilitarian justification (cf. *U*, II 23–25).

The strategic interpretation of a right applies this strategy conception of rules to liberties and holds that a rule protecting these liberties meets conditions (a) and (b). This generates a *strategy-right* to these liberties.

Mill can recognize strategy-rights to certain liberties. But his deliberative account of happiness provides a stronger conception of rights than the strategic conception does. The strategic conception recognizes moral rules with the dialectical force of trumps as a practical necessity or false target justified by our cognitive and affective limitations. But strategy-rights are not *counterfactually stable;* they do not apply in those circumstances in which we can reliably and efficiently detect (sub)optimific acts. And it seems that genuine moral and political rights should be counterfactually stable. Where an agent's claim to something is protected by a moral rule or a right, it would be wrong to deprive her of that thing, even if we are perfect and costless calculators of utility and departure from the rules here had no bad spillover effects on our behavior elsewhere.

By contrast, the account of rights provided by a deliberative conception of happiness seems counterfactually stable. We protect particular liberties, on this account, because these liberties are necessarily, and not just contingently or epistemically, connected with the realization of dominant components of value; we cannot maximize value without securing these liberties. And an objective version of the deliberative conception of happiness (Section 6) will secure greater counterfactual stability for rights to these liberties insofar as it does not hold the value of exercising deliberative capacities hostage to contingent conative facts.[33]

This interpretation of Mill's conception of rights is confirmed by his discussion of the connections among justice, rights, and utility in chapter V of *Utilitarianism:*

> Justice is a name for certain classes of moral rules which concern the essentials of human well-being more nearly, and are therefore of more absolute obligation, than any other rules for the guidance of life; and the notion which we have found to be of the essence of the idea of justice— that of a right residing in an individual—implies and testifies to this more binding obligation. (V 32; cf. V 33, 37–38)

That some of these "essentials of well-being" are necessary conditions of realizing value is clear in Mill's discussion of the foundation in security that many of our basic rights have (V 25). Just as security from attack is a necessary condition of pursuing other goods, so too are basic liberties necessary conditions for exercising those higher capacities whose exercise is a dominant component in human happiness.

A basic liberty can be infringed, according to this interpretation, if and only if its exercise would more seriously infringe other important intrinsic goods or other necessary conditions of intrinsic value (e.g., liberties or basic well-being) held by others or by the agent herself. These things too act as trumps over considerations of lesser goods, and so should be construed as rights; they constrain what the agent may do to herself or others.[34] Indeed, these restrictions on liberty apply in just those cases where the agent's exercise of freedom would constitute "harms," in Mill's technical sense. That is, he thinks that someone can have her basic liberties interfered with only if doing so is necessary to prevent her from depriving someone of interests in which that person has rights (*OL*, IV 3, 10, 12).[35] Though rights act as trumps, they are not absolute; they can be overridden if they conflict with other rights.[36]

14. The Distribution of Dominant Goods

Mill can represent certain liberties and goods necessary to the realization of higher capacities as trumping the promotion of lesser intrinsic and extrinsic goods. But perhaps this fails to recognize sufficiently robust rights. Mill's hierarchical theory of value allows basic goods to trump nonbasic goods; for instance, it allows basic liberties to trump mere preferences or pleasures. But while it allows trumping *across* ranks of goods, it does not allow trumping *within* a rank of goods. Mill must apparently allow one claim to pursue higher pleasures to be defeated by a greater number of claims to pursue comparable pleasures or another claim to pursue greater pleasures.

This objection is hard to assess in the abstract. While Mill must concede the possibility of conflicts among such liberties and goods, there seems nothing wrong with this in principle, because we do want to recognize the possibility of conflicts among rights. But some conflicts among dominant goods may not seem properly resolved by maximizing value. For example, Mill seems committed to allowing an intellectual elite to deprive others of basic liberties or goods in order to provide this elite with the leisure and resources to deliberate in ways that realize higher capacities. Provided the elite is large enough or exercises their rational capacities well enough, this sort of exploitation would seem to be permissible, indeed, obligatory. But surely genuine rights to basic liberties should constrain such exploitation.[37]

If Mill's theory cannot account for this, then it faces an important distributional problem.

As far as I know, Mill does not explicitly consider this worry. But he discusses related issues, and his claims here and his deliberative conception of happiness provide the resources for a reply. To block the sort of exploitation imagined in the example, Mill must claim that the value that the elite realizes in these circumstances could not outweigh the costs to themselves and others of denying others basic liberties and goods. Part of this reply relies on claims that we have already examined and defended.

First, in discussing Mill's deliberative conception of happiness (Section 5), we noted that the same sort of deliberative capacities can be exercised in a variety of different activities. For example, I exercise many of the same sort of capacities in organizing a charity benefit or a cooperative business enterprise as in organizing a bank robbery. If so, it is unclear whether a closed society enables the elite to exercise deliberative capacities that it could not exercise equally well in more socially harmonious ways. No doubt, the closed society enables them to engage in different activities, but this does not show that they exercise their rational capacities any more fully by these activities than they would by the activities allowed them in a free society. If so, it is not clear that the elite gain anything by their exploitation.

Second, by denying basic liberties to others the elite insulate themselves intellectually. But cooperative discussion and exchange exercise deliberative capacities (Sections 11–12). If so, the isolation of the elite deprives them of input from those they exploit, and so compromises the quality of their own deliberations. The exploited also lose the benefit of cooperative discussion with the elite. These two costs must be added to the more obvious damage done to the exploited when they are denied the goods and liberties necessary to exercise their deliberative powers effectively. This means that in a closed society the elite themselves lose and the exploited lose twice over, even if the elite gain in one way.

Third, we have seen that Mill can and should distinguish some liberties as more central to the exercise of higher capacities than others (Section 12). One way to understand the centrality of goods or liberties to the exercise of rational capacities is in terms of the number of rational activities to which those goods or liberties are necessary and the structural importance of those activities to the person's character and rational agency. If so, the goods and liberties denied the exploited in this closed society are much *more central* than those goods and liberties that the closed society enables the elite to possess. Freedoms of speech, association, and occupational choice and a level of material well-being necessary to secure physical and psychological health and stability just have a more central role in the exercise of people's rational capacities than do the leisure and resources that such an elite might use in the pursuit of rational activities that they could engage in only in such a closed society.

Mill can strengthen this defense of rights to basic liberties if he can argue that certain sorts of cooperative *social capacities* are among our higher capacities and that the sort of exploitation involved in the example is incompatible with the right sort of exercise of these capacities both on the part of the elite and on the part of the exploited. The relevant social capacities would presumably involve mutual concern and respect and would be realized in, among other things, cooperative activities conducted on terms of mutual advantage.

Mill does think that the exercise of such social capacities is a significant good. In various places he asserts the role of social sentiments and social relationships in the happiness of progressive beings (cf. B, 91; C, 120–24; U, II 18, III 10, V 20; A, V/106). And he appeals to this fact to address a related problem. In chapter III of *Utilitarianism* Mill addresses, among other things, the rational authority of utilitarian moral demands, in particular, the apparent conflict between the individual's own good and the other-regarding demands of utilitarianism (and other moral theories). He argues that the conflict is, for the most part, illusory by appealing to the role of social sentiments and cooperative social relationships in each individual's good. Mill thinks we come increasingly to recognize these social aspects of our nature and welfare as civilization advances (U, III 10). Indeed, he commits himself to a very strong claim about the interdependence of people's interests:

> In an improving state of the human mind, the influences are constantly on the increase which tend to generate in each individual a feeling of unity with all the rest; which, if perfect, would make him never think of, or desire, any beneficial condition for himself in the benefits of which they are not included. (U, III 10)

Here Mill describes how progressive beings increasingly come to conceive of the relations between their own good and that of others. But he presumably also intends to claim, and our objective interpretation of his conception of happiness licenses us in concluding, that their preferences are reliable evidence of what is good for them. And what is good for a progressive being, Mill believes, is good for human beings. So, even if these social components of a person's welfare will be fully recognized only as civilization advances, they are components of human welfare now.

Mill's claims here make his theory of value *distribution-sensitive*. If forbearing and cooperative social relations are a part of each person's good, then the inequalities in basic goods and liberties and social relations characteristic of the closed society cannot be a way of maximizing his set of weighted values, in part because they will frustrate an important component of the welfare of both the exploited and the elite.[38]

But we may wonder whether a moral theory that is distribution-sensitive can be teleological. For instance, Rawls claims that "if the distribution of goods is also counted as a good, perhaps a higher order one, and the theory directs us to produce the most good (including the good of distribution among others), we no longer have a teleological view in the classical sense."[39] This constraint follows from the assumption that teleological theories must define the moral property of rightness in terms of the promotion of some nonmoral value(s). And this assumption is sometimes taken to follow from the claim that teleological theories, unlike deontological theories, must specify the right in terms of the good and specify the good independently of the right.[40]

But teleological theories should eschew these constraints; they need only define the right in terms of the good and conceive of the good as *distinct* from the right. Unless the good is distinct from the right, defining the right in terms of the good will be circular. But if the right that the teleologist defines in terms of the good is all-things-considered obligation, then she can define the good in any other way, without circularity. In particular, she can define the right as the promotion of the good and give an account of the good in terms of distributional moral properties.

But not all teleological theories are utilitarian; utilitarian theories are teleological theories that take the good to be human (or sentient) welfare or happiness. If Mill's reply requires assuming that the distribution of benefits and harms to people is itself a good—in addition to the benefits and harms to people themselves—then it must have value that cannot be explained by its contribution to people's welfare or happiness. This would make Mill's commitments nonutilitarian, even if they are teleological.

Though Mill's theory of value is distribution-sensitive, the value of distribution is theoretically derivative. It is not that distribution is a good independently of any contribution it makes to human welfare; it is a good because it is a constituent of human welfare. Part of the good of a progressive being, Mill claims, consists in exercising his social capacities. If so, his doing well cannot be achieved at the expense of other people's welfare. Thus, certain distributional properties are intrinsically good, and they are so because of the role they play in human happiness. If so, a teleological theory that incorporates such assumptions will be utilitarian.

But even if this is a possible form of utilitarianism, its evaluative assumptions may seem ad hoc. Are these assumptions independently plausible? Mill thinks so. As we have seen, he thinks the correct conception of happiness must take the exercise of our higher capacities to be a dominant component. And Mill thinks that the sort of social capacities whose exercise we have been discussing are among these higher capacities. This is clear from the discussion in chapter III of *Utilitarianism*. There he asserts that mutual concern and commitment and common projects are characteristic of progressive beings and that this sort of social interaction is in large part responsible for the development of what we think of as civilization. This is a theme that Mill articulates in several other places as well. For instance, in his essay "Civilization" he writes that "wherever . . . we find human beings acting together for common purposes in large bodies, and enjoying the pleasures of social intercourse, we term them civilized" (C, 120; cf. C, 120–24). And in *Principles of Political Economy* Mill frequently remarks that economic development goes hand in hand with greater economic cooperation and interdependence and that these aspects of modern economic life create a school of social sentiments in which economic actors, especially laborers, develop common interests and deliberative powers (*PPE*, IV.vii.1/763; cf. II.3/205, IV.vii.6/792–94). These claims show that Mill's assumptions about the social components of human happiness reflect well-considered evaluative views that rest, in part, on his views of human nature and social theory.

On this view, Mill takes certain distributional properties to be good because of their relation to the social components of human happiness. And the exercise of the relevant social capacities may be part of our good as progressive beings in exactly the same way that the exercise of rational capacities is part of our good as progressive beings. But there would be even greater explanatory unity in Mill's view if the exercise of the relevant social capacities could be represented as an important special case of the exercise of deliberative capacities. In that case distributional considerations would be valuable because of their role in certain social relations, which would be valuable because of their role in the exercise of people's rational capacities.

Mill often says that social cooperation and interaction breed identity of interests (e.g., *U*, III 10). We can make sense of this claim if in the process of exercising these cooperative virtues we *extend our interests* by engaging in new and more complex forms of practical deliberation than those available to us individually.[41] When I interact with others on a footing of mutual concern and commitment, I learn of and share in their experiences and activities, and this allows me to participate in (if only vicariously) and benefit from a wider range of experiences and activities than I could on my own. This wider range of experiences and activities will expand my knowledge, but it will also expand and aid my practical deliberation about my own projects and activities in the future. For, as we have seen, Mill claims that deliberation and discussion of my own projects with others will force me to consider and assess new alternatives, and this will also enhance my deliberation about my own projects and activities. Furthermore, cooperation with others on projects of mutual advantage will allow me to pursue larger and more complex projects and goals than I could working on my own, and this will expand the range of my deliberative powers and control.

Indeed, these considerations argue for the kinds of social and political organization that Mill defends. As we have seen, Mill argues for a form of democratic equality, where democratic equality is understood to involve democratic institutions against a background of personal and civic liberties and comparative social and economic equality that establishes a decent minimum standard of living. And, in particular, he thinks that the principal justification of this sort of democratic government is that it improves the intellectual, deliberative, and moral powers of its citizens (*CRG*, esp. chaps. II–III). Now a society will extend the interests of its members roughly in proportion to the extent of its democratic equality. Democratic decision-making affords the opportunity for widespread participation in a process of mutual discussion and articulation of ideals and priorities. Because deliberation will be improved, and interests extended, by input from diverse perspectives, Mill rightly recognizes the role of proportional representation in a deliberative democracy (*CRG*, VII/260–62). Democratic processes thus establish common projects more widely and in so doing exercise new deliberative capacities in the members of such a society.[42] A background of personal and civil liberties with comparative social and economic equality makes possible more widespread development of individual talents and capacities, and this will expand the range of experiences, values, and perspectives that individuals can enjoy vicariously and draw on in their own deliberations.

In these ways, Mill might think that the right sorts of interpersonal and social interaction will expand the deliberative powers of parties to such interaction. He does not make all these claims explicitly. But they are available to him and lend a greater unity to his moral and political views than they would otherwise enjoy.

Whether we take the value of exercising these social capacities to be theoretically derivative from the value of exercising rational capacities or on a par with the exercise of rational capacities, their value will constrain the ways in which practical or theoretical deliberation can be pursued. Appeal to the higher value of fair and cooperative social relationships can serve as a tiebreaker. When, as we saw, the same set of rational capacities can be exercised in more and less socially harmonious ways, a commitment to the exercise of social capacities, as part of exercising one's higher capacities, will require the fair and cooperative realization of these rational capacities. Moreover, these social capacities have an importance not simply as a tiebreaker. So in our example, even if exploitative social arrangements can uniquely promote some aspects of rational deliberation, this higher-order value will be outweighed by greater higher-order costs. Both the exploited and the exploiters lose by their lack of cooperative interaction with each other, whereas at most only the exploiters gain.

In these ways, exploitation necessarily involves social and private higher-order costs to both exploiters and exploited that must offset any marginal higher-order benefits that exploitation uniquely permits exploiters to reap. If so, basic liberties do constrain would-be exploiters' pursuit of higher-order, deliberative goods. Does this mean that Mill's theory can represent rights that are constraints on the pursuit of the good? In one sense, no. Insofar as he is an act-utilitarian, he does and must represent the recognition of rights as part of maximizing the good, properly understood. But he can recognize rights as constraints on the pursuit of various *goods*. And this, I argue, promises to deliver a fairly robust account of rights. In particular, Mill's deliberative conception of the good allows him to respect important distributional aspects of rights that teleological theories are alleged not to be able to accommodate. This account does not represent rights as nonteleological side-constraints. But this fact cannot by itself be thought to be an objection to that account without begging the question against the possibility of an adequate teleological account of rights.

This discussion obviously raises large issues about the nature of deliberative powers and the social dimensions of these powers. But perhaps we have said enough about these issues to show that Mill's version of utilitarianism has no obviously insuperable difficulty accounting for the distributional character of rights.

15. CONCLUSION

Mill's deliberative conception of happiness drives his version of utilitarianism and accounts for its most distinctive features and resources. His version of utilitarianism promises to accommodate rights—both negative rights to particular liberties and to protection from harms and positive rights to the conditions of basic well-being. These positive and negative conditions are necessary to the realization of dominant goods, namely, the exercise of deliberative capacities. As such, claims to these conditions have the dialectical force of trumps in moral and political debate; this will be part of promoting Mill's weighted set of values. If so, Mill's deliberative views about happiness promise a plausible explanation of the logic and content of individual rights on a utilitarian basis. Here, his version of utilitarianism has resources not available to traditional (e.g., hedonistic) forms of utilitarianism. These resources make his moral and political theory both more distinctive and more coherent than is generally recognized.

NOTES

I would like to thank Michael Bratman, Joshua Cohen, Robert Fogelin, Terry Irwin, Diane Jeske, Derek Parfit, Robert Stalnaker, audiences at Dartmouth College and the University of Connecticut, and the Editors of *Philosophy & Public Affairs* for helpful comments. Work on this article was conducted during a period at the Center for Advanced Study in the Behavioral Sciences that was funded by an Old Dominion Fellowship from the Massachusetts Institute of Technology and by grants from the National Endowment for the Humanities (#RA-20037-88) and the Andrew W. Mellon Foundation. I am grateful to these institutions for their support.

1. See, e.g., Henry Sidgwick, *The Methods of Ethics,* 7th ed. (Indianapolis: Hackett, 1981), pp. 93n, 94, 121; T. H. Green, *Prolegomena to Ethics* (New York: T. Crowell, 1969), secs. 162–63; F. H. Bradley, *Ethical Studies,* 2d ed. (New York: Oxford University Press, 1927), pp. 116–20; G. E. Moore, *Principia Ethica* (New York: Cambridge University Press, 1903), pp. 71–72, 77–81; C. L. Ten, *Mill on Liberty* (New York: Oxford University Press, 1980), pp. 34, 39; cf. Jerome Schneewind, *Sidgwick's Ethics and Victorian Moral Philosophy* (New York: Oxford University Press, 1977), pp. 185–86.

2. See, e.g., Robert Paul Wolff, *The Poverty of Liberalism* (Boston: Beacon Press, 1968), pp. 19–20; Gerald Dworkin, "Paternalism," in *Morality and the Law,* ed. R. Wasserstrom (Belmont, Calif.: Wadsworth, 1971); Alan Ryan, *J. S. Mill* (Boston: Routledge and Kegan Paul, 1974), pp. 131–33; Ten, *Mill on Liberty,* pp. 6, 27, 34, 77; H. L. A. Hart, "Natural Rights: Bentham and John Stuart Mill," reprinted in his *Essays on Bentham* (New York: Oxford University Press, 1983), pp. 94–104; David Lyons, *Ethics and the Rule of Law* (New York: Cambridge University Press, 1984), pp. 172–77.

3. References, parenthetical or otherwise, to Mill's texts have the following form. References to *On Liberty (OL),* ed. E. Rapaport (Indianapolis: Hackett, 1978) and to *Utilitarianism (U),* ed. G. Sher (Indianapolis: Hackett, 1979) are to chapters and paragraphs in any edition. I will refer by both chapter and page number to *Considerations on Representative Government (CRG),* reprinted in *Three Essays,* ed. Richard Wollheim (New York: Oxford University Press, 1975); *The Subjection of Women (SW),* also reprinted in *Three Essays;* and the *Autobiography of John Stuart Mill (A)* (New York: Columbia University Press, 1924). Other references are to

natural divisions in the text (if any) and page numbers in the editions in the *Collected Works of John Stuart Mill* (Toronto: University of Toronto Press). I will refer by book, chapter, and section and page number to *Principles of Political Economy (PPE)*, in *Collected Works*, vols. II–III, and *A System of Logic (SL)*, in *Collected Works*, vols. VII–VIII. I will refer by page number to "Bentham" (B), in *Essays on Ethics, Religion and Society*, in *Collected Works*, vol. X; "Civilization" (C), in *Essays on Politics and Society*, in *Collected Works*, vol. XVIII; and "Chapters on Socialism" (CS), in *Essays on Economics and Society*, in *Collected Works*, vol. V.

4. My overall picture of Mill has benefited from Fred Berger's important study of Mill's moral and political thought, *Happiness, Justice, and Freedom* (Berkeley and Los Angeles: University of California Press, 1984), esp. chaps. 2, 3, and 5. But my interpretation differs from Berger's in significant ways, as will become clear. I have also benefited from James Bogen and Daniel Farrell, "Freedom and Happiness in Mill's Defence of Liberty," *Philosophical Quarterly* 28 (1978): 325–38.

5. This assumption should not distort my discussion; the reconciliation of utilitarianism and rights should be, if anything, most difficult on the sort of act-utilitarian assumption that I am making here.

6. Theories of value that are subjective in this sense need not be subjective in the further sense of claiming that a person's welfare is whatever he takes it to be. In *this* sense, hedonism and some desire-satisfaction theories are not subjective.

7. Cf. Richard Kraut, "Two Conceptions of Happiness," *Philosophical Review* 88 (1979): 176–96, and my *Moral Realism and the Foundations of Ethics* (New York: Cambridge University Press, 1989), pp. 220–31.

8. For example, Bentham seems to be a simple hedonist, while Sidgwick is a preference hedonist. Cf. Jeremy Bentham, *Introduction to the Principles of Morals and Legislation* (London: Athlone Press, 1970), esp. chap. IV, and Sidgwick, *The Methods of Ethics*, pp. 42–43, 127, 131.

9. The only difference between the two, as far as I can see, is that the intensity of a preference pleasure will be a function of the strength of the preference that it continue, while the intensity of a simple pleasure will be the vividness or intensity of the pleasurable sensation or feel.

10. Pleasures (the mental states) can perhaps be extrinsically, as well as intrinsically, valuable if they cause other pleasures. (However, we may wonder whether pleasures, as contrasted with rememberings or anticipations of pleasures, cause other pleasures.) So it is not certain that Mill's quantitative hedonist is discussing activities, rather than mental states. But surely what quantitative hedonists usually defend the greater extrinsic value of is certain kinds of pursuits and activities (things that have only extrinisic value).

11. Davidson considers a related worry about the individuation of actions in terms of their causes or effects. He argues that the first sort of epistemic dependence between cause and effect is compatible with the requirement that causal relata be independent. Donald Davidson, "Actions, Reasons, and Causes," reprinted in his *Essays on Actions and Events* (New York: Oxford University Press, 1980), pp. 10–11, 13–14. But this does not diffuse the worry about the dependence between cause

and effect that arises when we treat activities as constituents of the mental states they cause. This proposal implies that the cause (the activity) is a part of the whole that is the effect (the pleasure); as such, cause and effect are distinct, but not independent.

12. Mill seems to allow that higher activity can occur without producing pleasure, because he allows that higher activities can be attended with great discontent (*U*, II 5) and that Socrates' pursuit of higher activities might have left him dissatisfied (*U*, II 6). If so, this would be one objection to an alternative hedonist strategy that construes higher activities as rational activities that give rise to pleasure. This alternative strategy individuates activities in terms of mental states, rather than individuating mental states in terms of activities, and so is the mirror image of the strategy discussed in the text.

13. In fact, the objective reading of Mill's conception of happiness fits well with much of the structure of the proof. For the objective reading allows us to say that desire—especially appropriately informed desire—is defeasible evidence of what is objectively valuable (Section 6). This both explains how claims about what is desired or would be desired under certain conditions support claims about what is desirable *and* explains, in part, why Mill does not think that the evidential relation constitutes a proof in the usual sense (*U*, I 5).

14. One could claim that competent judges prefer A to B because they believe A is better or more dignified than B but insist that A is better or more dignified than B simply because competent judges prefer A. Though consistent, it would be peculiar for Mill to insist that competent judges are the measure of higher value but ignore the *evaluative grounds* for their preferences. I see no reason to interpret Mill's appeal to competent judges in this selective way.

15. This suggests that on a desire-satisfaction theory it is the satisfaction of desire as such that is intrinsically valuable, while the satisfaction of particular desires must be extrinsically valuable.

16. Cf. Bogen and Farrell, "Mill's Defence of Liberty," pp. 334–35, and Berger, *Happiness, Justice, and Freedom,* pp. 37–38.

17. Notice also that Mill explicitly asks us to distinguish happiness and the mental state of contentment (*U*, II 6).

18. Robert Nozick, *Anarchy, State, and Utopia* (New York: Basic Books, 1974), pp. 28–33; Ronald Dworkin, *Taking Rights Seriously* (Cambridge, Mass.: Harvard University Press, 1978), pp. xi, 184–205.

19. As I shall discuss shortly (Section 12), even Mill's blanket prohibitions on paternalism apply only when the individual whose liberty is in question is a mature adult whose rational faculties are sufficiently developed (*OL*, I 10).

20. This justification of censorship need not presuppose the infallibility of the censor, as Mill sometimes suggests (e.g., *OL*, II 3).

21. Cf. Alvin Goldman, "Epistemic Paternalism: Communication Control in Law and Society," *Journal of Philosophy* 88 (1991): 113-31.

22. Ten, *Mill on Liberty,* pp. 126–28, brings out the importance of (i) to Mill's defense of free speech. While (i) is sufficient to show that Mill is not merely defend-

ing free speech as a way of promoting true belief, (ii) does this and plays a greater role in Mill's overall defense of liberty in *On Liberty*. Cf. T. M. Scanlon, "A Theory of Freedom of Expression," *Philosophy & Public Affairs* 1, no. 2 (Winter 1972): 204–26.

23. Mill goes on to say that this threshold of rational development has been "long since reached in all nations with whom we need concern ourselves" (*OL*, I 10). Though this qualification can be read so as to signify the narrowness of Mill's concerns, it can also be read as signifying his belief that there are few such exceptions and so as signifying the breadth of his concerns.

24. Contrast my interpretation of the importance of liberty as a necessary condition of dominant value with suggestions that Mill thinks liberty and liberties are intrinsically valuable: Bogen and Farrell, "Mill's Defence of Liberty," and Berger, *Happiness, Justice, and Freedom*, pp. 41, 50, 199, 231–32. Though Berger discusses Mill's restrictions on the scope of the argument (pp. 269–70), he does not seem to see that they force Mill to deny that liberties have intrinsic value.

25. Though Berger does recognize limitations on Mill's defense of liberty, he seems to see that defense as a defense of liberty per se, rather than specific liberties; see *Happiness, Justice, and Freedom*, p. 230.

26. Mill was concerned with redressing inequalities resulting from arbitrary social and natural circumstances (*PPE*, II.i.3/207, V.ii.3/808; *CS*, 710–14). Though he generally defended equal taxation of earned income, he claimed that earned income below a certain minimum should not be taxed at all (*PPE*, II.xiii.3/374–75, V.iii.3/809–10, V.iii.5/830–31). He defended the use of inheritance taxes to limit social and economic inequality (*PPE*, II.ii.1/216, II.ii.4/225, V.ii.3/811, V.vi.2/868, V.ix.1/887). He also linked (unearned) rental income with inherited wealth and argued that it may be heavily taxed (*PPE*, V.ii.5/819). The case for thinking that Mill thought government should pursue egalitarian redistribution of wealth through taxation is made in further detail by Berger, *Happiness, Justice, and Freedom*, pp. 159–86.

27. Cf. Jeremy Bentham, *Of Laws in General* (London: Athlone Press, 1970), chap. VI, para. 4.

28. A familiar manifestation of this challenge is the worry within constitutional theory about how to reconcile the rejection of *economic* substantive due process (e.g., the rejection of Lochner v. New York, 198 U.S. 45 [1905]) with the acceptance of *civic* and *personal* substantive due process (e.g., the acceptance of "selective incorporation" and privacy cases such as Griswold v. Connecticut, 381 U.S. 479 [1965]). The reconciliation must explain why the liberty of contract is not a fundamental liberty, while personal and civic liberties are fundamental liberties; cf. Palko v. Connecticut, 302 U.S. 319 (1937). A deliberative conception of happiness and a theory about the conditions of exercising deliberative capacities begin to provide the basis for such a reconciliation (I hope to pursue these issues elsewhere).

29. However, Mill does claim that others can be compelled to supply some of these benefits, under the harm principle, because harm can result from inaction as well as action (*OL*, I 11); cf. David Lyons, "Liberty and Harm to Others," *Canadian Journal of Philosophy* 5 (suppl.) (1979): 1–19.

30. Mill also claims that taxes on necessities, which are necessary conditions of exercising one's higher capacities, require a sacrifice "that is not only greater than, but incommensurable with" the sacrifices imposed by taxes on luxuries (*PPE,* V.ii.3/809–10).

31. Cf. Rolf Sartorius, *Individual Conduct and Social Norms* (Encino, Calif.: Dickenson, 1975), esp. chap. 8, sec. 3; David Lyons, "Human Rights and the General Welfare," *Philosophy & Public Affairs* 6, no. 2 (Winter 1977): 113–29; Berger, *Happiness, Justice, and Freedom,* chaps. 3–5, esp. pp. 70–73, 131–34, 247–48, 271, 291; and John Gray, "John Stuart Mill on Liberty, Utility, and Rights," *Nomos* 23 (1981): 108–9.

32. This strategic reliance on moral rules is compatible with *act*-utilitarianism. Acting on the best strategic rules will result in some wrong acts; but because these acts will be part of an optimific pattern of behavior, an act-utilitarian can represent them as cases of *blameless* wrongdoing. If so, Mill's reliance on secondary principles does not imply rule-utilitarianism. Contrast J. O. Urmson, "The Interpretation of the Philosophy of J. S. Mill," *Philosophical Quarterly* 3 (1953): 33–39. However, the act-utilitarian account of secondary principles is incompatible with the link Mill sees between wrongdoing and blame (*U,* V 14; cf. Section 1).

33. As a general matter, Mill's reconciliation of utilitarianism and rights depend only on his deliberative conception of happiness and does not require the objective interpretation of the deliberative conception. Thus, a suitably informed desire-satisfaction interpretation of the deliberative account can effect much the same reconciliation. However, it would not provide the same degree of counterfactual stability for utilitarian rights. This may be an advantage of the objective interpretation.

34. I assume that people can hold rights against themselves; Mill certainly believes that people have duties to themselves (*OL,* IV 6).

35. This interpretation makes Mill's own harm principle and his acceptance of weak paternalism out to be just special cases of a more general harm principle that insists that liberty be restricted if its exercise would cause (or pose an imminent threat of causing) harm to *someone,* the agent or others. This interpretation threatens the self/other asymmetry that Mill appears to draw in *On Liberty.* But once we see his acceptance of weak paternalism and remember that he will count as a harm only damage to dominant goods, it is not clear that Mill's claims about liberty require any self/other asymmetry.

36. Cf. Dworkin, *Taking Rights Seriously,* pp. 191ff.

37. Cf. John Rawls, *A Theory of Justice* (Cambridge, Mass.: Harvard University Press, 1971), pp. 210–11, 329–30; Hart, "Natural Rights," pp. 96–97.

38. The theme that exploiters and oppressors are themselves harmed by exploitative relationships, because such relationships are inconsistent with beneficial personal and social interaction, is explicit in *The Subjection of Women* (*SW,* IV/522–25, 541).

39. *A Theory of Justice,* p. 25.

40. See William Frankena, *Ethics,* 2d ed. (Englewood Cliffs, N.J.: Prentice-Hall, 1973), pp. 14–17, and Rawls, *A Theory of Justice,* pp. 24–25, 30–31.

41. For fuller elaboration of this idea, see my "Rational Egoism, Self, and Others," in *Identity, Character, and Morality,* ed. O. Flanagan and A. Rorty (Cambridge, Mass.: MIT Press, 1990), esp. secs. 5–10; cf. T. H. Irwin, *Aristotle's First Principles* (Oxford: Clarendon Press, 1988), pp. 393–95.

42. Not coincidentally, Mill thought it a virtue of the sort of workers' associations that the Cooperative Movement supported that they would introduce democratic processes into the workplace and so expand common interests and deliberative powers (*PPE,* IV.vii.6/792–94).

Further Readings

Some Related Works by Mill

Original publication dates are shown; items are then located by volume in the *Collected Works of John Stuart Mill,* published by the University of Toronto Press. Note that many of Mill's writings are available in paperback editions.

"Remarks on Bentham's Philosophy" (1833, X).
Bentham (1838; X).
A System of Logic (1843; VII–VIII).
Principles of Political Economy (1848; II–III).
On Liberty (1859; XVIII).
Considerations on Representative Government (1861; XIX).
Utilitarianism (1861; X).
The Subjection of Women (1869: XXI).
Autobiography (1873; I).
Three Essays on Religion (1874; X).
Chapters on Socialism (1879; V).

Books on Mill or Utilitarianism

Berger, Fred R. *Happiness, Justice, and Freedom: The Moral and Political Philosophy of John Stuart Mill.* University of California Press, 1984.

Brandt, Richard. *A Theory of the Good and the Right.* Oxford, 1979.

Cooper, Wesley E., Kai Nielsen, and Steven C. Patten, eds. *New Essays on John Stuart Mill and Utilitarianism.* Canadian Association for Publishing in Philosophy, 1979.

Donner, Wendy. *The Liberal Self: John Stuart Mill's Moral and Political Philosophy.* Cornell University Press, 1991.

Frey, R. G., ed. *Utility and Rights*. University of Minnesota Press, 1984.

Kagan, Shelly. *The Limits of Morality*. Oxford, 1989.

Laine, Michael, ed. *A Cultivated Mind: Essays on J. S. Mill Presented to John M. Robson*. University of Toronto Press, 1991.

Lyons, David. *Rights, Welfare, and Mill's Moral Theory*. Oxford, 1994.

Moore, G. E. *Ethics*. Hutchinson, 1912.

Morales, Maria H. *Perfect Equality: John Stuart Mill on Well-Constituted Communities*. Rowman & Littlefield, 1996.

Packe, Michael St. John. *The Life of John Stuart Mill*. Secker & Warburg, 1954.

Regan, Donald. *Utilitarianism and Cooperation*. Oxford, 1980.

Riley, Jonathan. *Liberal Utilitarianism: Social Choice Theory and J. S. Mill's Philosophy*. Cambridge, 1988.

Ryan, Alan. *J. S. Mill*. Pantheon Books, 1970.

————. *The Philosophy of John Stuart Mill*. 2nd ed. Humanities Press International, 1990.

Scheffler, Samuel, ed. *Consequentialism and Its Critics*. Oxford, 1988.

Semmel, Bernard. *John Stuart Mill and the Pursuit of Virtue*. Yale University Press, 1984.

Sen, Amartya, and Bernard Williams, eds. *Utilitarianism and Beyond*. Cambridge, 1982.

Skorupski, John. *John Stuart Mill*. New York: Routledge, 1989.

Smart, J. J. C., and Bernard Williams. *Utilitarianism, For and Against*. Cambridge, 1973.

Sumner, L. W. *Welfare, Happiness, and Ethics*. New York: Oxford, 1996.

Utilitas. This journal specializes in utilitarian theory.

INDEX

action: character and, 108–9; consequences and, 3, 26–27; ends and, 12;
feelings and, 144n31; liberty of, 166;
type and token, 6. *See also* right action acts: beneficial, 49–50; connectedness of, 55; positive, 57; rightness
of, 101, 104. *See also* right action
acts: beneficial, 49–50; connectedness
of, 55; positive, 57; rightness of, 101,
104. *See also* right action
act-utilitarianism, 25–27, 34, 42n9, 51,
53, 58, 62nn20–21, 100, 117, 119–
20n13, 177, 179n5, 182n32; abandonment of, 52; actual-outcome,
119n5; character utilitarianism and,
104, 106; critics of, 99; duty and,
103; good and, 108; hegemonic,
106; liberty and, 33; maximizing
version of, 150; moral obligation
and, 31; motive utilitarianism and,
103, 104, 121n24; right/wrong and,
109–10; utility maximization and,
105, 107
Adams, Robert M., 101–3, 119nn9–12
Amish, education and, 72, 83n18
*Analysis of the Phenomena of the Human
Mind* (Mill), 48, 92
aretaic theories, 102, 112
"Are There Any Natural Rights?"
(Hart), 45
art, 14–15, 18
Art of Life, 9, 15, 86, 97n12, 143n25
"Auguste Comte and Positivism"
(Mill), 49

Austin, John, x, 62n21, 63n29
Autobiography (Mill), x–xi, 130

bad-making property, 151
Baker, John M., 25, 26
benevolence, imperfect obligations of,
39
"Bentham" (Mill), 129, 145n44
Bentham, Jeremy: desire and, 132; education and, 70, 71, 73–74, 83n14;
empirical naturalism and, 124; good
and, 123, 124–26, 130, 131, 136,
137, 138–39; happiness/pleasure
and, 128, 136; hedonism and, 85,
126; intrinsic value and, 125; liberty
and, 167; Mill and, 123, 126, 130,
131, 134, 135, 145n38; obligation
and, 38; psychology of, 131, 133–34,
138; pursuits and, 152; rights and,
30; sanctions and, 35; self-effacing
theory and, 123; social rules and, 36;
on teaching, 78; utilitarianism and, x,
61n19, 68
Bill of Rights, 29
Brandt, Richard, 140n4
breach of promise, 50
Brown, D. G., 57, 58

cause and effect, 154
censorship, 180n20; opposition to,
164–65
character, 118n2; action and, 108–9;
imagination and, 143n26; judgment
of, 117–18; moral evolution of, 106;

moral/nonmoral value of, 106;
    moral theory and, 117–18; norma-
    tive affirmation of, 106; social, 50
character utilitarianism, 99, 100–101,
    118; act-utilitarianism and, 104, 106
choices, 142n15, 171, 172; implemen-
    tation of, 166; motive-affecting, 103;
    self-destructive, 33
civilization, development of, 175
consequences: actions and, 3, 26–27;
    evaluation of, 52, 85
*Considerations on Representative Govern-
    ment* (Mill), 158
cooperation, 51, 74, 83n26, 176; facili-
    tating, 80; fairness and, 55–59; public
    goods and, 58; unstable, 56
Cooperative Movement, 183n42
costs, higher-order, 177
Chrestomathia, 70, 83n14
criminal law, 64n36, 163
critical theory, self-understanding and,
    139

decided preference criterion, 126–27
Declaration of Independence, 29, 38,
    40
Declaration of the Rights of Man, 38
deliberative conception: objective in-
    terpretation of, 159–62, 160–61;
    subjective interpretation of, 160
democratic processes, 176
deontology, 112, 115, 116, 117, 174
desirability: desire and, 88–90, 91, 95;
    good and, 96n7; happiness and,
    97n11, 98n24; intrinsic, 129
desire, 90, 92, 132; desirability and, 88–
    90, 91, 95; happiness and, 88; object
    of, 90, 91; pleasure and, 91, 92; satis-
    faction of, 16–17
desire-satisfaction theory, 150, 157,
    179n6, 180n15
Dewey, John, educational criterion and,
    73
Diggs, B. J., 25

dignity, 59, 160
Doctrine of Ends, 15, 16
"Dr. Whewell on Moral Philosophy"
    (Mill), 26
Dryer, D. P., 9, 60–61n11
Dualism of Practical Reason (Sidgwick),
    17–18
Durkheim, Emile, 74–76, 77, 79, 81
duty, 5, 45, 54, 55, 57, 60–61n11; act-
    utilitarianism and, 103, 120n15; all-
    things-considered, 105; imperfect,
    60n11; judgment of, 47; moral, 45,
    61n17, 109; motive utilitarianism
    and, 105; obligations and, 42n10; vi-
    olation of, 47
Dworkin, Ronald, on rights, 162

economic opportunity, 79–80, 176
education, 96, 167, 168; choice maxim-
    isation and, 76–77; conservative the-
    ory and, 74, 75; development
    maximisation and, 69; economic op-
    portunity and, 79–80; employment
    and, 71, 77, 78; function of, 73, 75–
    76, 79, 80; goals of, 71, 77; happiness
    and, 67–71, 72, 145n44; liberal, 67,
    78, 80, 81; religious, 74; social/polit-
    ical organisation and, 81; specialisa-
    tion in, 75, 79–80; theoretical,
    77–81; utilitarianism and, 68, 71, 73;
    vocational, 77–81. *See also* training
empirical naturalism, 139, 140n4,
    143n26, 146n47, 146n50; and Ben-
    tham, 123–24
employment: education and, 71, 77, 78;
    Greatest Happiness Principle and, 70
ends, 85; actions and, 3, 12; happiness
    and, 86, 90; moral rule and, 3, 6; ul-
    timate, 12–13, 86
Equality of Taxation, principle of, 59
experiments in living, 123, 124,
    130–34; empiricism and, 137–40;
    exploratory/critical parts of, 138;
    good and, 137; intuitionism and,
    137–40
exploitation, 171–2

fairness: cooperation and, 55–59; duty of, 57, 58; principle of, 45, 59, 60n3

fair play, 45, 46

feelings, 129, 158; action and, 144n31; judgment and, 144n30

fictions, theory of, 141n8

Frankena, William K., 102

freedom, 166; civil, 67; education for, 71–73; social boundaries of, 73–77

free speech, 166, 171, 172; defending, 164, 165; restrictions on, 167

general acceptance, notion of, 118n3

general happiness, 2, 53; good and, 93, 94; individual's happiness and, 88, 92–96; liberty and, 32

general welfare, 42n10; human rights and, 29–41; inequalities/injustice/exploitation and, 29; moral obligation and, 31, 34; moral rights and, 39; social rules and, 33

good, 136, 140n4, 174; basic, 43n15, 171, 172; conception of, 124–31, 137–39, 177; dominant, 171–72, 177; empiricist theory of, 139; experiments in living and, 137; extrinsic, 171; intrinsic, 111, 157, 160, 169, 171; maximization of, 108, 115, 125; nobler sentiments and, 135; pleasure and, 125; theory of, 134, 140

good-making property, 151

goodness, 119n10; intrinsic moral/nonmoral, 106; moral/nonmoral, 115, 117; pleasures and, 141n7; rightness and, 112; valoric accounts of, 117

Greatest Happiness Principle, ix, 6, 10, 151; Principle of Utility and, 11

Grote, George, 53, 54, 61n19

Grote, John, 21

happiness, 59, 82n6, 149, 174, 180n13; analysis of, 92, 161; attaining, 134; components of, 156–57, 168, 175;

conception of, 127–29, 142n23, 151, 175; deliberative conception of, 157–61, 168, 170, 171, 172, 177–78, 181n28, 182n33; desire and, 87, 88, 95, 97n11, 98n24; education and, 67–71, 72, 145n44; ends and, 9, 13, 18, 20, 22, 34, 86, 90, 91, 94; general and individual, 88, 92–96; higher capacities and, 158, 171; ideal of, 128; maximizing, 125; morality and, 95; objective conception of, 150–51, 161, 173; perfectionism and, 69; pleasure and, 20, 26, 96n9, 128–29; promotion, 6, 86, 95, 151; right to, 93–94; rules and, 53; subjective conception of, 150. *See also* general happiness

Hare, R. M., 140nn4–5; act-utilitarian theory and, 62n21

Hart, H. L. A., 45, 46

hedonism, 85, 88, 124, 126, 142n16, 145n38, 150, 161, 179nn6, 10, 180n12; ethical, 128, 143n27; higher pleasures and, 154, 155, 157; intrinsic goods and, 157; pleasures and, 153; preference, 151, 157, 161; psychological, 90–91; quantitative, 126–27, 135–36, 153; rejection of, 152; simple, 151

hedonistic utilitarianism, 149, 151–52

higher capacities, 160, 177; exercising, 171, 172, 175; happiness and, 158, 171

human rights, general welfare and, 29–30, 40–41

Hume, David, moral reasoning and, 18

ideal compliance, 118n3

imagination, 129; character and, 143n26

indicative-imperative criterion, 14–15

instrumental rules in force, 25

intellectual pursuits: extrinsic value of, 156; voluptuous pursuits and, 152, 155

interests, identity of, 175–76
intermediate generalisations, 6
intuitionism, 141n11; experiments in living and, 137–40; hedonism and, 126

Jackson, Reginald, 1
joint work, social interests and, 57
judgment, 56, 158; causal, 26; feelings and, 144n30; moral, 20, 34, 35, 36, 47, 48, 60n5, 64n42; rightness of, 104
justice, 5, 52–53, 60n1, 170; analysis of, 34, 48, 49, 50; distributive, 59; duties of, 50, 58; obligations of, 37; principles of, 30, 41, 59; rights and, 46–50; rules of, 46, 51–52, 54, 55, 58; sentiment of, 136–37; social, 117; utility and, 4, 46; violation of, 47

Kant, Immanuel, 1, 18; education and, 74; utilitarian arguments and, 7
knowledge, value of, 77

Later Letters (Mill), Venn letter in, 26
Leibniz, 1
Lewis, George Cornewall, 63n29
liberalism, education and, 67, 75
liberty, 30, 81, 174, 181n24; basic, 167, 171, 172; civic, 76, 176; defending, 149, 162–68, 173, 181n25; education and, 78; general happiness principle and, 32; personal, 176; political, 76; principle of, 32–33, 38; restrictions on, 46, 163, 167–68, 171, 172; right to, 162–63, 170; utilitarianism and, 33, 162–63, 169
life-styles, diversity/experimentation in, 158–59
Logic of Induction, 1
Lyons, David, 26, 60n1, 63n28, 64n30; on expectation/reliance, 61n16; on moral obligations/moral rules, 51; rule-related interpretation by, 63n27

Mandelbaum, Maurice, 25
Marmontel, 132
Marshall, John, 98n24
mental states, 155, 156, 157, 180nn11–12
Methods of Ethics (Sidgwick), 17
Mill, James, x, 97n16; Bentham and, 130; hedonism and, 145n38; pleasures and, 144n35
Mill, John Stuart: consistency of, 161–62; criticism of, ix, 1, 40–41; depression of, x–xi, 131, 138–39; interpretations of, 2–6; psychology of, 136, 139, 144n32; self-discovery for, 132; youth of, x
Mitchell, Dorothy: on desirable/good, 96n7
Moore, G. E., 97n11, 142n16; on general welfare/moral obligation, 31; on good, 140n4
moral assessment, 107, 111, 112, 113, 126; utilitarianism and, 114, 118
moral codes, 33, 36; rule-utilitarianism and, 118n2
moral discourse, 111, 115
morality, 4, 15, 34, 61n15, 97n18; adoption of, 61n17; criterion of, 86; happiness and, 95; prudence and, 17, 18; rights and, 53; theory of, 11, 62n20
morally bad/good, 113
moral obligation, 4, 37, 40, 61n17, 127; analysis of, 38–39; breach of, 35; general welfare and, 31; normative theories of, 102; obligation and, 5
moral principles, 40, 41
moral right, 30, 127; analysis of, 37, 115, 117; commitment to, 39; general welfare and, 39
moral rules, 39, 53–54, 61n17, 64n43; applicability of, 7–8; ends and, 3, 6–7; fundamental principle and, 7; as intermediate generalisations, 6; reasoning and, 4–5; role of, 50; as rules

of thumb, 25; secondary principles of, 26; strategy conception of, 169–70, 182n32

morals, foundation of, ix, 6, 11, 100

moral theory, 11, 45, 99, 115, 149, 174, 178; character and, 101, 117–18; empiricism in, 139–40; self-effacing, 123

moral values, 104, 112–13, 120n20

motives, 103–4, 144n31; assessment of, 102; moral value of, 104

motive utilitarianism, 101–4; act-utilitarianism and, 103, 104, 121n24; characterization of, 101; duty and, 105; valoric utilitarianism and, 121n24

Nagel, Thomas, on happiness/end, 20

neutrality, 72, 78–79, 80

nonhedonic values, 124, 125, 128; authenticity of, 134–37

nonmoral values, 113–14, 120n20, 121n23

Nozick, Robert, on rights, 162

obligation, 39, 112; all-things-considered, 105, 108, 111, 174; branches of, 57–58; duties and, 42n10; imperfect, 39, 46, 49, 50; moral obligation and, 5, 36; perfect, 46; rights and, 37, 53; theory of, 36–37, 62n19; virtues and, 37. *See also* duty; moral obligation

On Liberty (Mill), x–xi, 4, 7, 33, 56–59, 138, 149, 157, 158, 162, 165

"On the Logic of the Moral Sciences" (Mill), x

Origin of the Species (Darwin), 78

others, self and, 16–22

pain: absence of, 11, 12, 13, 20, 21, 87, 90, 92, 128, 129, 151; pleasure and, x, 92, 124, 144n31

Parfit, Derek, self-effacing theory and, 123

paternalism, 180n19, 182n35; liberty and, 168; opposition to, 32, 163–64; prohibition of, 166–67; weak, 166, 168

perfectionism, 69, 74, 119n10

Plato, 1, 18

pleasure, 12, 13, 21, 87, 90, 134, 136, 151, 157; attaining, 144n31; choice criterion of, 73; desire and, 91, 91; duration of, 152; good and, 125, 141n7; happiness and, 20, 26, 96n9, 128–29; hedonism and, 153; higher, 127–28, 149, 152–56, 159–62; intensity of, 152; kinds of, 151, 154–55; lower, 128, 153, 169; as motive, 130; objective, 153, 161; pain and, x, 92, 124, 144n31; preference, 154, 155, 179n9; promoting, 11, 129; quantity of, 93, 152; simple, 154, 155; subordination of, 129

poetry, 152; criticism of, 141n9; impact of, 131, 132–33, 139

Poor Laws, 167

Possibility of Altruism, The (Nagel), 20

practical reason, general theory of, 14–16

practice rules, 25

preferences, 142n15, 159, 160

preference-satisfaction theory, 150

principle of sympathy and antipathy, 125

Principle of Utility, 12, 21; formulation of, 9–10, 13, 22; Greatest Happiness Principle and, 11; as moral principle, 19; reasoning and, 14

Principles of Political Economy (Mill), 56, 59, 175

progressive beings, abilities of, 157

proof, 87, 89; direct, 85–86

prudence: morality and, 17, 18; Principle of Utility and, 21

psychology, nonhedonic values and, 134–37

punishment, 8, 49, 64n46, 74; justification of, 34, 50

Railton, Peter, 140n4
rational capacities, 176, 177
Rationale of Judicial Evidence (Bentham), x
Rawls, John, 25, 41, 60n3; on liberty, 46
reasoning, 48, 158; intellectual/practical, 165; moral, 8, 20, 25, 50, 51; moral rules and, 4–5; practical, 13, 14; Principle of Utility and, 14
right action, 52, 103, 105; analysis of, 49; ascertaining, 16; judgment of, 47, 116; strategic interpretation of, 170; testing, 11; theory of, 112, 150; utilitarianism and, 118; wrong and, 109–10, 113. *See also* moral right
rightness, 26, 51, 62n20, 110–11; goodness and, 112; judgment of, 116; moral, 9–10, 111, 112; questions of, 3; valoric accounts of, 115–16, 117
rights, 29; acknowledgment of, 31; analysis of, 37–38, 48, 56–57; conflicts among, 64n30, 171; defending, 40–41, 49, 63n29, 173; deliberative utilitarian account of, 168–71; distributional character of, 177; justice and, 46–50; legal, 54; moral, 53, 54, 162; obligations and, 37, 53; overriding, 53–54, 64n30; political, 162; positive/negative, 162; principles of, 30, 41; recognition of, 49, 55; strategy, 170; teleological account of, 177; theory of, 31–32, 54, 56, 57, 58, 169; utilitarianism and, 41, 54, 162–63, 179n5, 182n33; violation of, 31, 38, 47–48, 50, 55
rights theorists: consequentialism of, 81; education and, 73, 76, 77, 82n2; utilitarianism and, 77
Rousseau, Jean-Jacques, 77
rules, 169; happiness and, 53; ideal-if-adopted, 63n28; ideal-if-conformed-with, 63n28; justice and, 51–52; obedience to, 52; social, 35, 56–57;

utility of, 101; violation of, 64n43. *See also* moral rule
rule of the road, 55, 64n30
rules of thumb, 25, 26
rule-utilitarianism, x, 25, 31, 36, 51, 99, 100–1, 117, 150
Russell, Bertrand, 71, 113
Ryan, Alan, 9, 62n22

sabbatarian legislation, 56
sanctions, 42n8; external, 34, 36; internal, 34, 36, 39; justification of, 39; social, 35
Schneewind, J. B., 96n3; on Mill's proof, 85–86
science, art and, 14–15
secondary principles, 54, 83n14, 169, 182n32
self, others and, 16–22
self-effacing theory, 123, 134, 135, 146n48
self-expression, 47, 165–66
self-interest, 43n14, 47; virtue and, 18
self-protection, instinct for, 136
self-regarding conduct, 8, 62n20
self-respect, 158; education and, 82–83n14
self-understanding, 137; critical theory and, 139
sensuality, inordinate, 70
sentiments, 135, 139; education and, 145n44; ethical, 136–37; moral, 60n5, 145n44, 146n52, 147n54; nonmoral, 146n52; social, 173, 175
Sidgwick, Henry, criticism of, 17–18
slavery, 29, 41
Smart, J. J. C., 68
social capacities, exercising, 173, 176, 177
Social Contract, The (Rousseau), 77
social relationships, 174; cooperative, 57, 76, 173, 175, 176
social utility, maximization of, 130
social welfare legislation, liberty and, 167–68

Socrates, 73
Subjection of Women, The (Mill), x, 158
substantive due process, 181n28
summary rule, 32, 33
systemic interests, 55–56, 58
System of Logic, A (Mill), x, 14, 15, 25, 86

taxation, 182n30; wealth redistribution through, 167, 181n26
Taylor, Charles, empirical naturalism and, 124
Taylor, Harriet, x
teleology, 14, 15, 16, 174–75, 177
Theory of Justice, A (Rawls), 46
training, 145n44; on-the-job, 80; vocational, 78, 79, 80–81. *See also* education

unhappiness, analysis of, 92
Urmson, J. O., 25, 51
utilitarianism, x, 2, 39, 94, 174; criticism of, 21, 29, 46, 82n6; direct, 120n16; indirect, 116; interpretive problems with, 149–51. *See also* act-utilitarianism; character utilitarianism; hedonistic utilitarianism; motive utilitarianism; rule-utilitarianism; valoric utilitarianism
Utilitarianism (Mill), xi, 7, 8, 25, 45, 54, 93, 149, 151, 158, 161, 162, 173, 175; formulations in, 10–14; purpose of, 1–2
utility, 6, 61n19, 156; justice and, 4; moral duties and, 45; proof of, 9, 33–34, 86; rights and, 41, 54
utility maximization, 17, 31, 45, 46; act-utilitarianism and, 105, 107

valoric utilitarianism, 112–15, 117, 118, 121n23; motive utilitarianism and, 121n24
value judgments, 124–25, 142n15, 146n50; nonhedonic, 125, 128, 129, 130, 132–35, 141n8, 142n16, 146n47; refutation of, 139–40; universal, 141n9
values: distribution-sensitive, 173–74; extrinsic, 152, 154, 156; higher-order, 177; intrinsic, 125, 134, 152, 171; nonmoral, 174; theory of, 54, 171, 173–74; weighted, 178. *See also* moral values
Venn, John, letter to, 26, 62n21, 64n43
virtues, 144n34; obligations and, 37; self-interest and, 18
voluptuous pursuits, 156; intellectual pursuits and, 152, 155

wealth, redistribution of, 167, 181n26
welfare, x, 150, 151, 158, 174; intrinsic, 93; maximizing, 38; objective theory of, 150; pluralistic theory of, 169. *See also* general welfare
well-being, 59, 170–71
"Whewell on Moral Philosophy" (Mill), 63n22, 96n9
Williams, Bernard, on utilitarianism, 119–20n13, 120n18
Wordsworth, Mill and, 132–33
wrong, 5, 50, 52; analysis of, 11, 16, 49; blame and, 182n32; judgment of, 47, 116; moral, 3; right and, 109–10, 113
wrongness, 3, 26, 51, 62n20, 110–11; criterion of, 35, 61n16; moral, 9–10

ABOUT THE CONTRIBUTORS

Elizabeth S. Anderson is associate professor of philosophy and Arthur F. Thurnau Professor of Philosophy at the University of Michigan and the author of *Value in Ethics and Economics* (1993) and articles in ethics, political philosophy, and feminist theory.

F. R. Berger was professor of philosophy at the University of California, Davis, and the author of *Happiness, Justice, and Freedom: The Moral and Political Philosophy of John Stuart Mill* (1984) and *Freedom, Rights, and Pornography* (1991).

David O. Brink is professor of philosophy at the University of California, San Diego. His research interests lie in ethical theory, the history of ethics, political philosophy, and constitutional jurisprudence, and he is the author of *Moral Realism and the Foundations of Ethics* (1989).

D. G. Brown is professor emeritus at the University of British Columbia and the author of *Action* (1968) and several papers on Mill's moral theory, including "Mill on Liberty and Morality," *Philosophical Review* (1972), and "Mill's Criterion of Wrong Conduct," *Dialogue* (1982).

Amy Gutmann is Laurance S. Rockefeller University Professor of Politics at Princeton University. Her publications include *Liberal Equality* (1980), *Democratic Education* (1987), and most recently *Democracy and Disagreement* (1996, with Dennis Thompson) and *Color Conscious* (1996, with Anthony Appiah).

David Lyons is emeritus professor of philosophy and of law, Cornell University, and professor of law at Boston University. His most recent books are *Moral Aspects of Legal Theory* (1993) and *Rights, Welfare, and Mill's Moral Theory* (1994).

Peter Railton is professor of philosophy at the University of Michigan. He has written on various topics in normative ethics and ethical theory. His papers most relevant to Mill's *Utilitarianism* include "Alienation, Consequentialism, and the Demands of Morality," *Philosophy & Public Affairs* (1984), "Naturalism and Prescriptivity," *Social Philosophy and Policy* (1989), and "Pluralism, Determinacy, and Dilemma," *Ethics* (1992).

J. O. Urmson is emeritus professor of philosophy, Stanford University, emeritus Fellow of Corpus Christi College, Oxford, and the author of *Philosophical Analysis: Its Development between the Two World Wars* (1956) and *Aristotle's Ethics* (1988).

Henry R. West is professor of philosophy at Macalester College. He is co-editor (with Joel Feinberg) of *Moral Philosophy: Classic Texts and Contemporary Problems* (1977) and the author of "Utilitarianism" in the *Encyclopedia Britannica* and "John Stuart Mill" in *The Encyclopedia of Ethics*.